PROPHETIC
CULTURE

ALSO AVAILABLE FROM BLOOMSBURY

Technic and Magic: The Reconstruction of Reality, Federico Campagna
The Withholding Power: An Essay on Political Theology, Massimo Cacciari
Hypnosis between Science and Magic, Isabelle Stengers (forthcoming)

PROPHETIC CULTURE

Recreation for Adolescents

FEDERICO CAMPAGNA

BLOOMSBURY ACADEMIC
LONDON • NEW YORK • OXFORD • NEW DELHI • SYDNEY

BLOOMSBURY ACADEMIC
Bloomsbury Publishing Plc
50 Bedford Square, London, WC1B 3DP, UK
1385 Broadway, New York, NY 10018, USA
29 Earlsfort Terrace, Dublin 2, Ireland

BLOOMSBURY, BLOOMSBURY ACADEMIC and the Diana logo
are trademarks of Bloomsbury Publishing Plc

First published in Great Britain 2021
Reprinted in 2022, 2023

Cover image: *The Swing of the Polichinelles* (Altalena dei Pulcinelli)
by Giandomenico Tiepolo (1793)

A catalogue record for this book is available from the British Library.

Library of Congress Cataloging-in-Publication Data

Names: Campagna, Federico, author.
Title: Prophetic culture : recreation for adolescents / Federico Campagna.
Description: London ; New York : Bloomsbury Academic, 2021. |
Includes bibliographical references and index. |
Identifiers: LCCN 2020055525 (print) | LCCN 2020055526 (ebook) |
ISBN 9781350149632 (hb) | ISBN 9781350149625 (pb) |
ISBN 9781350149649 (epdf) | ISBN 9781350149656 (ebook)
Subjects: LCSH: Civilization, Modern–Philosophy. |
Civilization, Modern–Forecasting. | Future, The.
Classification: LCC CB430 .C36 2021 (print) |
LCC CB430 (ebook) | DDC 909.82–dc23
LC record available at https://lccn.loc.gov/2020055525
LC ebook record available at https://lccn.loc.gov/2020055526

ISBN: HB: 978-1-3501-4963-2
           PB: 978-1-3501-4962-5
           ePDF: 978-1-3501-4964-9
           eBook: 978-1-3501-4965-6

Typeset by Integra Software Services Pvt. Ltd.
Printed and bound in Great Britain

To find out more about our authors and books visit www.bloomsbury.com
and sign up for our newsletters.

Per Arturo, per la felicità.

CONTENTS

LIST OF FIGURES

ACKNOWLEDGEMENTS

I would like to thank those whose support, advice and creative work have significantly contributed to shaping this book.

Thank you to Arianna Casarini for her extraordinary work sourcing and designing the images in the book. Thank you to Franco Berardi, whose work has long been a great source of inspiration to me and whose afterword crowns this volume. Thank you to Prof Giuseppina Sciurba for sharing with me her sophisticated knowledge of art history and art theory. A special thank you to Rain Wu, who has accompanied me along the journey of this book since its beginning and beyond its conclusion.

Thank you to my dear friends Andrea Bellini, Father Paul Butler, Rebecca Carson, Francesco Fusaro, Adelita Husni-Bey, Timothy Morton, Manlio Poltronieri, Sarah Shin, Muge Sokmen, Francesco Strocchi, Eriko Takeno, Julian Tapales, Isabel Valli, Ben Vickers and Kevin Walker, who have advised me on the early drafts of this book.

Thank you to Roosje Klap and Niels Schrader for inviting me to teach in the Master of Nonlinear Narratives at KABK. A big thank you to my students: our long discussions gave me the opportunity to adjust large parts of my argument, to identify new directions and to clarify my ideas.

Thank you to my editor Liza Thompson for championing this project, to Lucy Russell for having accompanied it through the editorial process and to everybody at Bloomsbury for their work.

Thank you, always, to Elisabetta, Luciano, Nellina and Arturo, to whom this book is dedicated.

[Daumal]: When I was around six, I heard something about flies which sting you when you're asleep. And naturally someone dragged in the old joke: 'When you wake up, you're dead.' The words haunted me. That evening in bed with the light out, I tried to picture death, the 'no more of anything' ... For three years these nights of questioning in the dark recurred fairly frequently. Then, one particular night, a marvellous idea came to me: instead of just enduring this agony, try to observe it, to see where it comes from and what it is. I perceived that it all seemed to come from a tightening of something in my stomach, as well as under my ribs and in my throat. I remembered that I was subject to angina and forced myself to relax, especially my abdomen. The anguish disappeared. When I tried again in this new condition to think about death, instead of being clawed by anxiety, I was filled with an entirely new feeling. I knew no name for it – a feeling between mystery and hope.

[Sogol]: I can admit to you that I fear death. Not what we imagine about death, for such fear is itself imaginary. And not my death as it will be set down with a date in the public records. But that death I suffer every moment, the death of that voice which, out of the depths of my childhood, keeps questioning me as it does you: 'Who am I?' Everything in and around us seems to conspire to strangle it once and for all. Whenever that voice is silent – and it doesn't speak often – I'm an empty body, a perambulating carcass. I'm afraid that one day it will fall silent forever, or that it will speak too late – as in your story about the flies: when you wake up, you're dead.[1]

---

[1]R. Daumal, *Mount Analogue: An Authentic Narrative*, translated by R. Shattuck, San Francisco, CA, City Lights Books, 1971, pp. 34–5.

CHAPTER ONE

TIME

FIGURE 1.1 *Giovanni Domenico Tiepolo*, The Burial of Punchinello (*La sepoltura di Pulcinella*), c. 1800. © *The Metropolitan Museum of Art.*

PROLOGUE
JONS THE SQUIRE

FIGURE 1.2 *Hans Holbein the Younger,* Death and the Soldier, *copy from the* Todtentanz *engraved for Francis Douce by George Wilmot Bonner and John Byfield, 1833.*

Rare swimmers in the vast whirpool.[2]

A lonely castle in the Scandinavian north. Six people around a table in an empty room. Emerging from the aura of a torch, framed by a black hood, Death makes its entrance. Lady Karin bids her welcome, while her husband the knight mutters his last prayers. The blacksmith and his wife introduce themselves to the 'noble Lord', who has come to take them all away. The nameless Girl, a survivor of rape and famine, breaks into a smile.

> Jons: *I could have given you an herb to purge you of your worries about eternity. Now it seems to be too late. But in any case, feel the immense triumph of this last minute when you can still roll your eyes and move your toes.*
> Karin: *Quiet, quiet.*
> Jons: *I shall be silent, but under protest.*
> Girl (on her knees): *It's finished.*[3]

Jons the squire is the only one to rebel. He too, like the others, will skip at the rhythm of Death's dance. But Death won't win from him the consent of a subjugated heart. A grimace shall remain imprinted on his face, far longer than the vanishing of his flesh.

Until this final scene, the hero of Bergman's film *The Seventh Seal* seems to be the melancholic knight, devoured by doubts and guilt along his itinerant tournament with Death. By the end, however, when truth becomes *aletheia*, 'the unveiled one', it is his squire Jons who takes upon himself the mask of the hero. His heroism isn't that of the victor, nor is it the pious surrender of self-sacrifice. But it is Jons, and not his master, who remains faithful to that something, within each existent, which isn't subject to Death's worldly dominion.

The story of Jons's life remains mostly untold. We meet him at the beginning of the film, asleep on a rocky shore, back home at last, after years of reluctant crusading. We hear him sing his lust for the pleasures of life and his disenchantment towards the illusions of society. His defiance in the face of Death, however, gives us a clue

---

[2] *Rari nantes in gurgite vasto.* Virgil, *Aeneis*, I, 118, in Virgilio, *Eneide* (dual language edition), Turin, Einaudi, 2014, p. 8 – my translation.
[3] I. Bergman, *Script of The Seventh Seal*, translated by L. Malmstrom and D. Kushner, London, Lorrimer Publishing, 1972, p. 81.

about an earlier time in his life. If we follow its trace, it will lead us far to the south of his master's Scandinavian domains – to the origins of his education.

At the time when the events of *The Seventh Seal* are set, during the years of the first Crusade, a new esoteric sect had established itself in the territories at Orient of the Holy Land. Feared and respected by their neighbours, they were known as The Order of the Assassins.[4] From their stronghold of Alamut, their leader Hassan-i Sabbah commanded the secret emissaries who descended to punish whoever would try to subjugate the Order. High on a rocky cliff on the Caspian mountains, the walls of Alamut surrounded a citadel in the shape of a garden – a vision, or a dream, of Earthly Paradise.

The Assassins were Shia Muslims, belonging to Nizari Ismailism. Following the teachings of Hassan-I Sabbah, 'the Old Man of the Mountain', they had subjected their faith to the esoteric fire, and had radicalized the theological tenets of Ismailism.[5] Their esoteric ardour did not spare the sacred scriptures of Islam, and the thousands of books contained in the library of Alamut provided guidance on how to transcend the letter of the prophetic message. The true Quran is not written on paper, they claimed, but it lives

---

[4]For a historical overview of the Ismaili sect of the Assassins, see M.G.S. Hodgson, *The Secret Order of Assassins: The Struggle of the Early Nizârî Ismâî'lîs against the Islamic World*, Philadelphia, PA, University of Pennsylvania Press, 2005.

[5]'All esoterism appears to be tinged with heresy from the point of view of the corresponding exoterism ... What concerns us here is not so much the historic esoterisms – such as Pythagorism, Shivaist Vedanta, Zen – but esoterism as such, which we would willingly call *sophia perennis* and which in itself is independent of particular [religious] forms, since it is their essence ... Religious theses are certainly not errors, but they are cut to the measure of some mental and moral opportuneness ... Only esoterism can explain the particular "cut" or adaptation and restore the lost truth by referring to the total truth; this alone can provide answers that are neither fragmentary nor compromised in advance by denominational bias. Just as rationalism can remove faith, so esoterism can restore it ... Esoterism tends to realize [a state in which] subject and object coincide and in which the essential takes precedence over the accidental, or in which the principle takes precedence over its manifestation ... The man is saved who understands the purpose of human subjectivity: to be, in relativity, a mirror of the Absolute at the same time as being a prolongation of Divine Subjectivity. To manifest the Absolute in contingency, the Infinite in the finite, Perfection in imperfection ... Whereas exoterism is enclosed in the world of accidence ... esoterism is aware of the transparency of things.' F. Schuon, *Esoterism as Principle and as Way*, translated by W. Stoddart and Pates Manor, Bedfont, Perennial Books, 1981, pp. 7–45.

in the mind of the interpreter. God's constant presence, everywhere
and anywhere, endows His creatures with the ability to receive
His message ever-anew. God's final revelation, if it is ever to take
place, is not to be expected in a future Great Resurrection. The
eschatological event is always-already taking place, here and now.

For a few decades, their faith brew in the murmur of theory. Until
one day – which would have marked a historical date, if it had not
been outside of history – the Assassins drew their final conclusions
and aligned their lives accordingly. They abolished the Law, and
first of all that of Death's necessity. They stepped out of the rest
of the *Umma*, the community of the faithful, to establish a new
universal community, a new *ecumene* of indestructible existents.

> *On the 17th day of Ramadan in 559/8th August 1164, the*
> *Imam proclaimed the Great Resurrection (*qiyamat al-qiyamat*)*
> *before all the initiates assembled on the high terrace of Alamut.*
> *The protocol of that occasion has been preserved. What the*
> *proclamation implied was nothing less than the coming of a*
> *pure spiritual Islam, freed from all spirit of legalism and of all*
> *enslavement to the Law, a personal religion of the Resurrection*
> *which is spiritual birth, in that it makes possible the discovery*
> *and the living realization of the spiritual meaning of the prophetic*
> *Revelations.*[6]

During his time in the Holy Land, Jons might have crossed paths
with the Assassins. Perhaps he met them as prisoners of war, or
during their periods of tactical alliance with the Crusader states.
They might have taught him how to respond to a sky made sterile,
a scorched earth and dried up waters, by withdrawing to Alamut
rather than surrender. Judging by his defiance in the face of Death,
Jons must have brought their flame with him to the cold lands of
Northern Christendom.

The Assassins survived Jons by almost two centuries. In the year
1256, the citadel of Alamut fell to the assault of the Mongol armies
led by Hulegu Khan. Its secret garden was razed to the ground, the
library burned and scattered, the walls demolished. The Assassins

---

[6]H. Corbin, 'Shiism and Prophetic Philosophy: The Reformed Ismailism of Alamut',
in *History of Islamic Philosophy*, translated by L. Sherrard, Abingdon, Routledge,
2014, p. 95.

tried to re-establish their stronghold, but the Mongols defeated them again in 1276, and finally vanquished them in 1282.

Over the centuries, also the ruins of Alamut have crumbled off the rocks. Only faint traces, today, testify that a fortress ever existed on that mountain.

But the Assassins knew the art of occultation. They knew how to withdraw, when victory is impossible. 'One day – they said to Jons – a voice will rise again from the terrace of Alamut. One day, again, Death shall be abolished, and the Law will be forbidden. That day will be just another today. But as long as it will not be this today, you must continue to carry Alamut on yourself, hidden in your grimace, "closer to you than your jugular vein."[7] An amulet against worldly powers and the deception of the end.'

And death shall have no dominion.[8]

---

[7] *Quran*, 50:16.
[8] D. Thomas, 'And Death Shall Have No Dominion', in D. Thomas (ed.), *The Collected Poems of Dylan Thomas: The Centenary Edition*, London, Weidenfeld & Nicolson, 2016, p. 23.

A GREAT FUTURE BEHIND YOU

FIGURE 1.3 *Gabriel Rollenhagen,* Astra Deus Regit, *emblem from* Emblematum centuria secunda, *engraved by Crispijn de Passe the Elder, 1613. © Herzog August Bibliothek Wolfenbüttel.*

The Khazars believe that deep in the inky blackness of the
Caspian Sea there is an eyeless fish that, like a clock,
marks the only correct time of the universe.[9]

I was living in Milan and I was half-way through my first year of
bachelor's. By that point, it was dawning on me that I had made a
mistake. Studying economics was not for me. I couldn't see how any
of that could fit into the picture that I had of my own future. But it
was too late to change it. I didn't know that it was possible to give
up something without declaring existential bankruptcy. The only
strategy that I could devise was to lull myself into a state of denial,
as if none of it had ever happened. I ignored classes and assignments
and for a while I took on the habit of swapping day and night.

One afternoon, my father came home from work to find me,
yet again, asleep on the sofa. Swinging between dream and vigil,
I waited for him to desist from his protestations. When he finally
walked out of the room, I heard him say in a neutral tone, 'You have
a great future behind you.'[10]

Still lying down, I felt that there was something to my father's
oracle. The 'story of my life' that used to be my compass had already
become false – and I was bringing to a close also the new story in
which I was entangled. The futures that they had inscribed within
me also seemed to be ending (though none of them would have
been as great as my father believed).

The future was behind me – I realized with relief. But something
didn't add up. If the future was behind me, what time was it in
which I was living? My time had run out of thread, but all the same
I continued to live *in time*, or at least in some, post-ultimate time.
With my head on the pillow, I imagined falling in a fissure between
temporal plates, somewhere after the future and before the present.

That question has remained with me. Is it possible that the future
might run out? Can time finally end, and people still continue to
live after its demise? This is possible, of course, in the case of an

---

[9]M. Pavić, *Dictionary of the Khazars: A Lexicon Novel*, translated by C. Pribićević-
Zorić, New York, NY, Vintage, 1989, p. 144.
[10]Later, I discovered that it was a quote from Joyce's *Ulysses*: 'A sudden – at – the
– moment – though – from – lingering – illness – often – previously – expectorated –
demise, Lenehan said. And with a great future behind him.' J. Joyce, *Ulysses*, Oxford,
Oxford University Press, 2008, p. 137.

individual who has outlived a certain existential trajectory. But does the same apply also to the end of the future itself – to that story, which an entire social group calls 'time'?

This might sound like an academic question, and rightly so. For over two millennia, metaphysicians have investigated the strange weaknesses and inconsistencies of the notion of time. In the fifth century BC, the Eleatic school disproved the passing of time as a logical impossibility,[11] while Theravada Buddhist philosophers in the third century BC defined it as a phenomenon that is entirely mind-dependant.[12] A little over 100 years ago, the English metaphysician John McTaggart used logic to demonstrate 'the unreality of time'[13] and, more recently, quantum physicists have added their voice to destabilize further any fixed or 'real' notion of time.[14] The existence of time as a 'thing' in itself has been rejected by many due to it being a mere convention,[15] a purely subjective parameter[16], an inconsistent notion[17] or a concept that defies common sense.[18]

For all its failure to stand to a test of logical legitimacy, however, time remains present to our experience at every turn. Time is so innate to us that it appears to be a basic parameter of how we are able to perceive reality.[19] The flow of time is inextricably related to

---

[11]See Giorgio Colli's argument on Zeno as the inventor of logic before Aristotle in G. Colli, *Filosofi Sovrumani*, Milan, Adelphi, 2009, pp. 57–61.

[12]See A. Bunnag, 'Why Time Is Unreal: From Buddhism to J. E. McTaggart', *Veridian E-Journal International*, vol. 9, no. 5, 2016, pp. 83–94; and N. M. Thera, *A Manual of Abhidhamma*, Kuala Lumpur, Buddhist Missionary Society, 1987.

[13]J. McTaggart, *The Unreality of Time*, The Perfect Library, 2015.

[14]For a readable-yet-rigorous survey of quantum physics' studies on time, see C. Rovelli, *The Order of Time*, translated by S. Carnell and E. Segre, London, Penguin, 2018.

[15]See, for example, Henri Poincaré, *The Foundations of Science*, translated by G.B. Halsted, Washington, DC, University Press of America, 1982.

[16]As claimed already by Saint Augustine – see St, Augustine, *Confessions*, Book 11, translated by V.J. Bourke, Washington, DC, The Catholic University of America Press, 2008, pp. 325–66.

[17]See, for example, F.H. Bradley, *Appearance and Reality*, Oxford, Clarendon Press, 1930.

[18]See K. Gödel, 'A Remark about the Relationship between Relativity Theory and Idealistic Philosophy', in P.A. Schilpp (ed.), *Albert Einstein: Philosopher-Scientist*, New York, NY, MJF Books, 1970, pp. 555–62.

[19]I. Kant, *Critique of Pure Reason*, A30-2/B46-9, translated by M. Weigelt, London, Penguin, 2007, pp. 67–8.

the functioning of that machine, within a subject (be it collective or individual), which creates a 'world' out of the raw avalanche of perceptions.[20]

Aristotle's definition, perhaps, comes closest to capturing our paradoxical experience of time: the 'counting of change with respect to the before and after'.[21] If we consider it as the process of someone's 'counting' – rather than as an autonomous entity – then time loses its apparent absoluteness, varying instead on the basis of the modes of counting, and on who engages in this chronogenic (time-making) process.[22] Time is no longer presented as a thing that might be real or unreal, but as a process that is at once fully fictional and fully authentic – a limit-process, whose cosmological location is at the threshold between the reality that we can apprehend and what lies beyond it.

---

[20]The process of world-creation can be understood as a 'machine', in the sense given to this term by Deleuze and Guattari in their *Anti-Oedipus*. 'A machine may be defined as a system of interruptions or breaks (*coupures*) ... Every machine, in the first place, is related to a continual material flow (*hyle*) that it cuts into ... Each associative flow must be seen as an ideal thing, an endless flux, flowing form something not unlike the immense thigh of a pig. The term *hyle* in fact designates the pure continuity that any one sort of matter ideally possesses ... In a word, every machine functions as a break in the flow in relation to the machine to which it is connected, but at the same time it is also a flow itself, or the production of a flow, in relation to the machine connected to it .... Every machine has a sort of code built into it, stored up inside it. This code is inseparable not only form the way in which it is recorded and transmitted to each of the different regions of the body, but also from the way in which the relations of each of the regions with all the others are recorded ... [The chains of meaning produced by this code] are called "signifying chains" (*chaines signifiantes*), but these signs are not themselves signifying. The code resembles not so much a language as a jargon, an open-ended, polyvocal formation.' G. Deleuze and F. Guattari, *Anti-Oedipus*, translated by R. Hurley et al., London, Bloomsbury, 2013, pp. 38–41.

[21]Aristotle, *Physics*, IV, ch. 11, 219 b 1–2. See Aristotle, *Physics*, translated by R. Hope, Lincoln, NE, University of Nebraska Press, 1961, p. 80.

[22]'Numbering is what creates the idea of time. The qualitative heterogeneity of mathematical exponents: this is what makes room for numbering. The quantitative differences between exponents are in fact a projection of those qualitative onto the temporal sequence that was originated by the latter.' P. Florenskij, *L'Infinito nella Conoscenza, I Limiti della Gnoseologia*, translated by M. Di Salvo, Milan, Mimesis, 2014, p. 55 – my translation from the Italian edition.

Despite its efficacy, however, the metaphor of counting encounters an empirical problem: it implies that time-making is a much more conscious process than our experience suggests. In our daily life, we feel time flowing somehow laterally to reality – in the same way that a musician feels the rhythm of what they're playing. It is only seldom that we actively 'count' time, while most frequently it emerges together with the unfolding of things, events and situations that make up the tapestry of reality. The term 'narrating' might better evoke the subterranean quality of time. To paraphrase Aristotle, time could be described as the 'rhythm of a subject's narration of change, with respect to the before and after'.

To investigate this rhythmic/narrative quality of time, let us begin by observing the nature of that process of worlding, to which the birth of time is connected.

Upon opening our eyes in the morning, we are not immediately and automatically greeted by a comfortable world, made up of clear and distinct things among which we can navigate our way. The flow of perceptions that constitutes our experience of reality is more akin to the onslaught of an oceanic tide – immense, faceless and undivided. At each instant, our awareness attempts to canalize perceptions within the frame of sense of a 'world' (*kosmos, mundus*): a newly created landscape where our experience can unfold, and our intentions can be projected. Worlding[23] is a metaphysical process that creates discontinuities, separations between individual 'somethings', out of a plane of pure existence where no clear divisions are already inscribed.

---

[23]'Worlding' is a fairly recent addition to the philosophical vocabulary, whose origin can be traced to Martin Heidegger's *Being and Time*. According to Heidegger, 'worlding', as a generative process of world-creation, is consubstantial to the way in which a human consciousness (*Dasein*, 'being-there') exists in a 'world' that, to a certain extent, is of their own making. Heidegger doesn't offer an exhaustive definition of the process of worlding, since 'the world presences by worlding. That means: the world's worlding cannot be explained by anything else nor can it be fathomed through anything else. This impossibility does not lie in the inability of our human thinking to explain and fathom in this way. Rather, the inexplicable and unfathomable character of the world's worlding lies in this, that causes and grounds remain unsuitable for the world's worlding. As soon as human cognition here calls for an explanation, it fails to transcend the world's nature, and falls short of it'. M. Heidegger, 'The Thing', in M. Heidegger (ed.), *Poetry, Language, Thought*, translated by H. Hofstadter, New York, NY, Harper and Row, 1971, pp. 179–80. My use of the term 'worlding' does not wish to be a faithful adoption of Heidegger's notion.

Due to its immediate proximity to our awareness, like an object that is too close to the eye, this relentless process of worlding often runs undetected – and it is commonly reduced to a matter-of-fact reconnaissance of what is 'there' in 'the world'. Far from being the total data set of a survey of the existent,[24] however, the world that we see around ourselves at any moment is the outcome of an act of metaphysical poetics – it is a 'likely story',[25] whose narrative fabric is adopted by the subject as the 'stuff of the world'.

Just by looking around in a room, I can't avoid separating this from that, this table from this chair, my clothes from my body. Without such divisions, arbitrary as they may be, I would be unable to address anything, to take anything or to repel anything – reality would no longer be a world, but an uninhabitable, undivided ocean of perceptions. Ultimately, a subject cannot count on there being such thing as a world, existing undisturbed by itself: they must rely on the magic of a metaphysical storytelling, *standing as* a world for those who perform it.

Worlding is the creative act par excellence: the cosmogonic gesture separating the land of reality from the waters of the Real. Mediterranean theology describes it in these terms, when it refers to cosmogony (world-generation) as an act of creation, and to the Godhead as a creator – Latin *Artifex*, Arabic *Al Khaaliq*, Hebrew *Boreh* – who makes something emerge out of nothing.

However, against a frequent misunderstanding of the notion of 'creation', cosmogony isn't an event that took place once and for all

---

[24]My definition of 'world' differs from the two main theories of possible worlds in contemporary analytic philosophy: Alvin Plantinga's abstractionism (the world as a 'maximally comprehensive state of affairs') and David Lewis's concretism (the world as a 'maximal connected object'). See D. Lewis, 'Possible Worlds', in *Counterfactuals*, Oxford, Blackwell, 2001, pp. 84–90; D. Lewis, *On the Plurality of Worlds*, Oxford, Blackwell, 1986; A. Plantinga, 'Actualism and Possible Worlds', in M.J. Loux (ed.), *The Possible and the Actual: Readings in the Metaphysics of Modality*, Ithaca, NY, Cornell University Press, 1979, pp. 253–73; A. Plantinga, *The Nature of Necessity*, Oxford, Oxford University Press, 1982, pp. 44–163. My perspective on world and worlding shares some terrain with that proposed by Martin Heidegger, although the focus that I adopt is less oriented towards projectuality. See M. Heidegger, 'The Worldhood of the World', in J. Macquarrie and E. Robinson (trans.), *Being and Time*, I, 3, New York, NY, Harper, 2008, pp. 91–148.
[25]In the *Timaeus*, 29c, Plato defines his metaphysical narration as an *eikos mythos* (a likely story) – see Plato, *Complete Works*, edited by J.M. Cooper, translated by D.J. Zeyl, Indianapolis/Cambridge, Hackett, 1997, p. 1235.

at the earliest point in time. The activity of worlding is repeated at every instant, in the same way that Ash'arite theologians described the world as the fragile outcome of God's continuous and arbitrary re-creation.[26] Even the most seemingly solid and undisputable thing in the world remains vulnerable to be eradicated at any point by the twisting and turning of a subject's own metaphysical narration.

The rhythm of a certain process of worlding counts as 'time' for that world – and vice versa, time itself counts as the rhythm at which a certain world emerges out of the bedrock of wordless and timeless existence.

Harmony, whose movements are akin to the orbits within our souls, is a gift of the Muses ... to serve as an ally in the fight to bring order to any orbit in our souls that has become unharmonized ... Rhythm, too, has likewise been given to us by the Muses for the same purpose, to assist us.[27]

Understood in these terms, time is not just a relationship of before-and-after between events, but it is also the meta-narrative sequence of past–present–future[28] binding the narrative flow like the three movements of a classical sonata.[29]

---

[26]For an account of occasionalist thought in Al-Ash'ari (873–935), Al Juwayni (1028–85) and Al Ghazali (1058–1111), see D. Perler and U. Rudolph, *Occasionalismus: Theorien der Kausalität im arabisch-islamischen und im europäischen Denken*, Göttingen, Vandenhoeck & Ruprecht, 2000.

[27]Plato, 'Timaeus', 47 d-e, in J.M. Cooper (ed.), D.J. Zeyl (trans.), *Complete Works*, Indianapolis/Cambridge, Hackett, 1997, p. 1250.

[28]These two modes of understanding time are famously defined by John McTaggart, respectively, as B-series (earlier than–later than) and A-series (past–present–future). In his attack against the attribution of reality to time, McTaggart focused in particular on challenging the A series, which he considered essential to any plausible notion of time.

[29]"We have to read the myth more or less as we would read an orchestral score, not stave after stave, but understanding that we should apprehend the whole page and that something which was written on the first stave at the top of the page acquires meaning only if one considers that it is part and parcel of what is written below on the second stave, the third stave, and so on. [...] As a matter of fact, it was about the time when mythical thought passed to the background in western thought during the Renaissance and the seventeenth century ... that we witness the appearance of the great musical styles. [...] It is as if music had completely changed its traditional shape in order to take over the function – the intellectual and emotive function – which mythical thought was

A subject creates the world in the same way that a Greek rhapsode would have sung: a poetic composition arranged on a meter. As there used to be a meter for each form of poetry, so a unique *segment* of time[30] emerges for every instance of worlding. No two subjects can inhabit the same time, unless they sing the world together as a chorus. The same past, present and future will take shape for them only as long as they shall be singing in metaphysical accord.

It is a rare combination that different people may exist in the same time-segment, and to a great extent large social groups function as fundamental metronomes for worlding – suggesting the rhythm to which one's own metaphysical narration should adapt, if they wish to share a common historical time with their neighbours.[31] The tendency of new political systems to change the calendar is justified by the fact that, indeed, historical time is nothing but the rhythm of the metaphysics that is socially dominant. There is no time outside of the sound of a world-song.

---

giving up more or less at the same period. [...] There are myths or groups of myths which are constructed like a sonata, or a symphony, or a rondo, or a toccata, or any of all the musical forms which music did not really invent but borrowed unconsciously from the structure of the myth.' L. Strauss, *Myth and Meaning*, Abingdon, Routledge, 2001, pp. 39–41, 44–5. See also L. Strauss, *The Raw and the Cooked: Mythologiques*, vol. 1, Part One, *Theme and Variations*, translated by J.D. Weightman, Chicago, IL, The University of Chicago Press, 1969, pp. 35–80.

[30]The notion of time as a bundle of 'timelines' – prominent among current sci-fi thinkers – implies geometrically that such lines run infinitely, without a beginning or an end. If it is interpreted as the rhythm of an ongoing cosmogonic narration, however, time has the quality of a segment, with a beginning and an end (and perhaps, a phantasmatic afterlife) bound to the voice that tells 'the story of the world'. After all, the severing that cuts time into segments is implicit in the word, 'time' deriving from the Greek *temnein*, 'to cut' (from which also the word 'temple' derives, as the circumscribed area of the sacred).

[31]'A civilisation [is] the product and expression of a certain mental outlook common to a more or less widespread group of people, thus making it possible to treat each particular case separately as regards the exact determination of its constituent elements.' R. Guenon, *Introduction to the Study of Hindu Doctrines*, translated by M. Pallis, Hillsdale, NY, Sophia Perennis, 2004, p. 55.

And then, inevitably, the moment comes when the day grows old, the narrator becomes tired and storytelling slowly ends. Together with the closure of one form of worlding, its sequence of past–present–future also ends.[32] When the voice that sings 'the world' starts to fade out, the range of possibilities that made up its future also begins to evaporate. The end of a world is an apocalypse that reveals (*apokalyptein*) the nature of time, at the same moment in which it slaughters it.[33]

One single lifespan can host many apocalypses. The existential landscape of a subject usually resembles the layout of a Mediterranean city, overlaid with strata of ruins, more than the uniform architecture of a New Town. Each world-apocalypse is authentically an End Time, where the rhythm of a world fades out together with the voice that sustained its narration.[34] We have all had experience of these End Times in the course of our own life – for example, when losing a love that was capable of changing the very substance of a street, or in the passage from childhood to the next phase of growth.

In genuine tragedy
it's not the fine hero that finally dies, it seems,
but, from constant wear and tear, night after night,
the old stage set itself, giving way at the seams.[35]

---

[32]'Who could describe with words the horror of that night/who could explain the massacre, or equal the sorrow with their tears? An ancient city, a long-standing civilisation falls.' *Quis cladem illius noctis, quis funera fando/explicet aut possit lacrimis aequare labores?/urbs antiqua ruit multos dominata per annos.* Virgil, *Aeneid*, I–VI, 2.361–363, London, Bristol Classical Press, 2002, p. 36 – my translation.

[33]Sacrifice is here evoked as that process through which the world is maintained within existence. For a fascinating account on the cosmic function of sacrifice in Vedic culture, see R. Calasso, *Ardor*, translated by R. Dixon, London, Penguin, 2015. For an analysis of the broader social valence of sacrifice, see R. Girard, *Violence and the Sacred*, translated by P. Gregory, London, Bloomsbury, 2013.

[34]'Every disintegration of a certain culture is an eschatology, it is the death of an aeon and the end of a certain time; from this, ensues the disquieting feeling that it might in fact be the final closure of all times and the world itself.' P. Florenskij, *La Concezione Cristiana del Mondo*, translated by A. Maccioni, Bologna, Pendragon, 2019, p. 43 – my translation from the Italian edition.

[35]Joseph Brodsky, 'Lullaby of Cape Cod', V, in *A Part of Speech*, edited by Joseph Brodsky, Oxford, Oxford University Press, 1997.

A child's metaphysics is radically different from that which they shall develop later in life: a cosmogonic narrative where a toy, or the darkness of a room, is endowed with agency and entitled to constant negotiations, is an 'otherworld' to a cosmos where the boundaries of life and non-life, reality and un-reality are more harshly delineated. The child's experience of the present defines their perspective towards the future, setting the metaphysical parameters where all possible events are envisioned to take place. A child, like any subject, assumes that the world of the future will be metaphysically continuous with that of their present. Their every plan or decision is based on the idea of a predefined range and kind of the possible.

The embarrassment that typically accompanies the crumbling of a childhood world marks the experience of having somehow survived the End Time – only to find oneself in open sea, out of sight from a new segment of time. The old metaphysics no longer applies and there is no new narration as yet in place: the feeling of inadequacy of early teenage years points to a subject whose actions lack the support of a strong frame of sense, standing out as shameful inasmuch as they lack a 'legitimate' status within reality.

The young adolescent, as a post-apocalyptic subject, has to make do with any precarious form of worlding that they may be able to devise. They scavenge among the ruins of the lost world of childhood, searching for some inspiration; or they resort to imitating just about any available metaphysical narration, in the hope of a pseudomorphosis.[36] But post-apocalyptic subjects, too, live in a world and a time of sorts, although the contours of their

---

[36]In mineralogy, a *pseudomorph* (false form) is a mineral or mineral compound that results from a substitution process, in which the appearance and dimensions remain constant, but the original mineral is replaced by another. Oswald Spengler adopted this term to describe 'those cases in which an older alien Culture lies so massively over the land that a young Culture, born in this land, cannot get its breath and fails not only to achieve pure and specific expression-forms, but even to develop fully its own self-consciousness'. See O. Spengler, *The Decline of the West*, vol. II, translated by C.F. Atkinson, New York, NY, Knopf, 1926, p. 189.

existential landscape remain fleeting and permeable to the incursions of the Real[37] beyond reality. Things become more unstable, while the inexplicable liveliness of each particle of reality emerges in a threatening fashion.

Like the silence of organs signals to their functioning, and noise to their crisis, so the end of a world takes our process of worlding out of its silence, turning it into an activity proper. The aftermath of an apocalypse is a shivering expanse, where reality itself requires constant mending.

---

[37]The Real is one of the three registers of reality described by psychoanalyst Jacques Lacan, alongside the 'imaginary' and the 'symbolic'. The Real is the ineffable, underlying bedrock of reality, from which humans are severed by their entrance into language. Although Lacan's notion of the Real has changed over the course of his philosophical investigation, it is possible to gain a fairly synoptic vision especially in J. Lacan, *The Seminar of Jacques Lacan: The Ethics of Psychoanalysis 1959–1960*, Book VII, edited and translated by J.A. Miller, Cambridge, Polity, 1997.

THE AFTERLIFE OF
CIVILIZATIONS

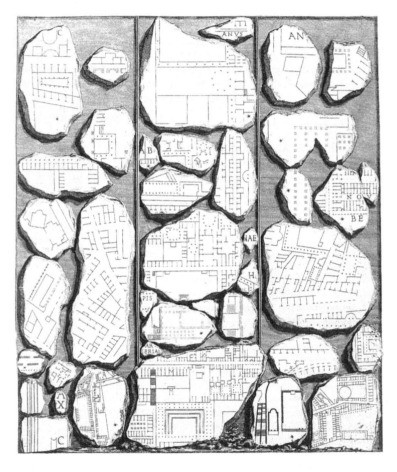

FIGURE 1.4 *Giovanni Battista Piranesi,* Map of Ancient Rome and
Forma Urbis, *from* Le antichità romane *(Roman Antiquities), t. 1, Plate
IV, 1756.*

Rising from the ruins
And facing the future.[38]

These traumatic moments of passage between worlds and times occur as often in the life of an individual, as in that of a collective.[39] When the closure of a world refers to the collapse of an entire civilization, historiography tends to define the following period as a 'Middle Age'. A scenario where life proceeds in the absence of a voice capable of narrating a stable world; a long winter when the material of history is in part congealed and, in part, slowly rots away. This is, of course, how these periods are seen and judged from the perspective of a more stable world – but such partiality is revealing of the difference between worlds with unequal narrative rootedness.

Instances of Middle Ages abound in the history of the past few thousand years. An early example is the so-called Hellenic Middle Age that followed the fall of Minoan and Mycenaean society in the twelfth century BC. Spanning for almost five centuries, the first recorded Medieval period in European history came at the close of a civilization that had flourished across a network of cities between the Argolis, Anatolia and Crete. The Minoan and Mycenaean era had been the time of Achilles, Hector, Minos, Orpheus, Herakles, Jason and all the heroes that populate Greek mythology. In his *Works and Days*, the poet Hesiod listed it as one of the five ages of the world: the Heroic Age.[40]

This spectacular society vanished suddenly, perhaps due to a series of environmental catastrophes,[41] and it was followed by

---

[38]*Auferstanden aus Ruinen und der Zukunft zugewandt.* Incipit of the 1949 anthem of the German Democratic Republic – lyrics by Johannes R. Becher, music by Hanns Eisler.

[39]'The entire operation of a historical era is established by the sense assigned by that era to the being-thing on the part of things. Indeed, the sense of what we call a "thing" is not stable.' E. Severino, *La strada: La follia e la gioia*, Milan, Rizzoli, 2008, p. 57 – my translation.

[40]Hesiod, *Works and Days*, 156–75, translated by D. Wender, London, Penguin, 1973, pp. 63–4.

[41]For a critical overview of the existing scholarship on the collapse of Bronze-Age civilizations in the Eastern Mediterranean, see the 'systemic collapse' approach suggested by archaeologist Eric H. Cline, in E. Cline, *1177 B.C.: The Year Civilization Collapsed*, Princeton, NJ, Princeton University Press, 2015.

half a millennium when even basic material culture dramatically diminished. Its two writing systems were lost and nothing came to substitute them until the adoption of the Phoenician alphabet, in the eighth century BC. Long-distance seafaring, mythically inaugurated by the Argonauts, ground to a halt. Even metallurgy, which had given the name to the Age of Bronze, before that of the Heroes, was abandoned until ironworking arrived from Anatolia.

The people who lived in those territories during the centuries following this collapse saw their spatial and temporal horizons shrinking. As ever during a Middle Age, the categories of time and space barely emerged from the surface of reality – leading to a rapid divestment from the infrastructures that used to reach into the spatial–temporal elsewhere.

Medieval subjects receive the elsewhere mostly passively, and for this reason all the more intensely. Past and future haunt a Middle Age like ghostly entities, severed from the context of the present. Threats and promises from an other, disjointed time, which is simultaneously long-lost and as-yet to come. The inner turmoil of a Middle Age, not taking place within a stable rhythm of time, relentlessly spins without advancing towards a future. A Middle Age is a period that is truly 'contemporary': it is a compressed world, whose present is confined entirely within its own bounds; a time that is defined only by its own coincidence with itself. It is an 'idiotic' age, in that its familiarity extends only to what is already *idios* (particular, private) to itself.[42]

In the same way as the post-Minoan and post-Mycenaean people, also the magma of local kingdoms that followed the liquefaction of the Western Roman Empire lost access to the infrastructures of their predecessors. Already in the fifth century AD, while travelling through the Italian peninsula ravaged by the Goths, the poet Rutilus Namatianus noted:

---

[42]As a corollary, we could add, encountering a civilization that calls itself Contemporary is a good indicator of a world at the tail end of its own narration, unconsciously readying itself for an incoming Middle Age – since trauma operates not only projectively, conditioning what happens afterwards, but also retrospectively: it already haunts a subject who is readying themselves to recognize it.

The monuments of an earlier age can no longer be recognised;
devouring time has wasted the mighty battlements away.
Traces only remain now among the crumbled walls:
under a wide stretch of rubble lie the buried homes.
Let us not chafe that human frames dissolve:
Here it is how cities too can die.[43]

By the eighth century AD, the material legacy of the Roman civilization had become so alien to the new Medieval landscape that an Anglo-Saxon poet could describe a minor complex of Roman public baths as 'the stones of giants', which had 'fallen to the ground broken into mounds' before their late discoverer could look at their 'treasure, at silver, at precious stones, at wealth, at prosperity, at jewellery, at this bright castle of a broad kingdom'.[44]

Not only public buildings were largely abandoned,[45] but also the inter-continental networks of roads and communications that used to supply the empire with people and materials rapidly fell into disuse.[46] Together with the infrastructures to expand through space,[47] the chronicling of life and history, to which Roman

---

[43]*Agnosci nequeunt aevi monumenta prioris:/grandia consumpsit moenia tempus edax;/sola manent interceptis vestigial muris,/ruderibus latis tecta sepulta iacent./ Non indignemur mortalia corpora solvi:/cernimus exemplis oppida posse mori.* My own translation. For further reading, see Rutilius Namatianus, *De Reditu Suo*, 409–14, in R. Namaziano, *Il Ritorno* (dual language edition), Turin, Einaudi, 1992, p. 30.
[44]Anonymous, *The Ruin*, in M. Alexander (ed.), *The Earliest English Poems*, London, Penguin, 1977, pp. 28–9.
[45]A prime example is the abandonment of aqueducts in the city of Rome for almost a millennium, from their destruction by the Ostrogoths in 537 AD until the Renaissance.
[46]'We choose [to travel by] sea, because all land routes/are flooded by rivers in the valleys and are covered by rocks on the mountains:/since the fields of Tuscia and the Aurelian road,/utterly devastated by the hordes of the Goths,/no longer tame the forests with inns, nor the rivers with bridges,/it is better to entrust the sails to the sea, however unpredictable it might be.' My own translation. For further reading, see Rutilius Namatianus, 'De Reditu Suo', 37–42, in *Il Ritorno* (dual language edition), Turin, Einaudi, 1992, p. 4.
[47]An emblematic case in point is the gradual but systematic destruction, after the fall of the Western Roman Empire, of the *Forma Urbis Romae* (Severan Marble Plan), a massive marble map of ancient Rome, created under the emperor Septimius Severus between AD 203 and 211.

civilization had entrusted its own projection towards the future, also decreased significantly. Literacy became scarce and writing withdrew into the sanctuary of small circles of ecclesiasts. Like the Hellenic Middle Age, also the so-called European Dark Age – from the fifth century to the Carolingian renaissance in the ninth century – has left behind very few material traces.

Nonetheless, in both cases, in the midst of a seemingly endless collapse, something remained of those stable worlds that once existed.[48] The relics of those lost civilizations continued to survive within the folds of a frayed time.

Carried by the voice and the memory of itinerant rhapsodes and *aoidoi*, the stories of the Minoan and Mycenaean age crossed the 'long night of the five hundred years'[49] of the Hellenic Middle Age, until they were formalized in the cosmological epics of the *Iliad* and the *Odyssey*.

Episodes like the combat between Achilles and the river Scamander, as recounted in the *Iliad*,[50] speak not only of the deeds of the heroes, but most importantly of the metaphysical settings of the world where they originally occurred. The Homeric cycle offers, not just the (inaccurate) description of a society, but more importantly a reproduction of the mind of a civilization in the act of constructing a fundamental frame of sense through which a world can take shape. Myths do not point to the hour of a civilization, but to its particular art of producing time. Like the three Moirai who spin the blank thread of a person's life, the voice of Homer unrolled

---

[48]To paraphrase Pessoa, what remains are 'all the dreams in the world', contained within a certain world-narration. 'I am nothing./I'll never be anything./I couldn't want to be something./Apart from that, I have in me all the dreams in the world,' F. Pessoa, 'Tabacaria', in F. Pessoa, *Selected Poems*, edited and translated by J. Griffin, London, Penguin, 2000, p. 111.

[49]*La larga noche de los quinientos años* was Subcomandante Marcos's definition of the Middle Age that befell indigenous populations in Central America after the Spanish invasion – and which continues to this day. The violence of the colonial enterprise can be measured, among other things, also by the devastating impact that it had on indigenous metaphysics – that is, on the possibility for the indigenous populations to perform a stable 'worlding' (and thus to produce a 'time-segment') in which they could live and flourish.

[50]*Iliad*, book 21, 200–381.

the time-segment of the Mycenaean–Minoan civilization – not the portrait, but the *frame* of a world.[51]

The works attributed to Homer reached into the ruins of a dead world to recuperate the materials for the foundation of what will later become the Classical Greek age.[52] Starting from the eighth century BC, the new generations of Archaic Greeks adopted the Homeric narration both as their ethical paradigm – crystallized by the notion of *arete* (nobility)[53] – and as their metaphysical understanding of the stuff that makes up 'the world' – a tragic assembly of gods and mortals under the aegis of *Ananke* (Divine Necessity). Centuries later, philosophers of the Classical Age still embarked on their explorations with an eye to the Homeric world as the fundamental benchmark against which their *logos* would be judged. This is particularly evident in Plato's work, where archaic mythology is always an implicit interlocutor in the discussions between Socrates and his counterparts.

The same process occurred again at the end of the European Dark Age, around the ninth century AD – when, among the ghosts still haunting Roman ruins, a new civilization sought some inspiration to start its own world-making narration. The Church played a crucial

---

[51]The Mycenaean and Minoan world, as sung by the rhapsodes, was a syncretic distortion both of the age past and of their own present. 'Homer and archaeology part company quickly. On the whole he knew where the Mycenaean civilization flourished, and his heroes lived in great Bronze Age palaces unknown in Homer's own day. And that is virtually all he knew about Mycenaean times, for the catalogue of his errors is very long. His arms bear a resemblance to the armour of his time, quite unlike the Mycenaean, although he persistently casts them in antiquated bronze, not iron. His gods had temples, and the Mycenaeans build none, whereas the latter constructed great vaulted tombs in which to bury their chieftains, and the poet cremates his. A neat little touch is provided by the battle chariots. Homer had heard of them, but he did not really visualize what one did with chariots in a war. So, his heroes normally drove from their tents a mile or less away, carefully dismounted, and then proceeded to battle on foot.' M.I. Finley, *The World of Odysseus*, New York, NY, New York Review of Books, 2002, pp. 39–40.

[52]For an examination of the foundational role of Mycenaean culture towards Greek Culture, see, for example, M.P. Nilsson, *The Mycenaean Origin of Greek Mythology*, Berkeley, CA, University of California Press, 1972.

[53]For an as-yet-unsurpassed account of the archaic notion of *arete* and of the role that it played in later in Greek culture, see W. Jaeger, *Paideia: The Ideals of Greek Culture*, vol. I, *Archaic Greece*, translated by G. Highet, Oxford, Oxford University Press, 1965.

role in the survival of the world of Rome, comparable to those Hellenic rhapsodes who offered their own voice as a living vessel for the lost Heroic Age. Embodied in the very structure, language and references of the Church,[54] Roman cosmology remained available to be rediscovered and exploited by a young civilization in the process of commencing their own cosmogonic narration.

When Charlemagne was crowned by Pope Leo III, on Christmas day in the year 800, he took upon himself the name of *Imperator Romanorum* (Emperor of the Romans) – a title which had lost all meaning almost four centuries earlier. Already at the court of Charlemagne's predecessors, Merovingian scholars had created the story of Francus, a mythical ancestor who had left Troy together with Aeneas but had gone northwards, towards the Rheine, to establish the Frankish people.[55] In its reconstruction of a world in which they could live, Carolingian society recuperated the legacy of the Roman civilization as the mythical foundation of its own institutional settings – that is, of the 'legitimate' power that regulates and predetermines the possible forms of action and knowledge in a certain world.[56]

---

[54]This is true also in the case of values that are at odds with Christian doctrine: it is mainly thanks to the extensive quotations reported in the works of early Christian polemicists, that substantial fragments of pagan theology managed to survive the fall of pagan society (a good example being Celsus's critique of Christianity, *On The True Doctrine*, which survived only thanks to its inclusion in the refutation written in AD 248 by the Christian theologian Origen of Alexandria, *Contra Celsum*). To appreciate the Church's embodiment of the lost Roman world, it is worth noting the emphasis placed by the Church on the figure of Constantine, the first Christian emperor, who long remained as the mythical model of the rightful ruler (see A. Barbero, *Costantino il Vincitore*, Rome, Salerno Editrice, 2016). See also the connection between Imperial Roman rituals of power, and early Christian religious rituals: 'In the festivals of the saints, crowds "swarm like bees" around the tomb [of the saint]; and the saint himself makes his presence felt all the more strongly by a ceremonial closely modelled on the *adventus*, the "arrival in state" of a Late Roman emperor.' P. Brown, *Society and the Holy in Late Antiquity*, Berkeley, CA, University of California Press, 1989, p. 7.
[55]The curious story of Francus was first presented in writing in the seventh-century *Chronicle of Fredegar*, and it was later developed in the eighth century in the *Liber Historiae Francorum*.
[56]I am adopting Michel Foucault's understanding of power and of institutions, as developed throughout his oeuvre, and particularly in M. Foucault, *Madness and Civilization: A History of Insanity in the Age of Reason*, translated by J. Murphy and J. Khalfa, New York, NY, Vintage Books, 2006.

Cases of strange resurrections, like those of the Mycenaean and of the Roman worlds, don't stand as historical exceptions. To find them, let us move to the south-east of the Mediterranean basin, where the wise elder of the ancient world used to reside:[57] the civilization of Egypt, already millennia old in Plato's days. In the fourth century BC, when Egypt fell to Alexander the Great's gallop towards the final frontier of the world, the land around the Nile had already endured centuries of Persian rule. In historical terms, the Egyptian civilization was, by then, a spirit deprived of a body – like the shadows of the Heroic Age preserved in the *Iliad*, it survived only as the remnant of a past future. But when the Macedonian conquerors coalesced with their new subjects into one people, they looked among the ruins of these two vanquished worlds for inspiration to start their own new cosmogonic narration. Mixed with a second adoption of the Homeric narrative, Egypt's hieratic and magic metaphysics produced the soil out of which the age of Hellenism grew.

To be sure, the Hellenistic reincarnation of these long-lost cosmologies subjected them to a process of reinterpretation and betrayal that substantially disfigured them. Creations like Serapis – the divinity invented by Pharaoh Ptolemy I Soter, from the syncretic combination of various Greek and Egyptian gods – would have probably appeared unacceptable to people living at the time of the earlier Pharaohs and of the Mycenaeans.[58] And

---

[57]"On one occasion, wanting to lead them [i.e. the Egyptian priests] on to talk about antiquity, he [i.e. Solon, one of the "seven sages" of Greece] broached the subject of our own ancient history. He started talking about Phoroneus – the first human being, it is said – and about Niobe, and then he told the story of how Deucalion and Pyrrha survived the flood. He went on to trace the lines of descent of their posterity and tried to compute their dates by calculating the number of years which had elapsed since the events of which he spoke. And then one of the priests, a very old man, said, "Ah Solon, Solon, you Greeks are ever children. There isn't an old man among you." On hearing this, Solon said, "What? What do you mean?" "You are young," the old priest replied, "young in soul, every one of you. Your souls are devoid of beliefs about antiquity handed down by ancient tradition. Your souls lack any learning made hoary by time."' Plato, 'Timaeus', 22 a-b, in J.M. Cooper (ed.), *Complete Works*, translated by D.J. Zeyl, Indianapolis/Cambridge, Hackett, 1997, p. 1230.
[58]By a fascinating coincidence, the head of Serapis was later adopted by Charlemagne as his own seal. See J. Seznec, *The Survival of the Pagan Gods: The Mythological Thought and Its Place in Renaissance Humanism and Art*, Princeton, NJ, Princeton University Press, 1972, p. 55.

the monstrosity[59] of these recuperations was only destined to increase – as it happened in the fifteenth century, when Italian Renaissance scholars combined the remnants of Hellenistic metaphysics with Cabbalism to produce in turn their own, new narration of the world.[60]

But the case of Hellenism wasn't dissimilar to the disfigured reincarnations of the Mycenaean–Minoan and Roman worlds. The historical inaccuracy of the heroes sung by Homer was doubled by the Greek appropriation of their model as the cornerstone of a new, 'tragic' mentality. And what could there be of more incongruous than a trousers-wearing barbarian, unironically taking on the title of Roman Emperor!

Such is the afterlife of a metaphysical narrative issued by a dead world: like a print left on a path, a new foot comes to fill it and to betray its boundaries. Indeed, if a world is ever to survive the end of its own historical body, it is through syncretic disfigurement rather than in the efforts of archival conservation. As in the story of Malinche – the Aztec woman who served as Hernan Cortes's translator and who mothered one of the first Mestizos[61] – betrayal

---

[59]I intend such monstrosity in the sense assigned to the figure of the monster by Georges Batailles. 'For Bataille, the monster is in some sense the very culmination of [Durkheim's notion of] the left-hand sacred – a formless figure that is paradoxically both useless waste and the mechanism of subversive operations, "uniting birth and death in the same rupture." Indeed, the very concept of monstrosity – with its contradictions, incompletions, and irrational effusions it implies – is itself monstrous; it is a tainted, wounded, maculate conception.' J. Biles, *Ecce Monstrum: Georges Bataille and the Sacrifice of Form*, New York, NY, Fordham University Press, 2007, p. 63.

[60]As it is well known, Italian Renaissance culture owed an enormous debt to the rediscovery of Hellenistic culture and especially to the re-introduction of Neoplatonism in Italy by Georgius Gemistus Plethon, via Marsilio Ficino. For an excellent account of the pervasive influence of Hellenistic and late-ancient Mediterranean thought on the Italian Renaissance, see R. Ebgi (ed.), *Umanisti Italiani: Pensiero e Destino*, Turin, Einaudi, 2016; and G. Busi and R. Ebgi, *Giovanni Pico della Mirandola: Mito, Magia, Qabbalah*, Turin, Einaudi, 2014 (where such 'Hellenism' reveals itself, in fact, as a form of philosophical pan-Mediterraneism).

[61]Born into Aztec high society, at a young age Malinche (also known as Malintzin or as Doña Marina) was sold into slavery by her stepfather. When she was a teenager, she was given as a gift to Hernán Cortés, whom she served as translator. She became Cortés's lover, and had with him a son and a daughter, who after Malinche's death

and translation, becoming-other and becoming-self are rendered indistinguishable in the twilight moment when a familiar world sets and an alien one begins to dawn.

This destiny might be hard to swallow for a civilization that still inhabits a living body. Whatever they might produce and however perfect their art might be, their only chance of transmitting their story to a living ear is by being misinterpreted, misunderstood, taken apart, pillaged and recomposed. Even then, though, something shall remain faithful to the original voice that sung out a world and its time-segment – a genetic echo, still resounding in their distant offspring. That 'something' is the small erotic detail, the *object petit a*,[62] that might catch the eye of those who shall live after the end of the future, and who might choose it as one among their own parents.[63]

---

grew up with their father's family. It is interesting to note how Aztec emissaries would address as 'Malinche' both Cortés and Malinche proper – as if the one was unthinkable without the other. The figure of Malinche remains an important icon of Mexican culture, where she is presented alternatively as a victim, a traitor, or the mother of the nation. For two different interpretations of her figure, see O. Paz, 'The Sons of La Malinche', in O. Paz (ed.), *The Labyrinth of Solitude and Other Writings*, New York, NY, Grove Press, 1994, pp. 65–88; and C. Townsend, *Malintzin's Choices: An Indian Woman in the Conquest of Mexico*, Albuquerque, NM, University of New Mexico Press, 2006.

[62]See Jacques Lacan's discussion of the *object petit a* (where *a* stands for *autre*, 'other') as the unattainable object of desire, in his seminars *Les formations de l'inconscient* (1957 – in J. Lacan, *The Seminar of Jacques Lacan: The Formations of the Unconscious 1957–1958*, Book V, edited and translated by J.A. Miller, Cambridge, Polity, 2017); *Le transfert* (1960–1 – in J. Lacan, *The Seminar of Jacques Lacan: Transference*, Book VIII, edited and translated by J.A. Miller, Cambridge, Polity, 2015); *L'angoisse* (1962–3 – in J. Lacan, *The Seminar of Jacques Lacan: Anxiety*, Book X, edited and translated by J.A. Miller, Cambridge, Polity, 2016); *The Other Side of Psychoanalysis* (1969–70 – in J. Lacan, *The Seminar of Jacques Lacan: The Other Side of Psychoanalysis*, Book XVII, edited and translated by R. Grigg, New York, NY, W. W. Norton, 2007).

[63]'Every great work of art has two faces: one toward its own time and one toward the future, toward eternity.' – Daniel Barenboim, in E. Said and D. Barenboim, *Parallels and Paradoxes: Explorations in Music and Society*, London, Bloomsbury, 2004, p. 52.

WESTERNIZED MODERNITY

FIGURE 1.5 *Mattheus Greuter,* Le Médecin guarissant Phantasie, purgeant aussi par drogues la folie, *1620.* © *Bibliothèque nationale de France, département Estampes et photographie.*

The end of culture should prepare us to the culture of the end.[64]

We have discussed how the form of 'the world' created by a civilization can fall in and out of darkness, in and out of a historical body. But this is not an automatic process, nor is rebirth assured to every form of worlding and every civilization. Countless cosmologies and metaphysical narratives have been lost in the course of history, either because their successors have shunned them as possible forefathers, or due to the rapid disappearance of their records. Many a world-form have failed to provide anything useful to the creation of a new world out of their ashes. Many others vanished together with the media to which they had entrusted their cultural output.

As seen from the standpoint of today's largest civilization on the planet – which we could call 'Westernized Modernity' – the possibility of an entire world-form being lost forever is cause for serious concern. Questions such as 'What will remain of us?' and 'What will stand the test of the end of our future?' are increasingly pressing on those – like the writer of these lines – who inhabit the world-song of Westernized Modernity. For an unfortunate coincidence, this civilization seems set to fail both the requirements of rebirth – and its world faces the prospect of an annihilation that isn't only historical, but absolute.

Before investigating its possible afterlife, however, let us gain a clearer idea of the traits of this civilization. I will start from the terms with which I have defined it. I used 'Westernized' – rather than the geographical 'Western' – to include all those areas of the world that have adopted a form of Modernity that has Western origins. By 'West', however, we shouldn't intend primarily Europe, with its old transatlantic colonies. The West is a specific concept, deriving from the geopolitical work of the US president James Monroe in the nineteenth century. As Carl Schmitt observed, the very emergence of the term 'the West' was a symptom of the United States' increasing hegemony over old Europe:

> *Strangely enough, the term 'Western Hemisphere' was opposed precisely to Europe, the old West, the old Occident. It was not*

---

[64]*La fine della cultura deve prepararci alla cultura della fine.* From the Autonomist wall-journal *Robinud*, Sesto San Giovanni, MI, Re Nudo, 1974.

opposed to old Asia or to old Africa, but rather to the old West. The new West claimed to be the true West, the true Occident, the true Europe. The new West, America, would supersede the old West, would reorient the old world historical order, would become the center of the earth. The West, and all that belonged to it in the moral, civilizing, and political sense of the word 'Occident,' would neither be eliminated nor destroyed, nor even dethroned, but only displaced. International law ceased to have its center of gravity in old Europe. The center of civilization shifted further west, to America. Like old Asia and old Africa before her, old Europe had become the past.[65]

If 'Westernized' tries to typify a certain, global-American stylistic quality, the term 'Modernity' has to be clarified a little more in detail. Every age is, to its own sense, a 'modern' age. If we had asked a twelfth-century English peasant at which time he was living, he would have certainly answered *'modo'* ('at present', the root of *modernus*). The present is always modern to itself, and thus the definition of modernity seemingly applies to any segment of history – if considered through its own eyes. However, there is a difference between the notion of modernity of the twelfth-century peasant and that of a Westernized-Modern subject. In earlier societies, the present (and by extension, time itself) was understood as a partial aspect of reality. The universe of that peasant would have included his own time-bound modernity, but at the same time it would have placed it alongside the a-temporal eternity of the Divinity. Earlier moderns were moderns only to themselves. Westernized Moderns deem themselves modern *absolutely*. To their civilization, time doesn't only coincide with itself, but also with the totality of what takes place within reality. The Universe of Westernized Modernity doesn't contemplate eternity, and thus within its world-structure there is no room for anything escaping time. Its modernity is not an indexical notion (like the terms 'here' or 'now', which change

---

[65]C. Schmitt, *The Nomos of the Earth: In the International Law of the Jus Publicum Europaeum*, part IV, translated by G.L. Ulmen, New York, NY, Telos Press, 2006, p. 290. For an insightful analysis of the distinction between Europe and the West, see C. Galli, 'Schmitt and the Global Era', in A. Minervini (trans.), *Janus's Gaze: Essays on Carl Schmitt*, Durham and London, Duke University Press, 2015, pp. 97–134 (especially pp. 108–9).

together with perspective), but it is the taxonomical definition of the only age whose time has conquered the Whole of reality.

To look more closely at the qualities of such an ambitious age, though, let us proceed beyond the level of definitions. Since we are observing it through the angle of worlding and of the type of metaphysics that characterize each world-song, let us consider the form of its *cosmos* – departing from the rules and parameters that govern its stage-machines.

Westernized Modernity has structured its mode of worlding around the principle of 'absolute language', acting as the basic benchmark for the totality of the existent. What holds together the civilization of Westernized Modernity, above and beyond its inner differences, is the axiom according to which what 'there is' in the world coincides with what falls neatly within the rules of linguistic classification.

As I have argued at length elsewhere,[66] the operating principles of 'absolute language' can be summarized as follows:

(1)   that language (of any kind, scientific, financial, etc.) is at least potentially capable of describing exhaustively all that there is;

(2)   that what exists is at least potentially describable through some form of language;

(3)   that what is impossible to describe exhaustively through language, does not exist;

(4)   that existence and language coincide, while outside language lies an abyss of pure nothingness.[67]

---

[66]See F. Campagna, *Technic and Magic: The Reconstruction of Reality, Technic's Cosmogony*, London, Bloomsbury, 2018, pp. 57–101.

[67]'The conviction that entities come from nothingness and return to it, that is, the conviction that entities – not-nothings – are nothing, is both supreme Folly and extreme Violence. ... [Such] Violence acts (or believes to be acting) on the basis of the conviction that it can annihilate and produce that which instead is impossible to annihilate, produce, or to create ... Extreme Violence and Folly are the hidden roots out of which grew the history of the West. Based on the faith that entities oscillate between being and nothingness, entities make themselves available to any forces pushing them towards nothingness and towards being: entities are seen as

As structured around the principle of absolute language, Westernized Modernity has produced a world where existence is deprived of any ontological autonomy, becoming instead entirely dependent on the historical, economic and political dynamics of language.

If we wish to explore further the essential character of this civilization, however, we should move even beyond the irradiating force of its first principle, towards the inner motion that animates it. Coherently with its insistence on language, the heart of its mode of worlding can be found at the level of logic: the 'law of non-contradiction', which Westernized Modernity has raised to the status of cosmogonic standard.

According to its earliest formulations, the law of non-contradiction states that 'it is impossible for the same thing to belong and not to belong at the same time to the same thing and in the same respect';[68] 'it is impossible to hold the same thing to be and not to be';[69] and that 'opposite assertions cannot be true at the same time'.[70] These were the rules for an 'orderly' way of thinking, and to this date they still constitute the bedrock of the philosophical discipline of Logic. If applied to existential possibilities, however, and not simply to the content of a proposition or to a concept, this injunction declares, for example, that a person cannot be at the same time human and non-human, female and male, local and foreign, worldly and otherworldly, alive and dead. Beings are arranged along a grid of clear-cut and mutually exclusive identities. It is on the basis of these butchered pieces of existence that Westernized Modernity has established the coincidence between what 'there is',

---

themselves demanding to be violated ... [Only on this basis] we can think of a limitless domination, production and destruction of entities; since, in their being dominated, their essence is not denied (that is, the essence assigned to entities by extreme Folly), while their most profound vocation is supposedly fulfilled. Nihilism is external Violence and Folly.' E. Severino, *Immortalità e Destino*, Milan, Rizzoli, 2008, p. 189 – I have partly used (and revised) the translation offered in E. Severino, *Nihilism and Destiny*, edited by N. Cusano, translated by K.W. Molin, Milan, Mimesis International, 2016, p. 21.

[68] Aristotle, *Metaphysics*, IV, 3, 1005b19–20.
[69] Aristotle, *Metaphysics*, IV, 3, 1005b24.
[70] Aristotle, *Metaphysics*, IV, 6, 1011b13–20.

and what is linguistically classifiable. And, as a corollary, between resistance to classification and a lower intensity of existence.[71]

The law of non-contradiction is a much earlier invention than the onset of Westernized Modernity. But even though it was widely employed by pre-modern Mediterranean scholars, it is only after the sixteenth century that this specialistic element of logic begins to shape the general consensus about what kind of stuff 'there is' in the world. The adoption of this metaphysical principle at the level of common sense marked an epochal shift, comparable to those passages between world-ages sung by mythologists. Indeed, the imposition of the law of non-contradiction upon the existent reshaped the field of what was possible to think, to do and to imagine,

---

[71]'A = A. That is the final answer. But this tautological formula, this life-less, thought-less, and therefore meaningless equality A = A, is, in fact, only a generalization of the self-identity that is inherent in every given ... The law of identity, which pretends to absolute universality, turns out to have a place nowhere at all. This law sees its right in its actual givenness, but every given actually rejects this law *toto genere* ... In excluding all other elements, every A is excluded by all of them, for if each of these elements is for A only not-A, then A over against not-A is only not-not-A. From the viewpoint of the law of identity, all being, in desiring to affirm itself, actually only destroys itself, becoming a combination of elements each of which is a center of negations, and *only* negations. Thus, all being is a total negation, one great "Not." The law of identity is the spirit of death, emptiness, and nothingness ... [The opposition between thing and person] consists in the fact that a thing is characterized through its outer unity, i.e., through the unity of the sum of its features, while a person has his essential character in an inner unity, i.e., in the unity of the activity of self-building, in that very same self-positing of I about which Fichte speaks ... But what is [the] thingness of a person? It is the vacuous self-equality of the person, giving to the person the unity of a *concept* that is self-confined in the combination of its attributes, i.e., the unity of a dead, fixed concept. In other words, it is nothing but the rationalistic "comprehensibility" of a person, i.e., the subordination of a person to the rationalistic law of identity. On the contrary, the personal character of a person, this living unity of his self-building activity, the creative transcending of his self-enclosedness, constitutes his nonsubsumability in any concept, his "incomprehensibility," and therefore his unacceptability for rationalism. It is the victory over the law of identity that raises a person above a lifeless thing and makes him a living center of activity.' P. Florensky, *The Pillar and Ground of the Truth: An Essay in Orthodox Theodicy in Twelve Letters*, translated by B. Jakim, Princeton, NJ, Princeton University Press, 2004, pp. 22–3 and 58–60.

in a similar way to the passage from the kingdom of Chronos the Titan to the regime inaugurated by the Olympian Gods.[72]

To have a clearer sense of the scale of this transformation, let us eavesdrop on the dialogue between Nephele the Cloud and her human lover Ixion, on the eve of the end of the reign of Chronos – imagining instead that it had taken place at the time of the establishment of the law of non-contradiction as a world-ruling principle.

> Cloud: *There is a new law, Ixion. The clouds are gathered by a stronger hand. [...] You can no longer mix yourself with us, nymphs of the streams and the mountains, nor to the daughters of the wind or the goddesses of the earth. Destiny has changed. [...] You were born under the old destiny, for you there are no monsters, only comrades. For you, death is only something that happens, like day and night. [...] You are wholly in your acts. But for them, the immortals, your acts have a meaning that lingers on. They touch everything from afar with their eyes, their lips and nostrils. They are immortals and can't live on their own. [...] And if you disgust them, if by chance you bother them in their Olympus, they storm on you and give you death.*
> Ixion – *So, we can still die.*
> Cloud: *No, Ixion. They will make a shadow out of you, but a shadow that longs for the life it lost and that can never die.*[73] – my translation.

If we were to elect a specific moment for this transformation – and for the creation of a new category of 'monsters' – we could locate it together with the establishment of modern International Relations.

---

[72]According to Greek mythology, the time of the Olympian Gods started after the end of two preceding ages. First came the kingdom of Ouranos, which came to a close when his son, the Titan Chronos, castrated and dethroned him. Then came the 'golden age', under the rule of Chronos, where illness and toil were unknown. The age of the Olympian Gods followed the battle between the Titans faithful to Chronos, and the Gods, Cyclops and Hecatoncheires (giants with one hundred hands) faithful to Zeus. The triumph of the Olympians and Chronos' exile effectively downgraded the world to the 'silver age' – only the first step, according to Greek mythology, in the world's descent towards the abyss of the present 'iron age', the last one before the final conflagration of the Universe and a new beginning.

[73]C. Pavese, 'La Nube', in *Dialoghi con Leucò*, Turin, Einaudi, 2014, pp. 9–11.

The date in question is as precise as only a mythic event: the year 1648, when the parties in the Thirty Years War assembled in the German region of Westphalia to put an end to the hostilities that had devastated the continent. Alongside the innovations introduced by the so-called scientific revolution, the new regime of international relations inaugurated in Westphalia managed to put an end to the turbulent period that followed the fall of the Theocratic Age[74] and to inaugurate a new form of worlding, which lasts to this day.

Among the principles affirmed by the treaties of the peace of Westphalia, central stage was given to the notion of sovereignty, which sanctioned the full autonomy of each state for matters concerning its own territory. On the basis of this principle, every state could advocate an exclusive power over its own subjects and denounce as interference any intervention in its own domestic

---

[74]I call Theocratic Age what is still commonly named Low European Middle Ages – roughly placeable between the eleventh and fifteenth centuries. A re-evaluation of the Medieval period was already ongoing during the Romantic period, but it is only in the twentieth century (arguably since C. H. Haskins's 1927 book *The Renaissance of the Twelfth Century*) that many historians have started to challenge the denomination of 'Middle Ages', as applied to the whole period between the end of Late Antiquity and the beginning of Modernity. Consensus among contemporary historians is that the very definition of 'Middle Ages', which is supposed to cover an entire millennium, should be discarded in favour of a more complex understanding. While I have retained the notion of a Dark or Middle Age to characterize the period between the fifth and the ninth centuries AD, I think that the age that spanned between the Carolingian Renaissance and the Italian Renaissance could be better described, in terms of its form of worlding, as the Theocratic Age. The rationale behind this appellation resides in the two elements that made up that particular world-form: *Theos* (God) and *Cratos* (Power). The time-segment of Charlemagne and of Dante saw the world emerge inside a frame where Heaven and Earth, Justice and Law, God and Power, Pope and Emperor represented two distinct, often conflicting yet complementary metaphysical principles. A similar understanding also subtends Ernst Kantorowiwcz's, *The King's Two Bodies: A Study in Mediaeval Political Theology*, Princeton, NJ, Princeton University Press, 1957, in that the king itself, like all elements in that world, was composed as much of an element of worldly power as of one of submission to, and continuity with, the utterly otherworldly. A clear examination by a contemporary can be found in Dante's 1313 political treatise *De Monarchia* – see Dante, *Monarchy*, translated and edited by P. Shaw, Cambridge, Cambridge University Press, 1996. The great massacres of the sixteenth and seventeenth centuries, both in Europe and in its American colonies, marked the end of that age and the arrival over the same territories of another Medieval interregnum – until the establishment of a new hegemonic form of worlding, after the peace of Westphalia.

affairs.[75] Perhaps the clearest expression of this notion can be found in Hegel's philosophy of the state:

> *The nation state* [das Volk als Staat] *is the spirit in its substantial rationality and immediate actuality, and is therefore the absolute power on* earth; *each state is consequently a sovereign and independent entity in relation to others. The state has a primary and absolute entitlement to be a sovereign and independent power* in the eyes of others, *i.e.* to be recognized by them. [...] *The state is the actuality of the substantial* will, *an actuality which it possesses in the particular* self-consciousness *when this has been raised to its universality; as such, it is the* rational *in and for itself. This substantial unity is an absolute and unmoved end in itself, and in it, freedom enters into its highest right, just as this ultimate end possesses the highest right in relation to individuals* [die Einzelnen], *whose* highest duty *is to be members of the state ... Since the state is objective spirit, it is only through being a member of the state that the individual* [Individuum] *himself has objectivity, truth, and ethical life.*[76]

The absolute power of each state over its territory translated politically the principle of non-contradiction. It became possible – if not required – to conceive of sovereign entities as entirely unbound by any external influence (whether that of *Ananke*, the Divine Necessity that rules all things, or of the universalism of Renaissance Humanism, or of any otherworldly divinity). It became standard policy to punish as treason any claim to multiple allegiances, and to deride as superstition the belief in ineffable presences that might defy the laws imposed by worldly powers. Everything in its right place – where the only possible 'right place' is as a unique placeholder in a well-defined series.

---

[75]The ham-fistedness with which supposedly universalist 'humanitarian' arguments have been instrumentalized to support various, recent military interventions testifies to the actual alienness of any universalist ethical notion to the politics of Westernized Modernity. For a critique of the contemporary pseudo-humanitarian arguments used to support military interventions, see E. Weizman, *The Least of All Possible Evils: Humanitarian Violence from Arendt to Gaza*, London/New York, Verso, 2011.
[76]G.W.F. Hegel, *Elements of the Philosophy of Right*, Section 3, *The State*, 331 and 258, edited by A.W. Wood, translated by H.B. Nisbet, Cambridge, Cambridge University Press, 2003, pp. 366–7 and 275–6.

On the basis of the metaphysical principles outlined in 1648, the civilization of Westernized Modernity proceeded to create even more stringent entities – from the naturalization of the idea of nation, which binds the entire world to a metaphysical (and not just political) grid of belongings, to the classification of the most minute sets of sovereign identities, mutually exclusive in their respective fields. Even religion, as reinterpreted through this perspective, was made to abandon its mystical dimension and to transform God from an ineffable mystery to yet-another sovereign power sui generis.[77]

Thanks to this metaphysical agreement disguised as a political treaty, then-emerging capitalism could count on a well-suited system of cataloguing, organization and stock-management – while newly born police forces had at their disposal an effective method of profiling, selection and control.[78] In the course of the time-segment inaugurated in Westphalia, the societies that adopted this cosmology have traversed a historical arch replete with technological marvels and scientific breakthroughs, and occasionally blessed by advancements in the field of civil and political rights. At the same time, however, this form of worlding has created the conditions for modern colonialism, the prison-industrial system, totalitarianism, total warfare, nuclear weapons and, most evidently, for a devastation of the global biosphere that has already led to a wave of mass extinctions.

Everything works; only the human no longer does.[79]

Like any other metaphysical narration – and indeed like any form of storytelling – also that of Westernized Modernity is not destined

---

[77]On the tension between Westernized Modernity and the ineffable notion of the divine, see in particular R. Guenon, *The Reign of Quantity and the Signs of the Times*, translated by Lord Northbourne, Hillsdale, NY, Sophia Perennis, 2002.

[78]The first centrally organized police force was created in 1667 by Louis XIV to control the city of Paris, while the first modern police force was inaugurated by the West Indies merchants in London in 1797. For a recent critical history of policing (in addition to the essential M. Foucault, *Discipline and Punish: The Birth of the Prison*, translated by A. Sheridan, London, Penguin, 1991), see M. Neocleous, *A Critical Theory of Police Power: The Fabrication of the Social Order*, London/New York, Verso, 2020.

[79]H. Ball, *Die Flucht aus der Zeit*, Munchen, Duncker & Humblot, 1927 – my translation from the Italian edition, H. Ball, *Fuga dal Tempo: fuga saeculi*, translated by R. Caldura, Milan, Mimesis, 2016, p. 125.

to last forever. The time-segment of its past–present–future is contained between a beginning and an end. For all its might and its hegemony over large parts of the globe, a multitude of elements seems to indicate that its historical arch might be reaching already the last stretch of its course. A feeling of the 'end of the future'[80] has already set the imaginative atmosphere of the past few decades of Westernized Modernity, while a growing number of global voices have soared to demand for its abolition. Among the more conservative strata of society, the awareness of an impending end has been phobically associated with phenomena such as the increasing technologization of the world, the loss of primacy of the human, the blurring of sexual and gender boundaries and the great movements of people crisscrossing the planet. It is worth considering these objects of concern – in part because there is some truth to their connection with the closure of this age and in part because of the disturbing political effects of such a conservative resistance to their arising.

Nostalgics of the heydays of industrialism often stress the risks posed to Westernized Modernity by the digitization of the economy, and by the substitution of robotic equipment to human workforce. Contrary to this view, however, these two phenomena in fact reinforce, rather than weakening, its metaphysical tenets. The replacement of the so-called physical sphere with digital environments falls perfectly in line with a world-structure that is faithful to the principle of absolute language. Likewise, the substitution of human agents with AI systems is merely the application of the notion of sovereignty to Capital – the successor on the same throne that used to be occupied by the State – and ensures that the autonomy of its dominion is guaranteed in every aspect.

The greatest imperilment to sovereignty, as elaborated after Westphalia, used to consist in the fractured form of human consciousness – always capable of doubting itself, questioning its allegiances, wishing its own annihilation and fleeing towards an implausible elsewhere. Substituting consciousnesses with the intelligence of artificial systems guarantees that today's hegemonic

---

[80]For a wide-raging exploration of how the idea of the 'end of the future' took hold of Westernized history after the 1970s, see F. Berardi 'Bifo', *After the Future*, Edinburgh, AK Press, 2011; and F. Berardi 'Bifo', *Futurability: The Age of Impotence and the Horizon of Possibility*, London/New York, Verso, 2017.

power gains at last full sovereignty over its own subjects. The AI worker constitutes the ideal inhabitant of Westernized Modernity, in the same way that the armed drone, incapable of feeling the consequences of their actions, fulfils the role of Modern soldier much better than its defective human colleagues. Ultimately, the suspicion harboured by many self-declared defenders of Westernized Modernity towards the latest technological developments is misplaced. The establishment of an autonomous robotic police force and the expulsion of the ineffable spark of consciousness from the world constitute the accomplishment, not the denial, of the metaphysics of this civilization.

Two other conservative concerns, however, come closer to the target. Both the phenomena which they address, although not new in themselves, have only recently acquired a significant status within the social discourse. These are the opening of contemporary metaphysics to the idea of 'non-human people',[81] and the diffused social praxis of challenging ingrained binary notions – typically those referring to gender and sexual identity. The former cultural position is gaining traction thanks to a growing awareness of the effects of Climate Change and of the urgency of tackling a problem that seems insoluble within the current metaphysical parameters. The movement towards a fluid understanding of gender and sexual identity, for its part, has succeeded in exploding the inner contradiction between the metaphysics of Westernized Modernity and the ideal of 'freedom' which for a long time has been heralded as its ethical foundation.

These two phenomena authentically challenge today's hegemonic form of worlding, and they propose to break with the rhythm of its time-segment. Signs of this metaphysical friction abound in contemporary culture, and they may be epitomized by a question routinely asked by journalists to people who have transitioned between genders – 'did you already feel like a man/woman before transitioning?' Such a question assumes a form of temporality that is linear, non-contradictory, and a metaphysics that is based on the coincidence between events and facts. The phenomenon

---

[81]I am borrowing this definition from Timothy Morton, currently the main theoretician in this field – see T. Morton, *Humankind: Solidarity with Non-Human People*, London/New York, Verso, 2017.

of transition presents a form of worlding that is incompatible with the one presently hegemonic, and thus it appears all the more incomprehensible to those anchored to the world-form of Westernized Modernity.

An equally strong blow to contemporary metaphysics comes from the personification of non-humans, which transforms the idea of person from a taxonomical notion (only such and such entities are people), to an indexical one (to exist means to inhabit, as a person, the centre of projection of a particular perspective towards the rest of the existent). As in the cosmology of Amerindian tribes like the Amazonian Yanomami:

> *Every existent being in the cosmos thus sees itself as a human, but does not see other species in the same way. (Needless to say, this also applies to our own species.) 'Humanity' is therefore at once a universal condition and strictly dietic, self-referential perspective. Different species cannot occupy the point of view of 'I' simultaneously, owing to deictic restrictions; in every confrontation here and now between two species, it is inevitable that one will finish by imposing its humanity on the other, that is, that it will finish by making the other 'forget' its own humanity. This entails that we humans (Amerindian humans, that is) do not see animals as humans. They are not human for us; but we know that they are humans for themselves. We know just as well that we are not humans for them ... Like all human beings – or more precisely: like all animals – Amerindians must eat or in some way destroy other forms of life in order to live. They know that human action inevitably leaves an ecological footprint. Differently to us, however, the ground on which they leave their footprints is equally alive and alert.*[82]

When non-contradictory identities cease to function as the absolute denomination of things, and subjectivity spreads across boundaries

---

[82]E. Viveiros de Castro and D. Danowski, *The Ends of the World*, translated by R. Nunes, Cambridge, Polity, 2017, pp. 70–1. For an account of Perspectivism, as read through an anthropological lens and in relation to the world-form of Amerindian cosmology, see E. Viveiros de Castro, *Cannibal Metaphysics*, edited and translated by P. Skafish, Minneapolis, MN, Minnesota University Press, 2014.

as the commonwealth of each and all, the cosmogonic narrative of
Westernized Modernity progressively grinds to a halt.

Thus, there is some truth to those reactionary discourses that
indicate (trans)gender theory and a post-anthropocentric sensitivity
as the nemesis of the civilization of Westernized Modernity. And
yet, their belonging to the sphere of culture touches conservative
sensibilities less deeply than the prime object of today's political
paranoia: the arrival of migrant 'others' from beyond the borders.

In political terms, this obsession with the danger of migrations
discounts the lesson of history. If we observe previous instances
of peaceful 'movements of people'[83] into the territory of a
civilization, the risks associated with it infallibly derived from
the failures and shortcomings of the civilization at the receiving
end – rather than from an innate danger posed by migrants. To
mention just the most renowned example, a dramatic event such
as the battle of Adrianople in AD 378 – where 20,000 Roman
soldiers and the emperor Valens himself were massacred by an
organized group of migrant Goths – ensued from a period of cruel
mismanagement of migration flows. For the first time after a long
period of intermingling, Gothic migrants had been imprisoned
within refugee zones along the borders of the empire, where over
the course of months they had been exploited and starved to such
an extent that they had started selling their own children and
themselves into slavery (with great profit of the Roman merchants
and landowners). The pressure of Hunnic raiders from the North,
and the sheer desperation in which these people versed, led to
rebellion and to the battle that inaugurated the final debacle of the
Western Roman Empire. The Roman world collapsed from within,
due to a series of internal economic and political failures, among
which featured the erosion of a system of open migration that had
been running for centuries.[84]

---

[83] *Völkerwanderung*, 'movements of people' (German translation of the Latin *migratio
gentium*), is the denomination assigned by German historians to the phenomenon
most commonly defined in textbooks as the 'barbaric invasions'.
[84] For a discussion of the context of the Battle of Adrianople and of its political
significance, see A. Barbero, *9 Agosto 378: Il Giorno dei Barbari*, Bari, Laterza, 2012.

Although the decline of Westernized Modernity cannot be attributed to the influence of migrants as a socio-political entity, the metaphysical impact on a civilization of other forms of worlding, arriving from beyond its frontiers, shouldn't be neglected. The increasing presence of people whose primary form of worlding is 'other' is already producing an early syncretic mix with the metaphysical model proposed by Westernized Modernity. In the long run, their combination will cause a dilution of both original forms – and this will constitute the best opportunity, for either civilization, to build a vessel on which to reach a new time after the end of their future.

The phenomena explored so far are all significant aspects of contemporary history, but their ability to prove the coming demise of Westernized Modernity remains limited. Ultimately, they reveal more of the phobic mindset of those who oppose them, than of the impending closure of the historical arc of an entire civilization. Unfortunately for those who have invested their paranoid energies towards them, the end of Westernized Modernity as a hegemonic form of worlding might occur much earlier than the full deployment of these cultural transformations.

The key to its collapse can be found in the symbiosis that this form of worlding has established with its own techno-economic system. If we listen to the voices singing out the cosmology of Westernized Modernity, we won't find them arising from the millions who suffer under its regime – and whose subservience to its metaphysics is not an endorsement, but a scar. For the reproduction of its narrative, Westernized Modernity relies entirely on a techno-economic system, spread across a planetary network of exchange, control and industry. The structure of its form of worlding, the specific separations which it imposes between things and the flow of its own particular time are embedded in the rhythm imposed on workers by the economic gatekeepers, on travellers by the controllers of the boundaries of citizenship and on all subjects of Modernity by the relentless cultural production of trainers and entertainers.

Such an enormous machine, bridling together countless energies into one complex mesh, is as hard to smash as it is easy to unravel. Was this techno-economic system ever to come to a long halt, the world-form which is presently hegemonic would rapidly find itself without rhapsodes singing its story: its spell over reality would remain orphan of a voice, and it would vanish together with the

time-segment that it has created. The sinews holding together its
metaphysical broadcast span over oceans and continents, reaching
into the depths of the Earth and in the recess of living consciousness.
The power of extraction and recombination deployed by this system
is impressive, but its extreme degree of intra-dependence makes
apparent an element of fragility. Like an organism, it is sufficient
that a single string of crucial connections becomes inoperative and
the entire system rapidly slows down to the point of stalling.

An event of catastrophic proportions, massive enough to break
or to suspend the infrastructures between the main nodes of today's
socio-economic system, would be sufficient to take away the
sustenance, not only of contemporary society, but also of its form
of worlding. We had a very mild example of this in 2020, with
the Coronavirus outbreak and its rippling effects on the economy
and society.[85] But that pandemic shouldn't be held as a benchmark
of future catastrophes. History teaches us that greater plagues are
always in store, while worse threats are already looming on the
horizon.

The new regime of scarcity inaugurated by climate change,
combined with the widespread availability of nuclear weapons,
already points to the growing probability of such an event in the
foreseeable future. In the absence of functioning international
mechanisms of mediation – a role at one point performed by the
assembly of the United Nations – increasing scarcity will seamlessly
turn into conflict, and this in turn will damage the infrastructures of
the global economy; and then again, *da capo*. Once the extraction
of materials necessary to keep going the world's technology and
its cosmogonic narration will have been suspended and the
infrastructure of its network broken, the desperate resort to nuclear
weapons will damage irreparably what shall be left of the system of
Westernized Modernity.

The metaphysical narrative of this civilization is destined to end
simultaneously with its techno-economic prostheses – not despite,
but precisely because of their impressive scale. And an interim
period of feeble and unstable worlding shall ensue. Reality will

---

[85]Both still ongoing at the time of writing.

show itself again in its rawest state: wordless, timeless, senseless, foreign. A new Dark Age shall cover the domains of Westernized Modernity, as widespread and distributed across the planet as these are today. Deprived of the technologies of the age of Westernized Modernity, the Dark Age to come will probably be a less destructive period than our present.

Less destructive, perhaps, but certainly more terrifying.

CHAPTER TWO

OTHERWORLDS

FIGURE 2.1 *Giovanni Domenico Tiepolo*, Punchinello Carried off by a Centaur (Pulcinella rapito da un centauro), *1791–1804*. © *Trustees of the British Museum, The British Museum.*

PROLOGUE
ANAMORPHOSIS

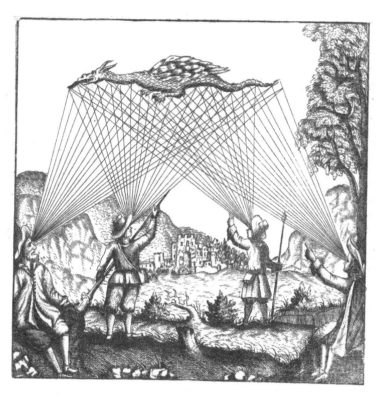

FIGURE 2.2 *Johann Zahn, illustration from* Oculus Artificialis Teledioptricus Sive Telescopium *(The Long-Distance Artificial Eye, or Telescope), 1685.*

Shadow, properly understood, is the diminution of light
applied to the surface of bodies, whose origin is
in the end of light, and whose end is in darkness.[1]

At age twenty, Leonardo da Vinci was working as an assistant in the bottega of the Florentine artist Andrea del Verrocchio. Legend has it that upon seeing that young man paint so prodigiously, Verrocchio abandoned painting and dedicated himself only to sculpture. But Leonardo was still waiting to show his talents outside of his boss's workshop. When a commission finally arrived for him from a small church just outside Florence, it was his first chance to cast a light of his own. The object of the painting had to be the Annunciation, that is, the moment when the archangel Gabriel descends on Earth to tell the Virgin Mary that she is expecting the son of God. A few months later, the painting (now in the Uffizi Gallery in Florence) was finally ready to be placed in a modest suburban church. As soon as it was raised to its assigned place, at mid-height on a side wall, Leonardo's painting suddenly lost a defect that had been visible throughout the stages of preparation: if seen frontally, the image of the Virgin Mary seemed deformed, with an arm too elongated and a broken wrist. Only when looked from below, and slightly to the right, the image acquires again natural proportions.

With his *Annunciation*, Leonardo recuperated a style of *anamorphosis* which had long remained an anecdotal oddity from ancient times. Roman author Pliny the Elder and medieval historian Ioannes Tzetzes spoke of a contest, which took place in the fifth century BC between the Greek sculptors Phidias and Alcamenes, to build a monumental statue of Athena. During the weeks of labour in the workshops, Alcamenes's statue had impressed the judges for its perfection, while Phidias's work had appeared monstrous in its grotesque proportions. Once both had been mounted on pillars, however, the decelerated perspective suddenly made Phidias's

---

[1] *L'ombra, nominata per il suo proprio vocabolo, e' da esser chiamata alleviazione di lume applicato alla superficie de' corpi, della quale il principo e' nel fine della luce, ed il fine e' nelle tenebre.* My own translation. For further reading, see Leonardo da Vinci, *Trattato della Pittura*, Che cosa e' ombra, 533, Catania, Brancato, 1990, p. 237.

Athena beautiful, and Alcamenes's ugly.[2] Unlike his rival, Phidias understood that the Divinity's 'true' beauty would have become apparent to human onlookers, only on condition of sacrificing its 'actual' perfection.

Leonardo's recuperation ignited an explosion of anamorphic drawings, engravings and paintings – spanning from Han Holbein's *The Ambassadros*, through Andrea Pozzo's astounding ceiling for the church of St. Ignatius of Loyola at Campus Martius in Rome, to modern Surrealist art and beyond.

> *[An early example is] a* Vexierbild *(puzzle-picture) by Erhard Schön (1491–1552), [which] is formed of four trapezoidal rows in which striped hatchings are continued by landscapes peopled with living figures. Town and hills, men and animals are reabsorbed and engulfed in a tangle of lines, at first sight inexplicable. But by placing the eyes at the side and very close to the engraving one can see four superimposed heads inside rectilinear frames. Perspective causes the apparent images to disappear and at the same time the hidden outlines to appear. The human figures are perfectly identifiable: the Emperor Charles V, Ferdinand I of Austria, Francis I and Pope Clement VII. German and Latin inscriptions which are executed in the same way give their names. Clear, precise profiles emerge from linear chaos. While preserving a thematic unity, the design combines two different pictures in one ...*
>
> *This superimposition causes a disconcerting phenomenon which takes on a symbolic meaning. The features of the hidden royal effigies disturb the topographical sites. They hover over countries and over scenes of historical vicissitudes like phantoms covering vast tracts of land. The vision takes place in an agitated landscape, marked by the sovereign power which it conceals. It is at once a drama and a piece of witchcraft.[3]*

---

[2]This story is recounted in several modern accounts, including J.F. Niceron, *La Perspective Curieuse*, Paris, 1638, p. 12; A. Kircher, *Ars Magna*, Rome, 1646, p. 192; A. Kircher, *Ars Magna*, Rome, 1646, p. 192; F. Blondel, *Cours d'Architecture Enseigne dans l'Academie Royale*, Paris, 1675–83, pp. 709–10; J. Baltrušaitis, *Anamorphic Art*, translated by W.J. Strachan, New York, NY, Harry N. Abrams, Inc, 1977, p. 8.

[3]J. Baltrušaitis, *Anamorphic Art*, translated by W.J. Strachan, New York, NY, Harry N. Abrams, Inc, 1977, pp. 11–12.

AESTHETICS AND ANNIHILATION

FIGURE 2.3 *Simon Fokke,* The First Flare in the Amsterdamschen Schouwburg, Happened on Monday the 11 May 1772 in the Evening Just after Half Past Eight, *1772. © Gemeente Amsterdam Stadsarchief.*

You are nobody mixed with nothing.[4]

A glitch is ignored; a disruption is co-opted within the system; a catastrophe devours everything beyond repair.

Delicate electronic hardware degrades fast, and its maintenance proves impossible without today's hyper-complex system of extraction and supply. Digital content corrupts even faster, dragging out of existence the possibility that any echoes might remain of the world from which it sprung. When the material conditions keeping its hardware operative will have collapsed, the digital archives to which this civilization has entrusted its cultural legacy will also vanish. As soon as the storages of contemporary culture will be deprived of a seamless supply of rare metals, electricity and skilled labour-force, they will become inaccessible once and for all – as absent as if they had never existed. More fragile than the papyri of the ancient world, the immense wealth of digitized culture hangs to a thread, depending for its survival on the continuation of the techno-economic settings of this civilization. The treasure of this society, obsessed with data, will be the first victim of annihilation, once its historical body will have exhaled its last breath.

More material media won't offer a safer shelter. The millions of books published in the past few decades won't be able to count on their paper for a long resilience. Already today, most paperback editions of the past century disintegrate at the touch. However well made, books will follow the typical destiny of their kind: in the best scenario, the survival rate of contemporary bookish culture will be comparable to the massacre that has befallen ancient culture.[5] After

---

[4]*Tu sì nuddu mmiscatu cu' nienti*, Sicilian insult.
[5]Only a very small percentage of literary works from classical antiquity has survived to the present day. 'According to Gerstinger [H. Gerstinger, *Bestand und Überlieferung der Literaturwerke des griechisch-römischen Altertums*, Graz, Kienreich, 1948, p. 10], about 2000 Greek authors were known by name before the discovery of papyri. But the complete works of only 136 (6.8%) and fragments of another 127 (6.3%) were preserved. Gerstinger counted, however, only authors whose names were known, not works known by their titles. The numerical relation between these and the works that are preserved wholly or partially would certainly even be much worse.' R. Blum, *Kallimachos: The Alexandrian Library and the Origins of Bibliography*, translated by H.H. Wellisch, Madison, WI, The University of Wisconsin Press, 1991, f. 34, p. 13.

the end of Westernized Modernity, only a microscopic fraction of the words, images and sounds currently accessible via electronic or paper support will remain available to be rediscovered ever again.

Unlike the monumental civilizations of antiquity, the world of Westernized Modernity will leave behind itself very little architectural legacy. Under a secular capitalist system, the materials employed for construction have long abided to the lowest possible denominator of quality and endurance. Left without maintenance, the forests of apartment blocks in contemporary cities are destined to crumble rapidly into mounds of concrete, plastic and rust. Even the towers of glass and steel – today's surrogate for the lacking monuments – will soon collapse into unwalkable fields of shards and spikes. Of this civilization, little will remain but the scars that it has inflicted on the natural environment. Islands of plastic across the oceans, garbage dumps, nuclear spills, man-made deserts will be the only rhapsodes left to sing the life and the metaphysics of billions of people and to testify for their legacy. Once the waste and residues of material culture will have taken over the absence of any other form of culture, the vision that tormented Andy Warhol will have achieved at last its grim realization.

Possibly, some will be relieved by the prospect of this annihilation. Aside from its bold technical conquests and its timid ethical progress – they might object – was there ever much else, in the metaphysical narrative of this world, that deserved to survive its historical arch? Immense has been the price for the modest advancements towards happiness that have been achieved by this age. A weirdly inefficient cost for a society that is devoted to the principle of efficiency.

Others, again, might respond with Miles Davis: 'So What.' What exactly is the problem – they might contend – if the inhabitants of this civilization will fail to deliver anything of use to the creation of a new world? Every subject has the power to leave behind themselves a desert, and to 'call it peace'.[6] No bearded divinity enthroned in the sky can decree that it should have been done otherwise.

---

[6]'They plunder, they butcher, they ravish and call it under the lying name of "empire". They make a desert and call it "peace".' Tacitus, 'Agricola', 30, in A. Birley (trans.), *Agricola and Germany*, Oxford, Oxford University Press, 1999, p. 22.

The problem at hand, however, has little to do with the worthiness of Westernized Modernity, or with the possibility of opportunistic behaviours in the absence of punishment. The reduction of the cultural legacy of an entire civilization to environmental pollution and mass-extinctions should concern anyone who is somehow bound to its fortunes. Aside from a narcissistic wish to survive one's own death, our very experience of life is already being affected by the proximity of this scenario.

To appreciate the urgency of this problem, it is necessary that we trace back the steps that connect the legacy of one's own culture with the inner mechanisms of our everyday metaphysics. Let us return for a moment to the way in which every subject creates for themselves the landscape of a world out of the barrenness of pure existence.

Creating a world for oneself implies establishing a set of metaphysics declaring 'this' and 'that' to be real, and the rest to be unreal. Reality is created by filtering the avalanche of ineffable perceptions, and these in turn are translated linguistically into the form of the world. The ongoing act of world-creation pulls the encyclopaedia of the world out of a state in which there is no language and no 'things'. Every act of worlding is an instance of creation ex nihilo (out of nothing): as when a piece of music starts, it breaks the silence with a sound that lacks any comparative. In its fundamental primitiveness, the song of the world is *the* aesthetic act par excellence. It has no previous logic or ethics to which it can appeal – rather, it creates them as the harmonic consequence of its own melody. Before the *sequitur* of logic, before meta-ethics[7] has even

---

[7]'[Metaethics] is not about what people ought to do. It is about what they are doing when they talk about what they ought to do.' W. Hudson, *Modern Moral Philosophy*, London, Macmillan, 1970, p. 1. On the distinction between ethics and metaethics, see this brief account by Alexander Miller: 'Normative ethics seeks to discover the general principles underlying moral practice, and in this way potentially impacts upon practical moral problems: different general principles may yield different verdicts in particular cases. [On the contrary, metaethics is] concerned with questions about the following: 1) Meaning: what is the semantic function of moral discourse? Is the function of moral discourse to state facts, or does it have some other non-fact-stating role?; 2) Metaphysics: do moral facts (or properties) exist? If so, what are they like? Are they identical or irreducible to natural facts (or properties) or are they irreducible ad *sui generis*?; 3) Epistemology: is there such

had a chance to cast its net, every system of sense requires an act of foundation that is axiomatic – and thus, aesthetic. The process that holds up a world, at any moment in our own life, is but an aesthetic endeavour. Like Euclid at the beginning of his discourse on geometry in the *Elements*, each of us at any moment bases the unfolding of their own cosmological narration over decisions taken by *arbitrium*.[8]

The act of foundation of the world – the *fiat lux* that brings a world out of the onslaught of raw perceptions – is not only the main aesthetic act, but also the most frequent. Repeated at each instant, it remains axiomatic in every distinction between things, subjects and landscapes. The process of worlding brings the subject to the immediate proximity of their own perceptions (*aisthetika*), and it allows them to reshape their landscape through intuition alone.

If living inside the phenomenon – cut away from the ungraspable 'thing itself' – amounts to a fall from grace, then aesthetics comes to our rescue like a benevolent demiurge. We owe aesthetics the substance of our days, and the metaphysics that we adopt to dissect them. And since aesthetics expresses itself through worlding, it endows this activity with the status of the ultimate ancestor of all tools.[9] Like an ancestor, the process of worlding demands to be

---

a thing as moral knowledge? How can we know whether our moral judgements are true or false?; 4) Phenomenology: how are moral qualities represented in the experience of an agent making a moral judgement? Do they appear to be "out there" in the world?; 5) Moral Psychology: what can we say about the motivational state of someone making a moral judgement? What sort of connection is there between making a moral judgement and being motivated to act as that judgement prescribes?; 6) Objectivity: can moral judgements really be correct or incorrect? Can we work towards finding out the moral truth?' A. Miller, *Contemporary Metaethics*, Cambridge, Polity, 2017, p. 2.

[8] The sudden and brutal realization of this arbitrariness and axiomaticity of the world emerges during anxiety and panic attacks, as well as in moments of inactive boredom – as discussed by Heidegger in his 1929–30 lecture series 'The Fundamental Concepts of Metaphysics', see M. Heidegger, *The Fundamental Concepts of Metaphysics: World, Finitude, Solitude*, translated by W. McNeill and N. Walker, Bloomington, IN, Indiana University Press, 2001.

[9] I use the term 'tool' here in the sense given by Georges Simondon to technology as a means to individuation – see G. Simondon, *On the Mode of Existence of Technical Objects*, translated by C. Malaspina and J. Rogove, Minneapolis, MN, University of Minnesota Press, 2017; and G. Simondon, *Individuation in Light of Notions of Form and Information*, translated by T. Adkins, Minneapolis, MN, University of Minnesota Press, 2020.

acknowledged – and like a tool, it requires users to recognize its agency and to follow its inner rules. In the same way that we have to respect the requirements of logic to be able to proceed with our intra-worldly arguments, so in igniting at each instant the very form of 'the world' we are bound to consider the one wish that belongs to the Genie of aesthetics.

This is a simple demand, perfectly in line with those of any other system of sense: the *conatus*[10] of aesthetics is for its own reproduction. Logic demands that its flow is kept crystalline and uninterrupted; and aesthetics asks its adopters that the light of creation is not smothered after the death of each spark. Differently from linguistic systems like logic or ethics, however, aesthetics doesn't reclaim for itself an infinite proliferation. It only asks for one more: another chance, after the end of a story, to start a different story anew; another possibility for the world to start again over the settled ashes of a catastrophe.

A true catastrophe awaits those who fail the only demand of the aesthetic machine. Its threat is much worse than that waved by the process of logic, whose betrayal leads to the impossibility of linearly directing one's thought and action. When the aesthetic machine ceases to function, it is not the subject who vanishes, but the world around them. An awareness that has become incapable of suspending its disbelief in front of their own projection of the world, and that has lost the ability to extract a narrative meaning from its own intuition, has become the prisoner of a game turned into torture. It is, literally, in Hell.[11] Aesthetics' demand to a civilization

---

[10]Intended in the sense of an innate wish of any agency to perpetuate its own being. 'Each thing, in so far as it lies in itself, endeavours to persevere in its being.' B. Spinoza, *Ethics*, part 3, prop. 6, translated by W.H. White and A.H. Stirling, Ware, Wordsworth Editions, 2001, p. 105.

[11]'[Julius asked his Master;] must not the Soul leave the Body at Death, and go either to Heaven or Hell?No, replied the venerable Theophorus ... The Soul has Heaven and Hell within itself already ...Here Julius said to his Master; This is difficult to understand. Doesn't it enter into Heaven or Hell, as a man enters into a House, does it not into another World?The Master spoke and said; No, there is no such kind of entering in; because Heaven and Hell are everywhere, and universally co-exist.' J. Boehme, 'Heaven and Hell', in *The Way to Christ*, translated by P.C. Erb, Mahwah, NJ, Paulist Press, 1977, p. 182.

and its inhabitants is utterly inescapable, lest the brief thrill of nihilism develops into catatonia. A world that was about to close its own story without an act of solidarity towards the world that will come would immediately unravel at its core. Like a tempest that's looming beyond anyone's reach, it would be impossible to inhabit it and unimaginable to escape it.

The wrath of aesthetics pushes its people towards a specific possibility of imagining the good. This is how aesthetics creates its own implicit ethics, and how the operational rules of its machine turn into existential directions. There is a term that has long been used to define this form of aesthetic ethics, although it has long lost that meaning: nobility (*aristeia*). To be aesthetically noble (*aristos*) doesn't mean turning one's own life into a closed work of art. As it happens to the adepts of spiritual chivalry,[12] living nobly consists in aiding the explosion of 'other' creations alongside and beyond one's own: to act as combustible in the aesthetic engine, out of which all possible worlds are projected.

At the time when a certain world-story still resounds strongly, aesthetic nobility demands that every subject sustaining that narration learns how to 'live well'. During such expansive stretches of time, the emergence of new stories is projected within the framework of a deep and wide future, where countless variations are still possible. Like the utopianists of mid-modernity, the noble living inside a strong world strive to keep the future open and to explore the canals that lead back to its reservoirs of dreams.

Upon those who live at the tail end of a world-form, however, nobility demands something a little more difficult. Aesthetics

---

[12]For a discussion of the *futuwwah* (spiritual chivalry) in Shiism, see H. Corbin, *History of Islamic Philosophy*, translated by L. Sherrard, Abingdon, Routledge, 2014, pp. 290–1, and 311–12; H. Corbin, *En Islam Iranien: Aspects spirituels et philosophiques*, vol. 3, *Les Fideles d'Amour, Shi'isme et Soufisme*, Paris, Gallimard, 1991; and P. Laude, *Pathways to an Inner Islam: Massignon, Corbin, Guenon, and Schuon*, Albany, NY, SUNY, 2010, pp. 156–8. A similar notion of spiritual chivalry animates also modern works such as R. Daumal, *Mount Analogue: An Authentic Narrative*, translated by R. Shattuck, San Francisco, CA, City Lights Books, 1971; H. Hesse, *The Journey to the East*, translated by H. Rosner, London, Peter Owen, 2007; and E. Jünger, *On the Marble Cliffs*, Harmondsworth, Penguin, 1970, among others.

imposes upon them the task of learning how to 'die well'. To master the art, not of opening the future, but of closing it.

As the world of Westernized Modernity moves to its final consumption – after a brief period of denial, disguised by the self-appellation of 'the contemporary'[13] – its story enters a stage where the only meaningful aspiration is to see beyond the approaching horizon of the end, towards that which shall come.

> *It is necessary to overcome the mournful situation – this is the command of the work of condolence. If this situation truly makes us prisoners, and the death of a loved one doesn't turn into our own choosing their death ... then we begin to die ourselves, together with what is dead. And in the impossible alternative of rolling back historical time we end up losing that moral power, which, by deciding on alternatives, makes possible our being-in-the-world. Who is unable to overcome a critical situation becomes its prisoner, and suffers its tyranny: a presence that is left without any margin before the mournful situation loses the fluidity, operability and planning of mundane becoming ... We become the dead, and our despair or our terror. The dead not killed by the living tend to return in an insolvent way, perhaps with a mask that makes them unrecognizable, and they contaminate the whole front of possible situations in real life.*[14]

To die well doesn't mean simply to abandon the stage of the world with the grace of someone who lets go: although a good medicine for those who can stomach it, this course of action is of little value to those who are left to keep on worlding. Learning how to die well requires the ability to mourn one's own death and to recognize, beyond the veil of time and of death, one same thread running through all forms of existence. It means including within one's own

---

[13]In a 'contemporary' time, death is negated by the freezing of time into the un-passing, contemporary 'now'. Eternity is denied and history is frozen in a moment where everything passes, but which in itself does not pass – but that is nonetheless locked within the movement of history.

[14]E. de Martino, *La Fine del Mondo: contributo all'analisi delle apocalissi culturali*, Turin, Einaudi, 2002, pp. 263–4 – my translation.

vision also the invisible presence of those who live – or shall live – in altogether 'other' worlds and time-segments. 'Those who are about to die' dedicate to these others the care that is usually reserved to one's own kin. The nobility of the *morituri* rests in closing their story in such a way as to create a possible trampoline for those who will have to start narrating a world anew. Such an injunction to 'die well' is immediately apparent in its ecological dimension – where responsibility requests that the environmental balance in the biosphere is neither devastated nor frozen, but that it is allowed to keep on changing again and again. In the same way and with equal urgency, however, it applies also to the cultural legacy that we will leave behind ourselves.

The urgent necessity of creating new works of 'traditional' culture should be understood in this sense. Like its root *tradere* (to hand over), 'tradition' has more to do with movement than with an archival conservation of past practices. Its realm is the inter-generational bridge of solidarity, where people from different worlds can aid each other to experience reality anew and as if for the first time.[15] Tradition touches upon the bare thread of reality, out of which every subject draws the form of the world and the rhythm of each instant. By leaving a legacy that might support the creation of a new story over the ashes of the old, a helping hand is stretched to those who will have to create a world ex nihilo, without the ease of living within a pre-existing frame of sense.

---

[15]A very important – although not unproblematic – work on the notion of tradition has been developed in the twentieth century by thinkers in the milieu of Perennial Philosophy. See in particular E. Zolla, *Che Cos'e' la Tradizione*, Milan, Adelphi, 1998; and R. Guenon, *Introduction to the Study of the Hindu Doctrines*, translated by M. Pallis, Hillsdale, NY, Sophia Perennis, 2004. Following the example set by the organizers of the Eranos summit, who always shunned his work and his ideas, I also refuse to include the fascist theorist Julius Evola in the Perennialist movement. On the history of the Eranos 'perennialist' summit and the Evola controversy, see H.T. Hakl, *Eranos: An Alternative Intellectual History of the Twentieth Century*, translated by C. McIntosh, Abingdon, Routledge, 2013.

A CHANCE
TO LIE

FIGURE 2.4 *Albrecht Durer,* Allegory of Eloquence (Allegorie auf die Beredsamkeit), *1514.*

Eusa says, 'Whats the diffrents if I done the acturel Bad Time
things my self or I dint?'
Orfing says, 'Wel if you dint do it then it aint on you is it.'
Eusa says, 'And if aint on me then what?'
Orfing says, 'Then youre free aint you. Nothing on you and the
worl in front of you. Do what ever you like.'
Eusa says, 'There you are and said it out of your oan mouf.
Which wud you rather? Have the worl in front of you and free
or have some thing hevvy on your back for ever?'[16]

What an excellent situation for cultural producers! It's not often that a handful of generations have a chance to invent not only an alternative present, but also a better past for themselves.[17] Once the digital and paper records of our culture will have vanished, very little will remain to contradict any alternative, invented versions of this time-segment. The looming end of the future endows the inhabitants of Westernized Modernity with a unique chance to lie.

For those of us who are 'en-worlded' within this dwindling cosmology, the task of learning how to die well begins with an exercise of downright falsity. Even if we were given the option of accurately conveying the form of the world in which we have grown up and lived, a sense of dignity and of parental care towards our post-future peers would advise us against it. Those who'll have face the daunting task of rebuilding a world ex nihilo don't deserve that we consign to them the metaphysical formula of a civilization whose impact on the planet has been exceptionally catastrophic. Before the curtain closes over this cosmology, those who are still living within it have the chance of leaving behind themselves something fertile: if it means to sacrifice truth, suffice it to remember that every foundation demands a sacrifice.

---

[16]R. Hoban, *Riddley Walker*, London, Bloomsbury, 1980, p. 52.
[17]That a therapeutic modification of the past is a legitimate form of tradition – if not its essence – is indirectly testified, with typical grace, by Jorge Luis Borges. In one of his many invented pseudo-bibliographies, Borges (together with his friend and co-author Adolfo Bioy Casares) attributes to a certain Adrienne Bordenave a book significantly titled *La modification du Passé ou la seule base de la Tradition* (Modifying the Past, or the Only Basis of Tradition). I side with Borges/Casares/ Bordenave's succinct thesis. See J.L. Borges and A.B. Casares, *Cuentos Breves Y Extraordinarios* – I have consulted the Italian edition, J.L. Borges and A.B. Casares, *Racconti Brevi e Straordinari*, Milan, Adelphi, 2020, p. 61.

Culture at the end of the future shouldn't linger on meditations about what should have happened but didn't – what kind of successes we could have achieved but missed, what kind of norms or behaviours we failed to develop. A lie that aims to create a fertile soil for the sprouting of new cosmogonies is not a form of utopia. More radically, it amounts to a complete rewriting of the world-frame that this society adopted as its own perspective towards existence. Its function is not to sketch the outline of a new social project, or to retrospectively correct the old one, but to substitute the existing narrative of 'time' and 'world' with a redeemed version that never was and shall never be. It is both an exercise in existential fiction and a form of metaphysical epic.

When good fortune decrees that a civilization dies without leaving any trace of its culture, other than the waste-products of its economy, the last of the artists and of the writers of that time have an opportunity that seldom appears outside of Borges's pages: to be truly creative, in the cosmogonic meaning of the term. To make public the job of worlding, as if giving the extreme unction to a time that is about to end. To live as if on planet Tlön, which flows directly out of the mind of its inhabitants.

> It is no exaggeration to state that the classic culture of Tlön comprises only one discipline: psychology. All others are subordinated to it. I have said that the men of this planet conceive the universe as a series of mental processes which do not develop in space but successively in time. ... In other words, they do not conceive that the spatial persists in time. The perception of a cloud of smoke on the horizon and then of the burning field and then of the half-extinguished cigarette that produced the blaze is considered an example of association of ideas. [...]
>
> The metaphysicians of Tlön do not seek for the truth or even for verisimilitude, but rather for the astounding. They judge that metaphysics is a branch of fantastic literature. They know that a system is nothing more than the subordination of all aspects of the universe to any one such aspect.[18]

---

[18] J.L. Borges, 'Tlön, Uqbar, Orbis Tertius', in J.L. Borges, *Labyrinths: Selected Stories and Other Writings*, edited and translated by D.A. Yates and J.E. Irby, London, Penguin, 2000, pp. 33–4.

It is at the level of metaphysical epic that the last cultural producers of the age of Westernized Modernity might find a solution to the plagues weighing on their world: the inability of its culture to survive the social body from which it has emerged, and the toxicity of what would have been its cultural legacy.

But let us proceed by steps towards this conclusion, beginning with the problem of which cultural media might be resilient enough to pass through the needle-eye of an apocalypse.

We can try using a self-reflecting question: What kind of media, in our own experience, guarantees the highest degree of survival to immaterial forms like those conveyed by culture?

If we look back at the immaterial forms and structures that have most profoundly conditioned each of us in the course of our life, like a branding mark impressed on our imagination, we can typically locate them in the field of events going under the name of 'trauma'. The loss of a loved one, the abuse received by a family member, the discrimination acted upon a person or a group by a crowd or witnessing an event that defies belief – these are all sudden challenges to a subject's ideas about their own personal boundaries as an entity, and about the geography of boundaries that exists within the world. Although trauma often derives from brutal facts, however, there is no necessity to associate it with violence and prevarication. Trauma can be interpreted more broadly as a profound modification within one's own fundamental metaphysics.

A traumatic narrative takes place at the threshold between the limits of a subject – the borders of what a subject can call 'myself' or 'my own' – and the weird or eerie presence of what transgresses these limits.[19] Trauma re-defines the idea of world and self that a subject has constructed until that point. The frequent oblivion of traumatic events indicates that they occur not within time, but somehow *before* the new time-segment which they inaugurate – they cannot be recollected among the facts of time, because they don't belong to their number.

Considering that metaphysical storytelling is always an ongoing process, the potential occurrence of traumatic events runs

---

[19]I am referring to the distinction between the 'weird' (what is there, but shouldn't be) and the 'eerie' (what should be there, but isn't) developed by the much-missed Mark Fisher – see M. Fisher, *The Weird and the Eerie*, London, Repeater, 2016. *Sit tibi terra levis.*

uninterrupted throughout a subject's life. Each instant that the world is created within a certain metaphysical perspective, there arises a chance for another traumatic shift. For people living within the strong narrative of a civilization, it is fairly easy to defuse the eruption of trauma by hiding it under the carpet of habits and common sense. But for those who happen to live in the gap between the end and the start of a world-story, reality teems at each instant with challenges to the stability of their geography of the existent. Metaphysical renegotiation is the traumatic terrain where one's own structures of sense and behaviour are rooted.

Immaterial forms that are capable of affecting a subject's way of worlding survive as part of the *gestalt* (form) of the subject's imagination – thus pre-emptively conditioning any logic or ethics that might ensue from it. Whenever culture cannot count on the support of external media for its survival, trauma provides a shelter where the most complex cosmological speculations can find refuge.

This was precisely what happened in the three cases of dead-and-reborn civilizations that were discussed a few pages ago.

What survived of the Mycenaean world – its entire cosmology hidden in the grain of sand of Homer's voice – amounted essentially to a meditation on the relationship between a subject and *Ananke*: the cosmic force which is capable of transgressing and re-designing all boundaries. The entire epic of the *Iliad*, which Simon Weil brilliantly interpreted as 'the poem of force',[20] has to do with the dilemma of how to face and to make sense of an external agency that is autonomous in itself, whose reasons are impenetrable, and that is capable of bending the frame of the world at any instant.

Likewise, the political and judicial vocabulary that allowed the Roman world-form to partly survive the disintegration of its society had to do with the experience of another liminal force: *potestas*, authority. Like the shamans who bridle the winds through their chanting, the formulae of Roman bureaucracy intervened at the level where power manifests itself as a social dynamic, challenging and defining a subject's own metaphysical and existential borders.

---

[20]See S. Weil, *Simone Weil's the Iliad or the Poem of Force: A Critical Edition*, edited and translated by J.P. Holoka, New York, NY, Peter Lang Publishing, 2006.

Also the destiny of the world of ancient Egypt – befitting that of Osiris, whose dismembered body was recomposed as a patchwork[21] – is traceable to the continuation of a similar thread in its cosmological narration. While the hieroglyphic records of Egyptian culture became completely inaccessible for centuries,[22] the tradition of Egyptian magic remained a powerful ally to more than one cohort of rebuilders of world – from Hellenism to the Italian Renaissance and beyond. Its living legacy consisted essentially in the liminal story about what falls in and out of visibility, in and out of life and death.

The same process is active well beyond the immediate region of the Mediterranean basin – for example, in the death-and-rebirth of the Vedic civilization in the Indian subcontinent. Spanning for

---

[21]A peculiar quality of ancient Egyptian gods is their mortality. Osiris, one of the greatest divinities in the ancient Egyptian pantheon, was murdered by his brother Set and was brought back to life by his sister-wife Isis. After his traumatic death and resurrection, Osiris developed an intensely compassionate attitude towards the creatures whom he accompanied into the Afterlife – but he also acquired a new, surprising appellative: The Tired God. 'Recitation: Awake, Osiris! Revise, O tired God! The God stands, the God takes possession of his body. The King awakes, the tired God revives.' *The Pyramid Texts*, 2092a–2094a N., quoted in J. G. Griffiths, *The Origins of Osiris and His Cult*, Leiden, Brill, 1980, p. 64.

[22]A case in point is the work of late-ancient Egyptian theologian/philosopher Horapollo, whose book on the meaning of hieroglyphs combines a profound symbolic reading, with an evident ignorance of their original semantic function. 'In 1419, Cristoforo de'Buondelmonti, a Florentine priest traveling over the island of Andros, bought there a Greek manuscript which he brought back with him to Italy. This was the *Hieroglyphica* of Horapollo Niliacus, an obscure Alexandrian of the second or fourth century A.D., who claimed in this work to set forth the hidden meaning of the sacred symbols used in ancient Egypt. Everyone believed that a real discovery had been made. In reality, all that Horapollo did was to sanction the mistaken view of hieroglyphics which had arisen by way of Apuleius, Plutarch, and Plotinus – namely, that they formed an ensemble of rebuses designed to make religious precepts incomprehensible to the profane.' J. Seznec, *The Survival of the Pagan Gods: The Mythological Thought and Its Place in Renaissance Humanism and Art*, Princeton, NJ, Princeton University Press, 1972, pp. 99–100. See also Horapollo Niliacus, *The Hieroglyphics of Horapollo*, translated by G. Boas, Princeton, NJ, Princeton University Press, 1993. For a wider discussion of the oblivion in which fell the hieroglyphic writing system – and of later, creative attempts at interpreting it – see R. Calasso, *I Geroglifici di Sir Thomas Browne*, Milan, Adelphi, 2019.

over a millennium, the Vedic world left behind a meagre harvest of archaeological evidence. But despite the fact that little survived in terms of its material legacy, the words of Vedic culture passed through the abyss of the apocalypse and established the cornerstone of Hinduism. Transmitted orally over the course of centuries before being systematized in writing, the Vedas provided a complex array of rituals and meditations on the function of sacrifice, as the means through which living beings can at each moment re-establish the contours of a world over the dark abyss of meaninglessness.[23]

In all these cases, what remains of a civilization is primarily its ability to help future generations to deal with their own existential limits vis-à-vis the disquieting presence of forces like necessity, power, death and the ceaseless crumbling of meaning. The echo of these world stories continued to reverberate in the existential trauma carried forward by those who came after their time-segment, and it proved essential for the reconstruction of a new cosmos over the ruins of the old. Indeed, there exists no other ruin, but what survives as part of a subject's daily struggle to create a 'world' where life might flourish. Whatever fails this task, however large and profound its marks might be on the environment, cannot be considered the ruin of a lost world, but it is merely an excremental trace.

At present, there is little evidence that the relics of Westernized Modernity might be able to avoid the oblivion of aesthetic failure. But a final chance to lie remains for the inhabitants of this dying world. A chance to redeem themselves, to learn how to die well and to aid the ignition of a new cosmogony. A slim chance.

---

[23]On the relationship between meaning and meaninglessness in Vedic rituals, see also F. Staal, *Ritual and Mantras: Rules without Meaning*, New Delhi, Motilal Banarsidass, 1996.

ARCHAIC
ADOLESCENTS

FIGURE 2.5 Head of Dionysus, c. 200 BC, Naxos, from the Canterbury Museum Collection. © The Warburg Institute, Iconographic Database.

Homeland will be when
we shall all be foreigners[24]

Fragile immaterial forms, like those conveyed by culture, can survive the collapse of their original body by embedding themselves within liminal existential experiences. As they reach the realm of trauma, they gain a chance to continue echoing after the end of the time-segment in which they originated.[25] Such liminal situations, however, are far from being a catalogue of stable events. Trauma varies on the basis of the subjectivity of those who experience it, and it depends on the context in which it takes place.

Thus, a dying world, striving to leave fertile soil to those who'll come after the end of its future, is bound to tackle the question of who exactly will be the recipient of its efforts, and what they will need: Who do we talk about, when we talk about 'post-future subjects', living between the apocalypse and dawn?

A clear answer is beyond anybody's divinatory ability. The distance between different forms of worlding impedes that the inhabitants of two separate *cosmoi* might gain a clear vision of each other. But although the inter-world fog renders the details invisible, it is still possible to imagine the general traits of the context where a post-future subjectivity emerges.

At the beginning of this chapter, while discussing the experience of surviving the end of a world, I used the example of an adolescent's embarrassment at finding themselves somehow still 'there', after the collapse of their childhood metaphysics. I referred to the difficulty for adolescents to create a spatial–temporal landscape where things might be again endowed with meaning, and to the brittleness of their position as world-makers.

The condition of an adolescent is not unlike that of an archaic people, coming after the end of a civilization. Archaic societies such as that of Homer or of Charlemagne came to life like newly

---

[24]*La patria sarà quando/tutti saremo stranieri.* F. Nappo, *Poesie 1979–2007*, Macerata: Quodlibet, 2007, p. 49.

[25]'Culture is what is left within us, once we have forgotten everything that we've learned.' *La cultura è ciò che resta in noi dopo che abbiamo dimenticato tutto ciò che avevamo imparato.* Letter from G. Salvemini to Lina Cavazza, 11 September 1907, in G. Salvemini and E. Gencarelli (eds.), *Carteggi, I, 1895–1911*, Milan, Feltrinelli, 1968, p. 363.

born giraffes, already able to stand. Similarly to adolescents, the Archaics focus their efforts on the reconstitution of some kind of metaphysical order over the raw flesh of reality. And in this endeavour, again like adolescents, the Archaics also remain mindful of the risk of creating excessively rigid metaphysical structures. Both of them are confronted by the paradox of freedom: on the one hand, they feel the necessity of living in a landscape of their own making, which compels them to actualize some of the countless possibilities that are available. On the other, though, they are aware that every actualized choice is destined to destroy all other possible futures that lie dormant in pure virtuality.[26]

The adolescent/archaic approach to world-building can be better appreciated alongside its two companion-figures: the child and the adult (and their metaphorical equivalents in the realm of civilizations).

Lacking a clear memory of the past and shielded from the possibility of a discontinuous future, children are drawn to a relentless activity of world-building. The world that surrounds them has barely any roots, but the child optimistically invests in the ability of their world-narration to keep everything from sinking back into the abyss. Facing the paradox of freedom, a child embraces without hesitation the promises of order.

In the old parlance of pre-structuralist anthropologists, the position of the child was often – and mistakenly – equated with that of so-called 'primitive' people, whose station within the great cosmogonic workshop appears to be at the very beginning of all things. Such a pristine position is, of course, a fantasy. Even in the absence of a human civilization before them, supposedly primitive people would have encountered the great non-human civilizations

---

[26]An adolescent relationship with freedom, and thus with creation, rests on a vital-yet-melancholic understanding of the infinite possibilities of metaphysics. Similar to Michelangelo's theory of sculpture, the adolescent on the one hand sees the cosmogonic potential of each action to bring about a unique world, while on the other (like the Tuscan artist) they sense the sudden anti-climax that befalls the actualization of any decision. 'Nothing the best of artists can conceive/but lies, potential, in a block of stone,/superfluous matter round it. The hand alone/secures it that has intelligence for guide.' M. Buonarroti, *The Complete Poems*, 151, translated by J.F. Nims, Chicago & London, The University of Chicago Press, 1998, p. 96. 'As by subtracting, my lady, one creates/from rugged mountain stone/an image of flesh and bone/developing even as the stone grows less … ' Ibid., 152, p. 96.

of the vegetable and animal kingdoms, with their own modes of life and metaphysical perspectives. This common misattribution of a childish nature to people from another world is a good indication of the Westernized Modern attitudes towards inter-worldly dialogue. As if they were talking to people who have no experience of anything, the Westernized Moderns often imagine that communicating with those who live at the beginning of a new world requires crafting messages that are plain, simple and fully explanatory.

This attitude is reversed, when Westernized Modern societies imagine the relationship with another kind of other-worldly subjects: aliens from outer space. In Modern narratives describing a possible contact with alien species, it is frequent to encounter their portraits as fully adult subjectivities. Whatever they might look like or whatever their intentions might be, outer space aliens are depicted as subjects that know exactly what they want. Like adults, they have a violent repulse for the order of the world, and an almost instinctive desire to break free from its structure and demands.[27] Hence, the caution with which aliens should be approached: in most science-fiction films, it is not a poet or an artist who is sent to meet them, but the military (and its scientific appendix) deployed in full strength. It is hardly a coincidence that the term 'alien' is used to define both those whom we fear might come to visit us from the outer space and the thousands of humans who are now being rejected from the militarized borders of many a contemporary Westernized nation.

Thinking of archaic people as *adolescent* subjectivities means disarming our imagination and setting the conditions for a relationship of solidarity towards those who shall come after us. An adolescent is neither a child nor an adult, nor is it the dialectic synthesis of the two. An adolescent is wary at the same time of order and of disorder, and their attitude towards the world does without the unlovingness of both children and adults. The brutality that is displayed at times by adolescents has very

---

[27]The adult subjectivity, as it is currently displayed by the majority of the electorate in most Westernized Modern countries, seems to deploy this attitude in a way that resembles Giovanni Verga's novella *La Roba* – where an ageing man prepares himself to his death by destroying as much as he can of what he created, while crying out loud, 'My stuff, you're coming with me!' (*Roba mia, vienitene con me!*). G. Verga, *Cavalleria Rusticana and Other Stories, Property*, translated by G.H. McWilliam, London, Penguin, 1999, pp. 167–72.

little in common with the totalitarian attitude of childhood, or with the adult taste for annihilation.

An archaic subjectivity looks towards reality with a combination of awe and terror. Its symbol could be the *kore*, the adolescent girl whose rigidity is balanced by an unsettling smile, the goddess whose three faces speak of one and the same death and rebirth.[28] Its attitude is tragic, like that of Achilles, the warrior boy who gave meaning to his adolescence as he died choking on his own blood. The world surrounding the Archaics teems with a disquieting kind of life, so close and yet so distant from human standards. Behind each entity, as if under a veil, lurks a pulsating abyss. The Sphinx still traverses their fragile landscape and her questions can reopen at any instant the distance between the world that is carved out of reality, and the wild avalanche of perceptions unceasingly outpouring from the Real.

For anyone living after the closure of a civilization's future, 'the world' and 'time' are tricky beasts to saddle. As in the myth of Bellerophon, the horseman who tamed winged Pegasus, it takes the intervention of a Divinity, and Her gift of golden bridles, to jump on the back of the world and to stop it from flying away. Adolescent Archaics seek the benign face of the sacred – a helping hand coming from the outside, to offer the reassurance of a magic formula or the spur of a riddle.[29] They look for it in the excesses of life that traverse all things, and especially among those corpses whose apparent death

---

[28]The three faces of the kore are those of Hekate, goddess of witchcraft, necromancy, and associated with crossroads and entrance-ways. For an insightful analysis of the figure of the Kore and its relationship with the Archaic mind, see C. Kerenyi, *Kore*, and C.G. Jung, 'The Psychological Aspect of the Kore', in C.G. Jung and C. Kerenyi, *The Science of Mythology*, translated by R.F.C. Hull, Abingdon, Routledge, 2001, pp. 119–208. For a discussion of the Greek Archaic mind, see the classic E.R. Dodds, *The Greeks and the Irrational*, Berkeley, CA, University of California Press, 2004; and, of course, the pioneering masterpiece of philology that inaugurated Nietzsche's career, in F. Nietzsche, *The Birth of Tragedy*, translated by S. Whiteside, London, Penguin, 1993.

[29]A similar attitude can be detected also in Mediterranean Late Antiquity, where the people living through the collapse of the Roman world – while struggling to build a new world for themselves – resorted to an ever-expanding cult of the saints: 'The growth of the cult of the saints in Late Antiquity ... was about people, and about the types of relationships that can be established between people. The relic is a person in a place; and, in that place, all that Late Antique men could value in unalloyed

is contradicted by a weird gleaming. During their walks among the ruins of what preceded them, the Archaics search for that spark, which distinguishes a sacred stone from any other identical pebble.[30] This indefinable 'something' is the minuscule force that saves, not by promising a better future to those who encounter it, but by offering them a better past. Mythical ancestors and civilizing heroes aren't professorial figures or judges of behaviours: they offer themselves as narrative suggestions on how to approach the *opera* of living.[31]

---

relations of friendship, protection and mercy in their society can come to be played out with liberating precision. Late Antique men had inherited a continuum of Mediterranean sensibility that longed for invisible and ideal companions. As Bishop Synesius of Cyrene wrote of his guardian angel: "and give me a companion, O King, a partner, a sacred messenger of sacred power, a messenger of prayer illumined by the divine light, a friend, a dispenser of noble gifts ... " Yet by the late fourth century the guardian angel tends to recede into the background; his position as an invisible friend and protector is taken over by the human figure of the saint ... Late Roman and early medieval men appear to be drawing a network of invisible fellow human beings ever closer around themselves. They work out a series of intense relationships with these, that are modelled with zest on what they consider to be good relationships in their ordinary life.' P. Brown, *Society and the Holy in Late Antiquity*, Berkeley, CA, University of California Press, 1989, pp. 14–15.

[30]'The radically new is the internal, concealed distinction in the externally identical – or, if you like, in the absolutely commonplace ... What is involved here is an absolute, infinite, concealed distinction, which can no longer be recognised as it does not display any outward sign, corresponding only to a choice that cannot be found on reason ... [The commonplace] acquires new justification as the site of an invisible, non self-evident difference, and of a doubt that cannot be ended by any self-evidence. The time of this doubt, moreover, is no longer an historical time, since it no longer displays any form of historical-dialectical reflection ... [It] corresponds to the unlimited doubt of a subjectivity that has also become unlimited. This doubt can only be interrupted by a leap, a decision, though even this does not finally abolish it.' B. Groys, *Introduction to Antiphilosophy*, translated by D. Fernbach, London/New York, Verso, 2012, pp. 9–11. See also Mircea Eliade's analysis of the phenomenon of *hierophanies* (manifestations of the sacred), in M. Eliade, *Images and Symbols*, translated by P. Mairet, Princeton, NJ, Princeton University Press, 1991, pp. 84–5.

[31]When visiting the site of old Troy to pay homage to his hero and role-model Achilles, 'Alexander the Great wept, not for Achilles in his tomb, but for himself.' B. Gracian, *The Pocket Oracle and the Art of Prudence*, 75, translated by J. Robbins, London, Penguin, 2011, p. 29. For a discussion of the role of mythical ancestors, see M. Eliade, *Images and Symbols*, translated by P. Mairet, Princeton, NJ, Princeton University Press, 1991. I have used the Italian term *opera*, to define the 'job' of living, both to avoid the squalid terminology of employment, and because the word *opera*, in all its meanings, conveys the sense of an activity which is innately collective, multifaceted and bigger-than-itself.

Once the veneer of the old world has vanished, a subject building a new age out of lifeless ruins encounters the ineffable dimension of existence more intensely than ever. When it is least bridled from linguistic parameters, pure existence manifests itself as a *mysterium tremendum et fascinans*, 'a mystery that terrifies and fascinates'.[32] The questions that it poses are different from those emerging within an already stable world: they are enigmas, rather than problems. As long as it stands, an enigma allows those whom it challenges to occupy a position that shares a common terrain with a Divinity. The paradoxical nature of reality, whose two faces are a veneer of meaning and an abyss of meaninglessness, reveals the presence both of something otherworldly within the world and, vice versa, of a linguistic frame surrounding any manifestation of pure existence.

The world-shattering voice of an enigma is equally capable of restyling a landscape, or of uprooting it entirely. The sheer intensity of living too near to the ineffable core of reality, where all meaning implodes, demands that an enigma must be resolved swiftly, even hastily. But success is met at a cost: once the Sphinx has been defeated and has thrown herself off the cliff, Oedipus falls victim to the new world which he created – the gods abandon him, and the internal contradictions of the new order drive him to despair.

Such is the curse that haunts the Archaic adolescent: either to be cast out of the company of the ineffable, or to lose their citizenship to the world itself. The onset of a new world, whether in one's own life or in the life of a civilization, is a threshold between these two catastrophic losses. As in many cosmogonic myths, the creation of a new world and of a new time demands a sacrifice that is personal and extreme.

When Prajapati had emitted the creatures, his joints became disjointed. Now Prajapati is the year, and his joints are the two junctures of day and night, of the waxing and waning lunar half-months, and of the beginnings of the seasons. He was unable to rise with his joints disjointed.[33]

---

[32] I am borrowing Rudolf Otto's famous definition of the sacred – see R. Otto, *The Idea of the Holy*, translated by J.W. Harvey, Oxford, Oxford University Press, 1958.
[33] *Satapatha Brahmana*, 1.6.3.35, translated by Brian K. Smith – quoted in B. K. Smith, *Reflections on Resemblance, Ritual, and Religion*, Delhi, Motilal Banarsidass, 1998, p. 61.

Even once the frame of sense of a new world has been created, the subject who brings it about remains in part excluded from their own creation. Archaic Greeks understood in these terms the races of gods and humans – always, fundamentally, foreigners to their own world. The Lord of the Olympians was Zeus *Xenios*, the protector of foreigners, and Himself the foreign guest par excellence within the world. And foreigners were both Dionysus, the god who came from the East, and Apollo the Hyperborean.[34] Millennia later, the Orthodox saint Andrei Rublev painted the mystery of the Trinity in the shape of the three angels who had come to the house of Abraham disguised as foreigners.

The vision of the raw kernel of existence, erupting ineffably through the mesh of the world, makes its beholders partake to its destiny, turning them into creatures that live at once within and without the world – entitled to everything and possessors of nothing.

Like the Archaics and the adolescents, foreigners too are afraid of both order and disorder: of being swallowed by the world that hosts them, and of remaining excluded from it.

To the cosmological foreigner who looks through the ruins of worlds past, searching for inspiration, only a remedy to both catastrophes seems of use – while everything else appears obsolete, in the same way that an adolescent feels the obsolescence of both childhood games and adult worries. If we are to imagine a cultural legacy that might assist the inventors of a new time, after the end of our future, we should think of a *pharmakon* that is simultaneously 'medicine and poison' to both order and disorder. A cosmological narration that contains them both, and that is opposed to either.

---

[34]Another divine figure occupying the position of the 'foreigner in the world' is the archetype of the trickster. See P. Radin, *The Trickster: A Study in American Indian Mythology*, New York, Schocken Books, 1972 (including the two Afterwords by Karl Kerenyi and C.G. Jung), and C.G. Jung, *The Archetypes and The Collective Unconscious, Collected Works*, 9, translated by R.F.C. Hull, Princeton, NJ, Princeton University Press, 1981. For a fascinating analysis of the trickster figure of Pulcinella, a quintessential foreigner to both life and death (as well as the character on the cover of this book, in a painting by Giovanni Domenico Tiepolo), see G. Agamben, *Pulcinella: Or Entertainment for Children*, translated by K. Attell, Kolkata, Seagull Books, 2015.

At the time of writing these lines, despite the growing social resentment that pervades the twilight of our age, it is already possible to feel this desire re-emerging in those contemporary narratives of Salvation – like those centred on an 'ecology without nature'[35] – which attempt to overcome the fragmentary notion of 'complexity', typical of Westernized Modernity, in favour of a holistic approach that comes 'not to bring peace, but a sword'.[36] It is this kind of *pharmakon* that the Archaic adolescents will seek, while scavenging through our defunct remains, in the time that will come after the end of our future.

---

[35]This definition was formulated and explored in depth by Timothy Morton, in T. Morton, *Ecology without Nature*, Cambridge, MA, Harvard University Press, 2007.
[36]Matthew, 10:34.

TETRAPHARMAKON

FIGURE 2.6 The Black Sun (Sol Niger), *illustration from* Splendor Solis, *attributed to Salomon Trismosin, c. 1532–5, from the collection of the Kupferstichkabinett Berlin.* © Staatliche Museen zu Berlin.

> *As people with chronic diseases when they have despaired*
> *of ordinary remedies turn to expiations and amulets and*
> *dreams, just so in obscure and perplexing speculations, when*
> *the ordinary and reputable accounts are not persuasive, it is*
> *necessary to try those that are more out of the way and not*
> *scorn them but literally to chant over ourselves the charms of*
> *the ancients and use every means to bring the truth to test.*[37]

It might be helpful to recapitulate the steps taken so far, in our discussion of the challenges (and the opportunities) for culture-making in the declining age of Westernized Modernity.

I began by examining the modes of operation of 'time' and 'world' as metaphysical *cosmoi*: non-natural, artificial structures of sense capable of shaping an existential landscape.[38] While looking at the characteristics of this artifice, I followed the similarity between world-making and musical storytelling – of which sung metric poetry, in the rhapsodic tradition, offers a prime example.

Then, I focused on that moment in the narration when the voice of the singer grows tired and the frame of sense of a certain age of the world begins to unravel. It is at that point that the rhythm of a world-song – which until then seemed time itself – is unveiled as the stretch of just one time-segment. To offer a few examples of what happens after the closure of a world-narration, I looked into the rich history of the Mediterranean basin – a region

---

[37]Plutarch, 'Concerning the Face Which Appears in the Orb of the Moon', in *Moralia*, XII, 920 B-C., translated by H. Cherniss and W.C. Helmbold, Cambridge, MA, Harvard University Press, 1957, p. 35.

[38]On the 'natural artificiality' of the world, see Sir Tomas Browne's theological argument: 'There was never any thing ugly or mis-shapen, but the Chaos; wherein not withstanding, to speake strictly, there was no deformity, because no forme; nor was it yet impregnate by the voyce of God: Now nature is not at variance with art, nor art with nature, they being both the servants of his providence: Art is the perfection of Nature: Were the world now as it was the sixt day, there were yet a Chaos: Nature hath made one world, and Art another. In briefe, all things are artificiall, for Nature is the Art of God.' T. Browne, 'Religio Medici', 1, 16, in T. Browne, *Religio Medici and Urne-Burial*, New York, NY, NYRB, 2012, p. 20.

where traces of recurring apocalypses are especially evident. The Minoans and Myceneas featured in the discussion alongside the Romans and the Egyptians, offering a picture of how civilizations frequently die, and of how strangely, at times, they happen to come back to life.

Moving between ages, I then passed to examining the form of worlding that is presently hegemonic over vast areas of the planet – what I called the civilization of Westernized Modernity. My own spatial–temporal location undoubtedly added an element of personal anxiety for the destiny of a form of worlding which – in and of itself – might not deserve such keen attention. Even in the absence of any concrete feeling of belonging, though, it is the very aesthetic nature of the act of worlding that compels every subject to ensure that the world-narration to which they partake doesn't end without providing something of use to the blossoming of other, alien acts of world-creation.

If this aesthetic imperative demands that a subject lies about the factual truth, so be it. It is better to invent from scratch a world-song that never was, and to consign it to those who shall come after the end of the future, rather than keeping a sterile record of the failures of an age. Thankfully, the extreme fragility of the cultural records of Westernized Modernity and their rapid vanishing after the demise of their society makes for an easier job of cultural fraud and of metaphysical redemption.

Any random lie, however, won't do. To calibrate cultural production at the end of an age, it is necessary to have some idea of those post-future people who might be the recipients of our efforts to invent a better past (for them and for ourselves). I developed this part of my discourse around the notion of trauma as the existential/cultural field where one's own fundamental metaphysics are negotiated and established; I identified the subjectivity of the adolescent – living at the threshold between an apocalypse and a new cosmogony – as the closest metaphorical equivalent to the position of an 'archaic' form of subjectivity.

The Archaics-to-come, like adolescents, shall seek a benevolent, mythical figure that might aid them in their daunting task of world-building by providing inspiration and a point of departure to establish a new metaphysics. It is towards the creation of this benign, mythical presence, that the cultural producers of the contemporary age should – I believe – concentrate their efforts.

It is now time to consider the traits of a cultural message that might be able to satisfy that aesthetic imperative befalling any subject living in a world. The discussion of this cultural message, as it will be developed in the closing pages of this chapter, shall serve as a footing for the next chapter – dedicated to the form of (prophetic) culture that might be able to convey it.

I have defined this type of cultural message as a *pharmakon* (medicine and poison), since it aims to act both as the enhancer of a new cosmogony and as an antidote to the fear and embarrassment of adolescent subjectivities. *Tetrapharmakon* (the four-folded *pharmakon*) is a term that I borrow from the Epicurean tradition, which identified in four principles the best possible cure to the anxiety and dread of finding oneself existing in a death-bound world of becoming.[39] Similar to the Epicurean remedy, this *pharmakon* is made up of four different elements and it is designed to tackle the existential paralysis that often accompanies a post-apocalyptic subject.

---

[39]The fourfolded ethical principle elaborated by Epicurus enjoined: 1. Don't fear god; 2. Don't worry about death; 3. What is good is easy to get; 4. What is terrible is easy to endure – see Diogenes Laertius, *Life of Epicurus*, in Diogenes Laertius, *Lives and Opinions of Eminent Philosophers*, vol. 2, Book X, translated by R.D. Hicks, Cambridge, MA, Loeb Classical Library, 1989. Aside from the Epicurean reference, I opted for a tetradic (fourfold) structure also in opposition to the typical triadic (threefold) structure of Westernized Modern dialectics. Following Pythagorean number-symbolism, it is possible to see how triadic dialectics moves from the number two (the numerical symbol of multiplicity) to the number three (transcendence), seeking the absolute at the cost of abandoning the realm of so-called 'illusions'. A tetradic structure, on the contrary, moves from transcendence (3) to the reconstruction of a world (symbolized by the number 4) which includes both ineffability and language, both the 'absolute' and the 'illusion', under one roof. For an examination of the symbolism of the number four, see Rene Guenon's essay *The Tetraktys and the Square of Four*, in R. Guenon, *Symbols of Sacred Science*, translated by A. Moore, Hillsdale, NY, Sophia Perennis, 2004, pp. 101–5; K.S. Guthrie, *The Pythagorean Sourcebook and Library*, Grand Rapids, MI, Phanes Press, 1988, pp. 28–30; Iamblichus, *The Theology of Arithmetic: On the Mystical, Mathematical and Cosmological Symbolism of the First Ten Numbers*, translated by R. Waterfield, Grand Rapids, MI, Phanes Press, 1986, pp. 55–64.

At first, the four elements that composite this *tetrapharmakon* might seem mutually incompatible – each of them presupposing a frame of sense that excludes the others. As in the afterlife of a civilization, though, it is only through a syncretic combination of apparent opposites, that a cosmological discourse can find both the means for its own survival and the ability to provide something aesthetically and cosmogonically fertile.

In mixing these four ingredients, the cultural 'pharmacist' has to consider their double relationship of enmity and friendship towards the forces haunting an archaic imagination: order and disorder. A cultural message launched beyond the future has to consider them both, counteract their power and simultaneously enhance them. Order and disorder – respectively, the vectorial pull of normative language and that of the ineffable bedrock of reality – shouldn't be denied or eradicated, but redeemed through a perspective that at once includes, mongrelizes and relativizes them within a wider angle. The Archaics might want to make a sacrifice to the god Fear (*Phobos*) before entering a field where anything can happen: this *tetrapharmakon* is meant as the offering to burn on that altar.[40]

The four components of this *tetrapharmakon* can still be found in the garden of Westernized Modern imagination. Some of them are flourishing vigorously, while others require a greater effort to be re-discovered under moss and rocks. Each of them describes, not so much a concept, but an attitude towards the activity of world-building. This *tetrapharmakon* is a collection of four figures who have been and can still be inhabited by anyone willing to artfully intervene on their perspective towards worlding. They are: the metaphysician, the shaman, the mystic and the prophet.

---

[40]The night before the battle of Gaugamela (1 October 331 BC), where Alexander's soldiers were to face Darius's much larger army, 'Darius kept his men in arms, and by torchlight took a general review of them. But Alexander, while his soldiers slept, spent the night before his tent with his diviner Aristander, performing certain mysterious ceremonies and sacrificing to the god Fear [*Phobos*].' Plutarch, 'Life of Alexander', in *Plutarch's Lives*, translated by J. Dryden, New York, NY, The Modern Library, 2001, p. 165.

In the closing pages of this chapter, I shall discuss the first three figures of this *tetrapharmakon*, while the fourth one will be the topic of the next chapter. This disproportion is partly balanced by the ground that I have already covered in another book, and it is due to the varying degrees of familiarity that contemporary culture entertains with them. While the figures of the metaphysician, the shaman and the mystic are fairly common features of contemporary imagination, that of the prophet still remains (aptly) foreign to cultural producers of this age.

Let us begin with the first figure, which is also the most prominent within today's mental landscape: the metaphysician. A metaphysician is not necessarily a philosopher who deals with a particular branch of the discipline: a scientist, a financial analyst or a software engineer also embodies the metaphysician. To the riddle of reality, the metaphysician responds by deploying a rigid net of receptors where the anxiety of nonsensicality can be captured, dissected, neutralized and re-packaged, so to be easily recombined at will. Metaphysical thought charms away the fear of disorder, by projecting a net of discontinuity over its field of vision. To exist is to be 'something': a thing that obeys the law of non-contradiction and that cannot be simultaneously itself and not-itself.[41]

The world of the metaphysician – and of those who reason along its lines – is a discontinuous expanse of blocks, bits and elements. Although devoid of a personality of their own, and despite being pre-defined by the grids through which they emerge, each of them retains its geographical uniqueness within the great frame of sense of the world. To the eye of the metaphysician, each existent, including themselves, is capable of responding to any taxonomical question with a binary 'yes' or a 'no', and to that respect each existent is 'this' existent, and not 'that' one – a man *or* a woman, a human *or* a non-human, a citizen *or* a foreigner,

---

[41]The metaphysician is, indeed, the incarnation of the principles of Westernized Modernity. Yet, as Pliny the Elder once observed, 'There is no book so bad, but some profit might be gleaned of it.' *Nullum esse librum tam malum, ut non in aliqua parte prodesset* – quoted in Pliny the Younger, *Letters*, vol. 1, III, 5.10, translated by W. Melmoth and W.M.L. Hutchinson, London, William Heinemann, 1931, p. 201.

alive *or* dead. The map of reality drawn by the metaphysician is an easily navigable realm, although a closer look suffices to reveal its homogeneity at every point.

Through the medicine of metaphysical thinking, disorder is chained and order is intensified to paroxysm. It is a powerful potion, but it doesn't lack its own share of risk. Taken on its own and a*b-solutus* (un-bound) from any external counterweight, a metaphysical gaze doesn't merely tame, but it castrates both order and disorder – reducing them to linguistic elements that depend on metaphysics' own system. Metaphysical order develops into paranoia raised to the status of organizing principle for the whole of reality. Metaphysical disorder, by the same token, is reduced to being mere 'complexity', that is, a challenge that has inscribed within itself metaphysics' ability to resolve it.

An excessive reliance on the metaphysician's mode of worlding has been among the causes of Westernized Modernity's failure to live up to its own ambitions of creating a 'happy' world in which to establish its kingdom. More is needed, if living subjects are to inhabit a reality that is at least as broad and multifaceted as their own lives.

The second figure of this *tetrapharmakon* might offer a balancing contribution. Unlike the metaphysician, this figure just about survives today at the margins of history, in conditions of extreme material precarity: the shaman.[42]

---

[42]My understanding of the figure of the shaman is indebted to the work of Eduardo Viveiros de Castro and to his notion of 'multinaturalism' in Amerindian cosmology. 'Cultural relativism, which is a multiculturalism, presumes a diversity of partial, subjective representations bearing on an external nature, unitary and whole, that itself is indifferent to representation. Amerindians propose the inverse: on the one hand, a purely pronominal representative unit – the human is what and whomever occupies the position of the cosmological subject; every existent can be thought of as thinking (it exists, therefore it thinks), as "activated" or "agencied" by a point of view – and, on the other, a real or objective radical diversity. Perspectivism is a *multinaturalism*, since a perspective is not a representation.' E. Viveiros de Castro, *Cannibal Metaphysics*, edited and translated by P. Skafish, Minneapolis, MN, Minnesota University Press, 2014, p. 72.

The world-building attitude of the shaman intervenes on the work of the metaphysician with the might of contradiction – precisely, with the betrayal of the law of non-contradiction. When the shaman wrestles with the raw avalanche of perceptions, their solution to existential anxiety steers away from the metaphysician's attempt to create a world around the notion of reality as a discontinuous field, made up of separate units and elements.[43] The shamanic approach to worlding develops on the assumption that reality is fundamentally a continuous field, binding all things together without confusing them. The reality narrated by the shaman takes the shape of a long, labyrinthine tunnel traversing every existent.[44]

From a shamanic perspective, each 'thing' is only partly a single and autonomous entity, and only temporarily so: anything can turn into everything, at least potentially. Movement – rather than metaphysical presence – is the principle controlling the existent. But the metamorphic movement of reality has to be carefully handled, lest reality will be deprived of any possible imaginary landscape in which a subject's life might take hold and grow. The shaman themselves, as a specialized figure within a certain form of society, presides over the harmonic flow of this movement, to which they personally take part.

---

[43]'According to Simone Weil, "since Greece, science is a sort of dialogue between the continuous and the discontinuous." An inevitable dialogue because "the discontinuous and the continuous are givens of the human mind, which necessarily thinks one and the other; and it is natural that it goes from one to the other." But it is a dialogue that can also turn into war. And war tends to manifest itself above all as an invasion of territories. Something can then happen that "is repugnant to reason, namely that the discontinuous is applied to magnitudes essentially continuous. And this is the case with time and space." Over seventy years later, the majority of physicists would disagree with Weil on this point. But there is another territory where the discrete has conducted a relentless invasion, encountering only scarce resistance: the territory of the mind, as well as that of consciousness.' R. Calasso, *The Unnamable Present*, translated by R. Dixon, London, Penguin, 2019, pp. 64–5. Simon Weil's quote can be found in S. Weil, 'À propos de la mécanique ondulatoire', in *Œuvres complètes*, vol. IV, book I, edited by A.A. Devaux and F. de Lussy, Paris, Gallimard, 2008, p. 493.

[44]The shamanic continuum resounds in the Old Testament vision of Jacob's Ladder, 'And he dreamed that there was a ladder set up on the earth, the top of it reaching to heaven; and the angels of God were ascending and descending on it.' Genesis 28:12 (*The New Oxford Annotated Bible*).

The shaman understands that everything in the world can be both 'this' *and* 'that', and their practice consists precisely in engaging with this endless movement across different identities. At the same time, however, the shaman feels the disquieting proximity of an utterly ineffable realm, lying underneath the twisting of language and of identity. The shaman stands as a living threshold between the edges of the world and its time-segment, and what defeats any attempt to establish any world or time. Ultimately, the shaman places their allegiance with the world, and their mission is to preserve both the inner fabric of the world and its autonomy from unravelling.

The shaman appeases *Phobos*, the god of fear, by embodying a living sacrifice to the abyss: their figure is a hollow marble, traversed by everything and nothingness at once, sliding along the edges of order and disorder. The intensity of this effort is immense, demanding that the shamanic subject engages in a ceaseless negotiation with all the forces emerging from reality's multiple dimensions. The shaman runs through the corridors of reality, ever on the verge of getting lost within the world, or to lose the world entirely – it is only their strength that keeps them in balance.

Although a shamanic approach to worlding appears close to resolving the archaic-adolescent's wariness of both order and disorder – which are composed in a broad understanding of reality as multi-dimensional – it should be noted that it places an enormous burden on its adopters. The specialization of shamanic figures within society, far from deriving only from the needs of social organization, points to the special training and energy that are necessary to embrace the activity of worlding exclusively on the basis of a shamanic approach. While democratic in its intentions, a

---

[45]The hiddenness of the sage is a frequent trope in philosophical and theological literature (think of Epicurus's exhortation to those aspiring to wisdom: *lathe biosas*, 'live in hiding!'), but it is especially developed in Shiism and Sufism. Shiism in particular has produced a rich body of thought around the figure of the *Mahdi*: the 'hidden imam' who will exit occultation at the end of time but who, at the same time, exists always and already in the heart of every faithful as their guide towards spiritual enlightenment (similarly to the figure of the 'pole' in Sufism). See H. Corbin, *L'Imam cache et la renovation de l'homme en theologie shi'ite*, Paris, L'Herne, 1960.

shamanic form of worlding risks, in practice, to become extremely selective in the way in which it can be enacted.

Among the mix of stimulants provided by the metaphysician and the shaman, the third ingredient of the *tetrapharmakon* comes like a calming herb. The figure that represents it, today as ever, exists in a state of hiding: the mystic.[45] Its relaxing properties don't derive from its surrender to *Phobos*, but to a movement beyond the dichotomy between order and disorder. If the cosmology of a metaphysician decrees that things in the world are 'either this or that', and if the shaman claims that everything can be in fact 'both this and that', the solution adopted by the mystic revolves around the notion of 'neither nor'.[46] The mystic is neither a figure of the world nor of the unworldly; neither an element or language nor an agent of the ineffable; neither human nor non-human; neither living nor dead.[47]

The figure of the hidden mystic-guide of Islam finds a mythical embodiment in the trickster-like figure of *Al-Khidr* – often identified with the prophet Elijha and with the mysterious companion of Moses mentioned in the Quran, Sura 18. On the figure of Al-Khidr, see H. Talat Halman, *Where the Two Seas Meet: Al-Khidr and Moses: The Qur'anic Story of Al-Khidr and Moses in Sufi Commentaries as a Model for Spiritual Guidance*, Louisville, KY, Fons Vitae, 2013; and F. Schuon, *Understanding Islam*, Bloomington, IN, World Wisdom, 1998, pp. 86–7 and 173–4 f.76.

[46]When considering mysticism, *vis-à-vis* metaphysics or shamanism, 'two striking aspects mark its contradiction of the ritualization of time: instead of capturing time within a liturgy, the drive is towards escaping time itself; instead of introducing one's own personhood within the act of the rite, all action is abolished. Rituals of askesis aren't active, but they are disciplinary; they don't place the human in relation with time; by stripping it of everything, they bring the human closer to the nakedness of its nothingness'. A. Neher, *L'Essenza del Profetismo*, translated by E. Piattelli, Genova, Casa Editrice Marietti, 1984, p. 68 – my translation from the Italian edition.

[47]Simone Weil's notion of 'decreation' is especially important to appreciate this 'divine' quality of the mystic: 'On God's part creation is not an act of self-expansion but of restraint and renunciation. God and all his creatures are less than God alone. God accepted this diminution. He emptied a part of his being from himself. He had already emptied himself in this act of his divinity; that is why Saint John says that the Lamb had been slain from the beginning of the world. God permitted the existence of things distinct from himself and worth infinitely less than himself. By this creative act he denied himself, as Christ has told us to deny ourselves. God denied himself for our sakes in order to give us the possibility of denying ourselves for him. This response,

While the metaphysician and the shaman posit themselves as subjects, the mystic perfects the art of being an object. In the way in which they operate as a world-builder, the mystic takes on the character of a reflecting surface where the ineffable dimension of reality can catch a glimpse of its own face. The world-making narration of a mystic is a seamless cloth, where the external boundaries between reality and the Real are devoid of any value.[48]

According to a mystical cosmology, the boundaries of the world lie within, not around, the existent. Language and the ineffable, intertwined with each other, reside within the very nature of each being. Both of them, as attributes, are merely facets of pure existence, which is in itself beyond all possible conceptualization. Indeed, for the mystic, the fundamental kernel of reality is beyond any attribution to 'this' or 'that' identity. Any mistaken attempt to declare the existence of 'this' and 'that' would automatically disprove itself, due to its dependence on an existentiating force that transcends such categories. If pure existence ever shows itself – thus claims the mystic – it does so out of its own inscrutable erotic desire, and not with the aim of creating a world.[49]

Little matters of the world to the mystic, aside from the love that they see within its joints and between its parts. The mystic gives nothing to *Phobos*, because their world is a living declaration that

---

this echo, which it is in our power to refuse, is the only possible justification for the folly of love of the creative act.' S. Weil, *Waiting for God*, translated by E. Craufurd, New York, NY, Harper and Row, 1973, p. 145.

[48]'When the soldiers had crucified Jesus, they took his clothes and divided them into four parts, one for each soldier. They also took his tunic; now the tunic was seamless, woven in one piece from the top.' John, 19:23 (*The New Oxford Annotated Bible*).

[49]The relationship between mysticism and eroticism recurs in traditions spanning from Tantrism to Teresa of Avila. However, it has seldom found a more beautiful and precise expression than in the language of Islamic mysticism – where it is often presented through the metaphor of the love between a nightingale and a rose – and above all in the words of fourteenth-century Persian poet Hafiz and of thirteenth-century Turkish poet Rumi. For a critical overview, see A. Schimmel, *Mystical Dimensions of Islam, the Rose and the Nightingale: Persian and Turkish Mystical Poetry*, Chapel Hill, NC, The University of North Carolina Press, 1975, pp. 287–343.

nothing can truly be lost: pure existence is an eternal attribute of each being, and as such it is the true subject within each object.

Mysticism gives rise to no world, but it signs a truce between all parties involved in the struggle to impose order over disorder. Taken by itself, the herb of the mystic makes its user eventually forget the world, and thus also the aesthetic imperative of allowing new world-creations.

None of these three ingredients, on their own, suffices to aid the malady of having to face reality in its barest state, and to build a new world over the ruins of the old. Each of them is only a partial remedy to the difficulties of living in an archaic age, at the beginning of a new time. To extract some benefit from their properties, it is necessary to grind them to a fine powder and to combine them.

The overlapping of the three world-filters of the metaphysician, the shaman and the mystic offers a spectacle of reality in which everything appears to be always in excess to itself. As seen simultaneously through this multi-focal lens, the worldly dimension of reality appears to be only an island within a much larger ocean. Much more lies off the shore of what language can combine into the form of a world. There is always a part within each thing in the world that resides elsewhere – where it is always-already saved from the vicissitudes of the world, and from where it can come back, as a subject, to intervene on the world and to modify its assets.

The combined worlding methods provided by the first three ingredients of the *pharmakon* offer a possible trampoline that might give Archaic adolescents some inspiration and the confidence to start their own, unique narration of another age. But even that is not sufficient. As with any medicine, it needs to be assimilated by the organism. And the absorption of these methods of world-building by an Archaic mind risks to be immediately blocked by the reciprocal incompatibility of their languages.

It takes a fourth element to render the *tetrapharmakon* effective. To this fourth figure, I have dedicated the entirety of the next chapter. Alongside the metaphysician, the shaman and the mystic, the prophet provides that particular style and language which might be capable of holding together such an eclectic combination of contradictions – and to allow for their assimilation by a subject standing between the end and the beginning of the world. Within the voice of the prophet, the three ingredients considered so far resound simultaneously – but it is only the special tone, modulation and cadence of prophetic singing that might succeed in creating ruins capable of speaking to post-future subjects.

CHAPTER THREE

PROPHETIC CULTURE

FIGURE 3.1 *Giovanni Domenico Tiepolo*, Punchinello's Farewell to Venice (L'addio di Pulcinella a Venezia), *1798–1802. © National Gallery of Art, Washington, DC.*

PROLOGUE
THE ENIGMA

FIGURE 3.2 Map of the Walls of Jericho, *illustration from the* Farhi Bible, *written by Elisha ben Abraham ben Benvenisti (known as Elisha Cresques), between 1366 and 1382.*

> *We know very well that reality transforms language.*
> *But also, that language can transform reality.*[1]

'The origins of Greek philosophy, and thus of Western thought, are mysterious' – this lapidary statement opens Giorgio Colli's 1975 book *La Nascita della Filosofia*.[2] In that short volume, Colli explores the relationship between the origins of philosophy and the event of an enigma.

To thinkers like Heraclitus and Parmenides, reality emerged in the shape of a divine labyrinth – as intricate and inescapable, as it was imperative for those who encountered it to reach its centre. The enigma was the style in which the Gods communicated their paradoxical wisdom, bestowing it upon humans as both a gift and a challenge. In the time of the *sophoi* (the wise) who lived before *philo-sophia*, wisdom consisted in an agonistic relationship between Gods and humans – where the position of the latter was, inevitably, that of tragedy.

Compelled by their own 'political nature' to communicate their wisdom, the *sophoi* struggled to put down in words the solutions that each of them had unveiled in their own depths. Hence the necessity to speak in riddles, whose obscurity hinted to the dimensions of reality which are non-conceptual and beyond language.

Then, around the fifth century BC, a new wind began to sweep through the mind of Greek society. Orality declined in favour of writing and the last relics of shamanism succumbed to an

---

[1] '*Sappiamo bene che la realta' trasforma il linguaggio. Ma il linguaggio puo' trasformare la realta'.*' A/traverso, Bologna, December 1976.
[2] See G. Colli, *La Nascita della Filosofia*, Milan, Adelphi, 1975. Giorgio Colli (1917–79) was one of the main philosophers, philologists, historians of philosophy and translators of philosophy in the twentieth century. Alongside his translation of Aristotle's complete works into Italian and his own original work on the philosophy of expression, Colli dedicated a great part of his intellectual life to recuperating both philosophically and philologically the works of so-called 'pre-Socratic' thinkers – including mythological figures like Apollo, Dyonisius and Orpheus, whose words he painstakingly recuperated from the wider body of Greek literature (see G. Colli, *La Sapienza Greca*, 3 Vols., Milan, Adelphi, 1990–3). Among Colli's most notable achievements there is the compilation, together with philologist Mazzino Montinari, of the first official German edition of Friedrich Nitezsche's *oeuvre* – which finally corrected the malicious mishandling of Nietzsche's legacy by his Nazi-sympathizing sister Elizabeth.

increasingly institutionalized religion.[3] The Gods seemed to have abandoned the world and their enigmas ceased to glare from within each sound, leaf or pebble.

It was at that point, Colli concludes, that the agonistic field of knowledge shifted from a tragic relationship between Gods and humans, to an all-out competition among humans alone. Oracular riddles were substituted by the persuasive discourses of rhetoricians, whose power over their audience derived from an unrelenting logic combined with a charming prose. Until, ultimately, *sophia* gave way to *philo-sophia* – and specifically, to philosophy as a literary genre.

Yet, this major transformation didn't entirely shut the passage towards the ineffable dimension that hides at the heart of reality. Even in its philosophical form, the discourse (*logos*) that humans need to deploy to make sense of their own existence can still maintain an element of its archaic, wild clarity.

Such a passage to the divine realm is not to be found in the muscular power of formal logic, nor in the seductions of a rhetorical style, but in those elements within the *logos* that don't fall for the temptation of thinking themselves as absolute and coincident with the Truth. It is in its recognition of the weakness that comes with being a form of literature, that philosophy still holds a bundle of the thread leading back to the mysterious kernel of reality.[4]

Precisely in its being literature, rather than an impartial description of 'things as they are', philosophy is still able to hear the same enigma that the *sophoi* received from Apollo.

The Lord whose oracle is in Delphi neither speaks out nor conceals, but gives a sign.[5]

---

[3]G. Scholem, *Major Trends in Jewish Mysticism*, New York, NY, Schocken Books, 1995, p. 7.

[4]'[Philosophy is] signification and communication of what is not representable in itself and that, in the course of this process, is preserved only in part while in part it flees and is lost.' *Significazione e comunicazione di ciò che in sé non è rappresentabile e che in questo processo, solo in parte è conservato, e in parte sfugge e si perde.* G. Colli, *La Ragione Errabonda: Quaderni Postumi*, edited by E. Colli, Adelphi, Milan 1982, p. 248 – my translation.

[5]Heraclitus, B93, in G.S. Kirk et al., *The Presocratic Philosophers: A Critical History with a Selection of Texts*, Cambridge, Cambridge University Press, 2005, p. 209.

STUTTERING[6]

FIGURE 3.3 *Gabriel Rollenhagen,* Lingua Quo Tendis, *emblem from* Emblematum centuria prima, *engraved by Crispijn de Passe the Elder, 1613.* © *Herzog August Bibliothek Wolfenbüttel.*

---

[6]For an excellent contemporary discussion of stuttering that is very different (and in part opposed) to mine, see the essay by Miri Davidson, *Speech Work*, first published in *We Do Not Believe in the Good Faith of the Victors*, 2019, a one-off publication by Fraile Press, London, online at: https://socialtextjournal.org/speech-work/

I have placed prophetism at the crossing point
of a three-folded encounter:
that between tradition and life;
that between existence and essence;
that between the City of Humans and the City of God.[7]

One day, while tending the flock of his father-in-law, Moses reached the far side of the wilderness and came to Horeb, the mountain of God.

There the angel of the Lord appeared to him in a flame of fire out of a bush; he looked, and the bush was blazing, yet it was not consumed. [...] God said to Moses, 'Thus you shall say to the Israelites, "The Lord, the God of your ancestors, the God of Abraham, the God of Isaac and the God of Jacob, has sent me to you."'[8]

According to the Old Testament, with these words God invested Moses with the role of acting as His prophet, the one who would bring His message to the tribe of Israel. But Moses protested; he objected God's demand with counterarguments. He knew for a fact not to be the best suited for the task:[9]

But Moses said to the Lord, 'O my Lord, I have never been eloquent, neither in the past nor even now that you have spoken to your servant; but I am slow of speech and slow of tongue. [...] O my Lord please send someone else.'[10]

Moses had a stammer. He couldn't possibly persuade an entire people with a stunted rhetoric as his only means, especially when

---

[7]A. Neher, *L'Essenza del Profetismo*, translated by E. Piattelli, Genova: Casa Editrice Marietti, 1984, p. 3 – my translation from the Italian edition.
[8]Exodus, 3:2; 3:15 (*The New Oxford Annotated Bible*).
[9]A recent theoretical examination of Moses's fragility can be found in J-C. Attias, *Moise Fragile*, Paris: Alma Editeur, 2015 (somewhat incorrectly translated in English as *A Woman Called Moses* – see J.-C. Attias, *A Woman Called Moses*, London/New York, Verso, 2020).
[10]Exodus 4:10; 4:13 (*The New Oxford Annotated Bible*).

carrying a message from outside the world. But God cares little
about facts. Moses wasn't given an option: he had *already* become
a prophet, even before receiving the command. It happened the
moment he looked at the burning bush and saw that it was not
consumed. His fate was sealed as soon as he heard the voice rising
from the bush and recognized the impossible within the possible,
eternity within time, the face of reality as an enigma. Experience
made him a mystic, and mysticism grew into prophecy as soon as it
met his heart, bound to the *politeia* (community) of those around
him. He had seen the unspeakable, and he was compelled to talk
about it. From that point onwards, his destiny was to become a
public cartographer of the unseen.

Beckett's formula, 'I can't go on. I'll go on,' is perhaps the
briefest definition of tragedy, but it is just as apt a description of the
condition of the prophet. Tragedy arises whenever a 'political animal
endowed with language'[11] encounters the ineffable dimension of
reality. A hero hit by tragedy sees their life moving from the field
of measurable activity to a theatrical stage where events diverge
from facts. Their voice, coming from behind the mask of tragedy,
resounds like the stammering of a prophet.

Such inner workings of prophecy are already implicit in the
term *prophanai* (to speak in front). Etymologically, prophecy has
its roots in the verb *phainein* (to show), and the soil that sustains it
in the noun *phos* (light). The prophet shows what they have seen,
not by representing it, but by shedding a light on it in front of other
people.

The light of prophecy, however, is of a paradoxical kind: it is
cast over an object that is made invisible by an excess of luminosity.
The prophet has to speak about the silence that constitutes the very
condition from which language can emerge. They need to bring
into the house of the phenomenon its very foundations, regardless
of whether the whole edifice might collapse. Indeed, any form of

---

[11]*Zoon logon echon* (animal endowed with language) and *zoon politikon* (political
animal) are Aristotle's definitions of the human being, at various points in the *Ethics*
and in the *Politics*. Today, as the idea of a human exclusiveness of the opera of
worlding is finally being successfully challenged, it is possible to apply them also to
other life-forms endowed with different forms of *logos*.

language that is burdened with the task of speaking beyond itself is destined to implode.[12]

Moses had a stammer, because a prophet *has* to have a stammer. It is a matter of optics: an excessive light-source can be brought into the range of the visible only by obfuscating its blaze. A prophet's stammer is a smoked-up mirror, where the ineffable might become visible precisely where the reflecting surface is at its most opaque – in the uncertainties, the hesitations, the excessive pauses of language.[13] But a prophet's stammer is not enough to make a prophecy, unless

---

[12]It is possible to observe a technical similarity between the stuttering of a prophet, with its connection to the ineffable, and what linguistic Roman Jacobson called the 'apex of babble' in the linguistic development of very young children. 'A babbling child can accumulate articulations which are never found within a single language or even a group of languages: consonants with the most varied points of articulation, palatalized and rounded consonants, sibilants, affricates, clicks, complex vowels, diphthongs and so forth.' R. Jacobson, *Child Language, Aphasia, and Phonological Universals*, The Hague, Mouton, 1968, p. 21. Daniel Heller-Roazen's comment is enlightening in this regard: 'Perhaps the infant must forget the infinite series of sounds he once pronounced at the "apex of babble" to obtain mastery of the finite system of consonants and vowels that characterize a single language. Perhaps the loss of a limitless phonetic arsenal is the price a child must pay for the papers that grant him citizenship in the community of a single tongue.' D. Heller-Roazen, *Echolalias: On the Forgetting of Language*, New York, NY, Zone Books, 2005, p. 11.

[13]An interesting visual elaboration on prophetic stammering can be found in the visionary works of fourteenth-century Italian mystic cartographer Opicinus de Canistris. Working as a priest for most of his life, Opicinus was tormented by obsessive doubts about his own ability to perform his sacramental duties. In particular, he feared mixing up or mispronouncing the words of ritual formulae, thus rendering inoperative his actions as a priest. As a consequence, he developed a form of stammer, which he tried to compensate through an equally obsessive production of mystical cartographies of the cosmos and of his own self – often presented as one and the same thing. 'One of the meanings that Opicinus attributes to his own name is connected to the Greek verb *opizein*, as it is adopted in Latin with the meaning "to stammer". Opicinus thus presents himself as the one who chews or shortens words (*frendens nomine*) ... If stammering was not among the causes of his sacramental panic, it might well have been one of its consequences.' S. Piron, *Dialectique du Monstre*, Brussels, Editions Zones Sensibiles, 2015 – my translation from the Italian edition, S. Piron, *Dialettica del Mostro: Indagine su Opicinus de Canistris*, translated by A.G. Nissim, Milan, Adelphi, 2019, p. 162. By an interesting coincidence, also eleventh-century Byzantine philosopher and theologian Michael Psellos (a famous commentator of the *Chaldean Oracles*), owes his surname to another Greek word for stammering, *psellizein*.

the audience has learned how to make their hearing stammer, too. Even the clearest prophecy remains entirely impenetrable, if the receiver is unable to hear the silences and hesitations within it.

Let's think of the anecdote retold by the thirteenth-century Cistercian monk Albericus Trium Fontium in his book *Chronicon*.[14] Back in the Roman days, Albericus recounts, a soldier went to consult the oracle of the Sybilla on the eve of a battle. 'Will I return from the field tomorrow?' he asked the oracle, trepidant. The reply of the Sybilla was nothing short of exhaustive: *Ibis redibis non morieris in bello*, 'You will go you will return not in the war you will perish.'

Her reply lacked literally nothing: a pause between words. Depending on whether a pause was placed before or after the *non*, her oracle could be interpreted to predict survival or death. If he was to understand the words on which his very life depended, the soldier needed to hear the unwritten rests gaping between sounds.

Albericus doesn't tell us if the soldier ever managed to unlock the oracle. If he did, however, chances are that the question that had brought him to the Sybilla had already ceased to bother him. To be able to hear the hidden rests within reality, one has to shift their position so radically that perishing or surviving ceases to be worthy of an anguished concern.

Using the license granted by the literary nature of philosophy, let us imagine that the soldier succeeded in attuning his hearing to the hidden stammer of reality, and that he finally solved the riddle. Whatever the response that he uncovered, we can see him the night before battle, sitting at the light of a campfire, carving on his shield one image and a few words – what in the Renaissance shall be known as a person's *impresa*. Perhaps anachronistically, the engraving that shall glare under the morning light will be the same that centuries later Isabella D'Este actually chose for herself. Above, the image of a musical pentagram filled only by signs of rest, symmetrically arranged. Underneath, a brief motto in Latin: *nec spe*

---

[14]See Paulus Scheffer-Boichorst (ed.), *Chronica Albrici Monachi Trium Fontium*, in *Monumenta Germaniae Historica: Scriptorum*, vol. 23, Leipzig, Verlag Karl W. Hiersemann, 1925, pp. 631–950.

nec metu, 'without hope without fear.'[15] Fearless and hopeless like a prophet, that soldier would have accepted the impossible task of partaking to history, while focusing on the rests that give rhythm to the partiture of reality.

> *Maybe the only thing that hints at a sense of Time is rhythm; not the recurrent beats of the rhythm but the gap between two such beats, the grey gap between black beats: the Tender Interval. The regular throb itself merely brings back the miserable idea of measurement, but in between, something like true Time lurks. How can I extract it from its soft hollow?*[16]

Our imaginary soldier swapped the predictive value of the Sybilla's oracle for an opportunity to develop a prophetic attitude towards language and its silent shadow.

Such a passage from prediction to prophecy might serve us, here, as an important disclaimer against a frequent confusion between the two processes. For most people – today as ever – the term 'prophecy' brings to mind the claims of fortune-tellers and the ambitions of forecasters of any kind. Indeed, it is not infrequent to encounter cases of prophetic utterances dealing with aspects of the future – that of the Sybilla, recounted by Albericus Trium

---

[15] A popular personal mark among aristocrats at the time of the Renaissance, an *impresa* was usually composed by a visual element (*res picta*) and by a motto (*inscriptio*), integrated at times by a few verses (*subscripto*). *Nec Spe Nec Metu* is an *inscriptio* without a visual body; the *res picta* of the rests on a pentagram (still visible in her *studiolo* in Palazzo Ducale in Mantua) lacks a verbal voice: combined, they produce one complete impresa. An *impresa* should always be read as a direct emanation of the personality of its owner, rather than as an abstract *bon mot*. In the case of Isabella d'Este, however, we have to do with a living human archetype – a Vitruvian woman in flesh and blood, among the most powerful creators of Renaissance style and sensibility. Her composite *impresa* is not only an element in her biography – it can be observed also as the portrait of a universal existential possibility. For an enlightening and erudite study of *imprese* in the Italian Renaissance and beyond, see M. Praz, *Studi Sul Concettismo*, Milan, Abscondita, 2014. For a new, fascinating interpretation of emblems in the light of a contemporary eco-philosophical sensibility, see poet Lucy Mercer's PhD thesis, *Speculative Emblematics: An Environmental Iconology*, Royal Holloway, University of London, 2020.

[16] V. Nabokov, *Ada, or Ardor: A Family Chronicle*, London, Penguin Classics, 2011, p. 421.

Fontium, being only one example. Whatever the temporal horizon of a prophetic utterance, however, it is important to realize that its message excludes, or at least greatly belittles, any concerns about the chain of events within one historical time-segment.

The opposition between prophecy and prediction is already evident in the original forms of these two terms: *pro-phanai* (to speak in front) is not *pre-dicere* (to speak in advance).

Prediction consists in the ability to see the succession of events within a certain time-segment, before they take place. A predicter is firmly set in a certain present, and from there they look at the seamless stretching-forward of time towards the future. An aspiring predicter requires, not only to be able to read the direction of the present, but also that no apocalypse ever comes to interrupt the narration of its particular time-segment.

Prediction, as a kind of interior design of the future, can flourish only as long as the chronogenic and cosmogonic song of the world keeps on flowing from the voice of a certain civilization. At a historical time when the future is about to run out, however, prediction fails to gain much of an insight into a time that is simply not going to be there to fulfil it.

This is especially evident today, when the society of Westernized Modernity has finally achieved a good technological mastery over the process of prediction within its own time-segment. As that particular time is oozing its last drops, the field of vision that is available to prediction is progressively crushed by the approaching wall of the horizon. Any ambition to predict under these circumstances – such as those that are engineered within machine-learning AI systems – amounts to a metaphysical fantasy, or, more simply, to an ever-diminutive achievement.

On the contrary, the prophet 'speaks in front' both of the present in which they live and of the chain of future events. To prophesize means to speak from the position of the 'end time': from a standpoint where time is recognized in its internal finitude, as a puzzle made of segment-upon-segment.

Time is a legitimate feature of reality for both predicter and prophet – but while the former sees it unfold along one sole avenue, where the observer is at once traveller and paving stone, the latter looks at time as if from the side of the road. Predicter and prophet stand at different levels of identification with time – one absolute and the other relative – and from their respective positions they create entirely different ways of engaging with the chain of events that are recorded in history.[17]

Whenever prophetic culture speaks of future events, its real message consists in the assertion that there is an outside to history, where the very notions of past–present–future appear irrelevant. Prophecy directs our attention to the spatial and extensional nature of time, describing the course of history like a physical object whose different portions we call past, present and future – in the same way that portions of our arm may be called wrist, forearm or elbow.

Being unable to speak directly about the ineffable realm of eternity, prophecy speaks of history *as if* from the standpoint of eternity. The brash facility with which prophecy treats notions of past, present and future is not a trick in a spectacle of prediction, but a symptom of its implicit relativizing time. In the words of twentieth-century Romanian theologian Dumitru Staniloae:

> *To rise above the things of the world does not mean that these disappear; it means, through them, to rise beyond them. And since they remain, the apophatic [i.e. negative] knowledge of God does not exclude affirmative rational knowledge … In apophatic knowledge the world remains, but it has become transparent of God. This knowledge is apophatic because the God who now is perceived cannot be defined; he is experienced as a reality which transcends all possibility of definition.*[18]

---

[17]Emanuele Severino paradoxically collapses this distance from prediction in his prophetic notion of philosophy (and of Greek tragedy) as connected to the Whole of reality: 'In thinking about nothingness, philosophy evokes the most extreme form of pain and of anguish – and Greek tragedy is the most powerful form of this evocation. But both philosophy and tragic thought are also the remedy to the danger that they have unearthed. If anguish derives from the unpredictability of the future, and if prediction bridles pain within meaning and renders anguish bearable, then philosophy, as the knowledge of the truth of the Whole – that is, as the true knowledge that see the arche, where all beings are generated and where they eventually dissolve – emerges as the Supreme Prediction, which alone can see the Sense of the world.' E. Severino, *La Filosofia dai Greci al Nostro Tempo: La filosofia antica e medioevale*, Milan, Rizzoli, 2004, pp. 36–7 (ebook edition) – my translation.

[18]D. Staniloae, *The Experience of God: Orthodox Dogmatic Theology*, vol. 1, translated by I. Ionita, Brookline, MA, Holy Cross Orthodox Press, 1989, p. 99.

Yet, how can one talk about events taking place within time, while standing in a position that is external to time itself? The prophet has no choice but to stutter about time, *nec spe nec metu,* publicly attempting an impossible performance.

A prophet's vision of historical events is as blurred and inaccurate, as their understanding of time's essence is crystalline. For an aspiring forecaster, there is little of use in a prophet's oracular utterances about what the future has in store. This is precisely the point: to avoid looking at prophecy as if one was handling a form of prediction. With regard to the future, a prophet jumbles up their words into an apparent riddle – which, once resolved, reveals itself as a joke. When prophecy engages itself with the future, it does so as if replying to an elbow that anxiously asks, 'when will the wrist arrive?'

> *Don't you ask, Leuconoe – the gods do not wish it to be known –*
> *What end they have given to me or to you, and don't meddle with*
> *Babylonian horoscopes.*[19]

Prophecy challenges, not the possibility of answering the demand for prediction issued by the voice of the present, but the anguished sense of urgency that usually accompanies such questioning.[20]

---

[19]Horace, *Tu ne quaesiris* – in Horace, *The Complete Odes and Epodes, Odes,* I, XI, translated by D. West, Oxford, Oxford World Classics, 2008, p. 34.

[20]In the *Chaldean Oracles,* a prophetic text par excellence, the injunction against any attempt at engaging with prediction is rather stricter: 'Do not cast into your mind the huge measure of the earth, for the plant of truth does not exist on earth. Do not measure the extent of the sun by joining rods together, for he is borne along by the eternal will of the Father and not for your sake. Let be the rushing motion of the moon; she forever runs her course by the action of Necessity. The starry procession has not been brought forth for your sake. The wide winged flight of birds is never true, nor the cutting and entrails of sacrificial victims. All these are ... the props of commercial fraud. Flee these things, if you would open the sacred paradise.' *The Chaldean Oracles,* fragment 107, edited and translated by R. Majercik, Leiden, E.J. Brill, 1989, pp. 90–1. The *Chaldean Oracles* are a series of sapiential formulae and invocations composed around the second/third century BC by the Roman/ Mesopotamian philosopher Julian the Theurgist. These often-obscure verses had

It is possible to interpret along these lines also the distance that runs between future-oriented utopian projects and the post-future approach of prophetic culture.

The utopic form belongs entirely to Modernity. [...] The elements that it shares with prophecy cannot hide the difference between the two: for the prophet, the whole of history is divine manifestation. [...] His activity is neither pre-vision nor pre-diction, but it is rather an affirmation here-and-now, en parrhesia, of what he heard from his Lord, and which He asked him to repeat to the people. [...] [Prophecy] is paradoxical hope, certain hope, irreducible to that which is presented by utopia. [...] On the other hand, modern utopia is a rational construct that doesn't presuppose the possibility of the divine breaking within history in such a way as to determine an absolute discontinuity. Utopia is essentially the idea of an evolution of history towards a future that, however not precisely calculable, can function as a paradigm directing present activity. This is a future that man is supposed to be able to pursue and to reach, by obeying only his own reason and his own nature. [...] Utopia concerns actual subjects and energies that proceed iuxta propria principia to the realization of intra-worldly goals.[21]

The discourse of prophecy points towards a dimension of existence cutting across the time of history, while remaining fundamentally alien to it. The infinitely recurring event of this reciprocal penetration

---

a powerful impact on later Neoplatonism, especially on Proclus and Iamblichus, who considered them as a very ancient – possibly millennia-old – equivalent to the esoteric aspects of Plato's teachings. Interest in them revived in the Italian Renaissance, especially in the circle of Marsilio Ficino and of Pico della Mirandola. They survive today only in small fragments (mostly thanks to the commentaries dedicated to them by eleventh-century Byzantine theologian Michael Psellos). On the pan-Mediterranean 'theological *koine*' inaugurated by the Chaldean Oracles, see P. Athanassiadi, 'The Chaldean Oracles: Theology and Theurgy', in P. Athanassiadi and M. Frede (eds.), *Pagan Monotheism in Late Antiquity*, Oxford, Oxford University Press, 1999, pp. 149–84.

[21]M. Cacciari, 'Grandezza e Tramonto dell'Utopia', in M. Cacciari and P. Prodi (eds.), *Occidente Senza Utopie*, Bologna, Il Mulino, 2016, pp. 65–7 – my translation.

between eternity and time, ineffability and language, enlivens the array of symbolic figures that populate works of prophetic culture.

If one was to remove the dimension of eternity from the horizon of prophecy, reducing it to a realm that can be mapped linguistically, prophecy would entirely lose its prophetic character. Once reduced to prediction or to utopia, prophecy's cosmological tale takes the same traits as all other forms of language, locked within the constraints of their own grammar.

THE GROTESQUE

FIGURE 3.4 *Jean Berain and Gabriel Ladame (after Hugues Brisville), Diverses Pieces de Serruriers, page 4 (recto), engraving, c. 1663. © The Metropolitan Museum of Art.*

*In addition to the normal phonological system, many languages
have still other, special phonological elements. To these
belong in particular 'foreign sounds', that is, the phonemes
that are borrowed from the phonological system of a foreign
language ... Usually these foreign phonemes are not realized
in exactly the same way in the particular foreign language, but
[they] are assimilated to the native system ... Furthermore,
[they] are not always pronounced in their 'proper place' once
they have entered the language. They are a sign of foreignism.*[22]

Prophetic stories often sound ridiculous. Not just because of the
number of absurdities that they contain, but because of the way
in which these are put together. The language of prophecy is so
distorted to be funny and disquieting at once. It is a form of *pictura
somnium* (dream painting),[23] resembling the style that is known
since the Renaissance as 'the grotesque'.

If there is one term that defines the relationship between prophetic
culture and the metaphysics that it conveys, this is 'grotesque'.

To gain an image of this key stylistic element of prophetic
language, let us move back to late-fifteenth-century Rome – precisely
to the slopes of the Esquiline hill, then a semi-rural area of the city.
One day, while tending his flock a young shepherd fell through the
foliage covering a hole in the ground. 'Falling down what seemed
to be a very deep well',[24] he found himself inside a large vaulted
hall, partly flooded by soil and debris. When he ignited his linchpin,
he noticed that the room was covered floor to ceiling in bizarre,
monstrous paintings, starkly drawn against a white background.
There were figures that were all things and none at all: a satyr that
half-way became a leaf, which in turn became a pillar, then a satyr
again, then a fish ...

---

[22]N.S. Trubetzkoy, *Principles of Phonology*, translated by C.A.M. Baltaxe, Berkeley,
CA, University of California Press, 1971, pp. 207–8.

[23]The disparaging definition given in 1556 by architect Daniele Barbaro to the newly
re-discovered Roman 'grotesque' paintings – quoted in A. Chastel, *La Grottesca*,
translated by S. Lega, Milan, Se, 2010, p. 22.

[24]L. Carroll, *Alice's Adventures in Wonderland and through the Looking Glass,
Alice's Adventures in Wonderland*, London, Penguin, 2003, p. 10.

The shepherd had inadvertently discovered the buried ruins of Emperor Nero's palace, the *Domus Aurea*. News of his discovery spread across Renaissance Italy and scholars and artists from all over the peninsula rushed to be lowered into the hole on the Esquiline hillside, to see for the first time that old–new style of painting. Since they had been found in a place resembling a grotto, these paintings were named *grottesche* – and their style became known as 'the grotesque'.[25]

This re-discovered style of Roman painting[26] succeeded in rekindling the same mix of excitement and repulsion which it had first attracted at the time of its creation. The description offered by the ancient Roman architect Marcus Vitruvius Pollio, who discarded it as 'senseless ornaments',[27] was echoed in the Renaissance by the foremost art theorist Giorgio Vasari, for whom they were nothing but 'a vulgar and ridiculous style'.[28] During the Tridentine period, many a conservative thinker like Cardinal Gabriele Paleotti

---

[25]This was the explanation given by Benvenuto Cellini in his famous autobiography: 'The curious discovering them in such places (since the level of the ground has gradually been raised while they have remained below, and since in Rome these vaulted rooms are commonly called grottoes), it has followed that the word grotesque is applied to the patterns I have mentioned. But this is not the right term for them, inasmuch as the ancients, who delighted in composing monsters out of goats, cows, and horses, called these chimerical hybrids by the name of monsters; and the modern artificers of whom I speak, fashioned from the foliage which they copied monsters of like nature; for these the proper name is therefore monsters, and not grotesques.' B. Cellini, *Autobiography*, Chapter VI, translated by J. Addington Symonds, New York, NY, Cosimo Classics, 2009, p. 63.

[26]Presently known as the Third Style, or Ornate Style, of Roman painting.

[27]'For example, reeds are substituted for columns, fluted appendages with curly leaves and volutes take the place of pediments, candelabra support representations of shrines, and on top of their roofs grow slender stalks and volutes with human figures senselessly seated upon them.' Vitruvius, *Ten Books on Architecture*, VII, 5.3, translated by M.H. Morgan, Cambridge, MA, Harvard University Press, 1914. Other vocal critics of this style were Pliny the Elder and Petronious, who lamented the demise of good old naturalism in favour of such nonsensical pictorial styles as there were in their time.

[28]G. Vasari, *Le Vite de' più eccellenti pittori scultori e architetti italiani*, vol. 1, XXVII, Firenze, Sansoni, 1966, p. 143 – my translation.

attacked the *grottesche* as 'capricious figments of the imagination',[29] underserving of a legitimate place in the catalogue of the arts.

The hostility with which the grotesque style was met by its cultural critics referred not only to its immediate aesthetics, but especially to its metaphysical implications.

> *We can show its originality [i.e. of the grotesque style] through its two laws … : the negation of space and the fusion of different species, the lack of gravity in every shape and the insolent proliferation of hybrids. At first [it is] a vertical world that is entirely defined by the game of graphics, without thickness or weight, a mix of rigour and inconsistency that brings to the mind a dream. In this linear emptiness, wonderfully articulated, semi-vegetal forms, semi-animals, figures "without a name" rise and merge into one another, along the elegant, windy movement of the ornament. From this, comes a double feeling of liberation; from concrete extension, as ruled by gravity, and from the order of the world that governs the distinction between beings. … The field of the grotesque is thus almost the exact antithesis of that of representation.*[30]

Despite this opposition,[31] however, the grotesque style enjoyed enormous success in European art, lasting until the Victorian era and resuscitating now and then ever since. Grotesque ornaments can be found almost ubiquitously, retaining in all their instances the fundamental traits of 'doubleness, hybridity and metamorphosis'.[32]

---

[29]G. Paleotti, *Discorso Intorno alle Immagini Sacre e Profane, diviso In cinque libri*, Bologna, 1582 – cited here from the reprint of books 1–2 in P. Barocchi (ed.), *Trattati d'arte del Cinquecento fra Manierismo e Controriforma*, vol. 2, book 2, ch. 37, Bari, Laterza, 1960–2, p. 425.

[30]A. Chastel, *La Grottesca*, translated by S. Lega, Milan, Se, 2010, pp. 32–3 – my translation from the Italian edition.

[31]One example above all: in the Medici Chapel, planned and built by Michelangelo, the grotesque ornaments produced by Giovanni da Udine were pitilessly whitewashed in 1556 by Giorgio Vasari (following a previous authorization by Pope Clement VII Medici). See David Summers, 'Michelangelo on Architecture', *The Art Bulletin*, vol. 54, no. 2, June 1972, pp. 146–57: 151.

[32]See R. Astruc, *Le Renouveau du grotesque dans le roman du XXe siècle*, Paris, Classiques Garnier, 2010.

To an attentive observer, however, grotesque figures are something more than simple hybrids. Their proliferation is virtually limitless, and their repetition signals to the depersonalization at their heart.

Like a minotaur, or a mermaid, or a cyborg, the grotesque is not one thing or the other, and this boundary creature roams the borderlands of all that is familiar and conventional. [...] First, the grotesque is best understood by what it does, not what it is. It is an action, not a thing – more like a verb than a noun. [...] Second, what the grotesque does best is to play or, rather, to put things into play. [...] And most important, the grotesque is best understood as something that creates meaning by prying open a gap.[33]

Suspending one's own metaphysical habits in front of a grotesque ornament allows the ridiculous to surface together with the vision of another, possible structure of reality. The 'moment of judgement' (*krisis*), when a subject draws distinctions within the unbroken avalanche of raw perceptions, is here resolved otherwise than it is commonly the case in Westernized Modernity. The line between a leaf and the hand that touches it no longer runs as a border separating two entities, but is indefinitely postponed.

This grotesque form of metaphysical geography can be found already in earlier mixed-technique artworks, where the flat surface of a canvas or of a panel is broken and expanded by the introduction of three-dimensional features. Carlo Crivelli's *Saint Peter*,[34] for example, confronts the viewer with a narration that takes place simultaneously on multiple levels: the dimension of the painting, expressive and stylized in the manner typical of Crivelli, opens up

---

[33]F.S. Connelly, *The Grotesque in Western Art and Culture: The Image at Play*, Cambridge, Cambridge University Press, 2012, pp. 1–2.

[34]The panel of *Saint Peter* is part of the so-called '*Demidoff Altarpiece*', painted by Carlo Crivelli for the Church of San Domenico in Ascoli Piceno in 1476, now at the National Gallery in London. Another notable example from the same time is Sandro Botticelli's used of this combination of two- and three-dimensional media in his *Portrait of a Man with a Medal of Cosimo the Elder* (1475) at the Uffizi in Florence. An example of a more popular use of the same method of depicting grotesquely a sacred scene is the *Mourners and Christ on the Cross* (1520–30), by an anonymous local artist, which can be found in the Palazzo Comunale in San Gimignano.

to the register of a bulging set of keys made of plaster, where the mode of representation is substituted by that of embodiment.

It can also be found in religious paintings from the European Theocratic Age,[35] when the combination between different realms of existence was expressed with remarkable clarity. When artists of that age depicted the infant Christ as a monstrous-looking baby in the lap of a beautifully idealized Mary, they were employing the grotesque method to depict a child who was no normal child, and a God who was not simply an abstract divinity but an incarnate mystery. Likewise, in *Fondo Oro* (golden background) paintings, they represented the inhabitants of the world as two-dimensional figures floating over an utterly alien landscape – a monochrome surface of gold foil, symbolizing what exceeds any possible figuration.[36]

> *The light of an icon is the prime symbol of the gratuitous overflowing of the Good ... No obstacle can block its irradiation, and no darkness can dissipate it. This is the essential theological reason for the refusal of perspective figuration: The Light, in its creative irradiation, cannot obey any other force but its own, and it cannot arrange itself according to the 'necessity' of the 'natures' which it encounters. It doesn't only illuminate the forms, but it creates them.*[37]

Their apparent failure to follow the rules of pictorial perspective should also be reviewed in the light of the grotesque style. A painting endowed with proper 'perspective' – from *perspicere* (to look ahead) – is that which allows its viewer to see as far 'ahead' as it is possible. Works constructed around a geometric notion of

---

[35]See *intra*, footnote 73.

[36]'Gold, which by the diffused light of day is barbaric, heavy and devoid of content, comes to life in the flickering light of the icon lamp or candle, for it sparkles with a myriad flashes in every direction, conveying a presentiment of other, unworldly lights, filling a heavenly space. Gold, which is the conventional attribute of the celestial world and which in a museum is something contrived and allegorical, in a church with flickering icon lamps and a multitude of burning candles is a living symbol, it is representation.' P. Florensky, *Beyond Vision: Essays on the Perception of Art, The Church Ritual as a Synthesis of The Arts*, edited by N. Misler, translated by W. Salmond, London, Reaktion Books, 2002, pp. 101–11: 108.

[37]M. Cacciari, *Tre Icone*, Milan, Adelphi, 2007, pp. 19–20 – my translation.

perspective (as endorsed for example by Brunelleschi) propose to the viewer a horizon that is enclosed within the limit-concept of infinity: their world remains within the boundaries of measurability and of language. Conversely, paintings like those on *Fondo Oro*, which seemingly lack any proper perspective, offer to their viewer a point of perspective from which they can look ahead, not only to infinity, but towards the eternity symbolized by gold. Their perspective is radically more generous, and thus by definition more accomplished, than the conic angle offered by geometric grids.[38]

The grotesque style endows a cultural producer with a multidimensional form of expression, which abides to a vision of reality where each speck of existence and each individual object are fields that exceed their own metaphysical boundaries.

The abstract tone of these arguments shouldn't lead the reader to believe that they are confined to the speculations of theologians and of philosophers. Experiences of this co-existence of impossibly different registers of reality within one same image abound in our everyday life, like as many 'profane illuminations'.[39] To define them,

---

[38]'Does perspective in actual fact express the nature of things, as its supporters maintain, and should it therefore be always and everywhere viewed as the unconditional prerequisite for artistic veracity? Or is it rather just a schema, and moreover one of several possible representational schemas, corresponding not to a perception of the world as a whole, but only to one of the possible interpretations of the world, connected to a specific feeling for, and understanding of, life? ... The absence of linear perspective among the Egyptians, as also in a different sense among the Chinese, demonstrates the maturity of their art, ... it demonstrates the liberation from perspective, or a refusal from the very beginning to acknowledge its power ... For the task of painting is not to duplicate reality, but to give the most profound penetration of its architectonics, of its material, of its meaning ... [And] there are realities, i.e., there are centres of being, something in the nature of concentrates of more intense being, that submit to their own laws, and each of which therefore has its own form. Therefore, nothing that exists can be seen as indifferent and passive material for fulfilling whatsoever kind of schemas, still less taking into account the schema of Euclidean-Kantian space. And so forms should be apprehended according to their own life, they should be represented through themselves, according to the way they have been apprehended, and not in the foreshortenings of a perspective laid out before-hand.' P. Florensky, *Beyond Vision: Essays on the Perception of Art, Reverse Perspective*, edited by N. Misler, translated by W. Salmond, London, Reaktion Books, 2002, pp. 197–272: 207–9 and 218.

[39]W. Benjamin, 'Surrealism: The Last Snapshot of the European Intelligentsia', in *One Way Street and Other Writings*, translated by E. Jephcott and K. Shorter, London, NLB, 1979, pp. 225–39: 231.

German writer Ernst Junger coined the notion of a 'stereoscopic gaze' – and to convey their mundanity, he used the example of being able to see a face inside the landscape of the moon, like children do, while not renouncing the scientific knowledge of adults. As Junger wrote in his beautiful *Sicilian Letter to the Man in the Moon*:

> *It is certainly true that the lunar landscape with its rocks and valleys is a surface that creates a task for astronomical topographers. But it is equally certain that it is simultaneously accessible to magical trigonometry ... – that it is at the same time a domain of spirits, and that the fantasy that gave it a face understood ... the language of daemons with all the profundity of a child's glance. But what was unprecedented for me in this moment was to see these two masks of one and the same Being melt inseparably into each other. Because here, for the first time, a tormenting dichotomy resolved itself for me ... It was not that an Either/Or changed into a Both/And. No, the real is just as magical as the magical is real. Here it was, the miraculous quality that had delighted us about the twofold images that we observed as children through a stereoscope: in the very moment they fused together into a single image, a new dimension of depth emerged from within them.*[40]

This peculiar method of worlding – presented by grotesque imagery in a compressed form – can be approached more evidently in examples of prophetic literature. Sacred texts in virtually every religious tradition apply the grotesque treatment, not only to creatures belonging to one same plane of existence (humans, animals, plants, objects), but also to figures coming from altogether different dimensions of reality. Humans and angels mingle with the phantasmatic and the inorganic, while the vertical plane of the Divine – as ineffable as a golden background – pierces the landscape at each point.

The lens of the grotesque is also indispensable to interpret the prophetic narrations of historical events. The evangelic tale of Christ's death and resurrection, for example, is an attempt to

---

[40]E. Jünger, *The Adventurous Heart: Figures and Capriccios*, translated by T. Friese, Candor, NY, Telos Press, 2012, pp. 129–30.

convey narratively the mass of events that were taking place in multiple dimensions of reality within the space of one sole moment in history. Only some of those events could be detected at a factual level – yet, this doesn't delegitimize their place within a complete account of reality. However keenly historians and archaeologists will look for proof or disprove of the narration of the Gospel, their discoveries will be limited to a restricted field of what is 'there' within existence.[41]

Likewise, when the Quran tells of thousands of angels descending from Heaven to join forces with the Muslims against the Quraish during the battle of Badr in 624 AD,[42] the grotesque narration of this event attempts to convey in one sole text a total-picture which is irreducible to words. If one was to search for proof of the passage of the angelic host in the archaeological deposits buried under the soil, they would miss the implicit message that the realm of factuality is only one, among the dimensions that simultaneously compose reality.

Both geographical and historical facts possess a symbolic validity that in no way detracts from their being facts, but that actually, beyond this obvious reality, gives them a higher significance. (This can be compared to the multiplicity of meanings according to which the sacred texts are interpreted, and which, far from opposing or destroying one another, on the contrary complement and harmonize each other in the knowledge of integral synthesis.)[43]

---

[41]'Many people think one can decide whether a miracle occurred in the past by examining the evidence "according to the ordinary rules of historical inquiry." But the ordinary rules cannot be worked until we have decided whether miracles are possible ... For if they are impossible, then no amount of historical evidence will convince us.' C.S. Lewis, *Miracles*, London, HarperCollins, 2002, p. 2. For a disputation of Naturalism (i.e. the idea or belief that only natural, as opposed to supernatural, laws and forces operate in the world), see in particular chapter 3 – in the version rewritten by C.S. Lewis after his debate with G.E.M. Anscombe in 1948.
[42]See Quran, 3:123–5.
[43]R. Guenon, *The Lord of the World*, translated by A. Cheke et al., Moorcote, Coombe Springs Press, 1983, p. 66.

Factuality, understood as the recording of facts (from *facere*, 'to do'), is only concerned with the products of language's 'doing'. A fact recorded by history or by science is an event whose contours coincide with the limits of a linguistic definition. It is the application of a certain linguistic label, singling out an event or state of affairs: the more precise the linguistic definition of the fact, the more intense the factuality assigned to the event.

Conversely, prophecy locates itself at the level of language's fundamental undoing. While it often describes its object in seemingly factual terms, prophecy adopts a form of factuality that doesn't assign absolute agency to language. Prophecy reinterprets the notion of 'fact', presenting it as an open limit that is available to being contaminated by multiple influences. To do so, prophecy speaks of imaginal entities as if they belonged to the context of linguistic factuality: it places angels and demons alongside animals and molecules. It speaks of sacred events as if they shared the same temporality as historical events. It depicts the ineffable face of God as if it was the same as a human face – and vice versa.[44]

Cyclically recurring sacred events, by the same token, are presented by prophecy as irreducible both to the world and to what completely exceeds any world: every Christmas, for example, is always the same exact event and the same a-temporal 'now', taking place in different historical presents. Its essence is as a point of contact and of passage between the poles of time and of eternity.

It is true, Jesus Christ was born only once, and it was a unique [historical] event. Yet, the liturgic festivity around his birth is repeated every year. [This is because] sacred liturgy reflects

---

[44]This trait of prophetic culture is especially evident in the literary genre of the fable, which, as Cristina Campo observes, contains and condenses within itself the same process and message of mystical journeys of initiation. 'In every century, the heroes of the absolute fable, of the fable of fables, have been the Saints ... Fables like *L'Histoire de Blondine, de Bonne-Biche et de Beau-Minon* and *Le Bon Petit Henri* are indeed perfect mystical itineraries ... [Thus,] a fable has to be read simultaneously on all its different plains, lest each of them remains at all implausible ... The fable's intermediate province, between trial and liberation, is a world of mirrors ... The hero of a fable is called since the start to read the watermark of the ulterior worlds [that lie within the page]. The hero is asked to do nothing less than to partake simultaneously to both worlds.' C. Campo, *Gli Imperdonabili, Della Fiaba*, Milan, Adelphi, 2019, pp. 29–42: 31–3 – my translation.

an event that, although already 'past' together with a certain moment in time, is nonetheless determined before time and eternally existing. It is an event that simultaneously lies beyond time, while also belonging to time as a specific historical event.[45]

The linear temporality of history is traversed by the eternity of the sacred, so to produce the effect of a recursive cycle. Prophetic events function as thresholds that shouldn't be considered solely through the logic of one of the dimensions traversing them.

The prophetic overcoming of historical time finds an iconic – although oblique – formulation in one of the letters sent by Antonin Artaud to his doctor Gaston Ferdière in the psychiatric hospital of Rodez:

And this means, dear Dr. Ferdière, that since 1934 there has truly been a break in the succession of time and thus that 1943, that 1943 in which we are living at present, cannot be located within time, as 9 years later than that 1934 when we gambled our destiny, but it is a year that stands in space as strangely close to that year, and that can be said to be parallel to it.[46]

The language of prophecy, thus, includes those of history and of archaeology – but only as pitches within a larger chord. Although it is possible to move between the registers of history and of prophecy, and to find traces of one within the other, this narrow passage opens only to those who know how to navigate a realm that includes both factual and non-factual kinds of truth.

That great mystic and ascetic, Blessed Heinrich Seuse, the Dominican, implored the Eternal Wisdom for one word affirming that He was love, and when the answer came, 'All creatures proclaim that I am love,' Seuse replied 'Alas! Lord, that does not suffice to a yearning soul.' Faith feels secure neither with

---

[45]P. Florenskij, *La Concezione Cristiana del Mondo*, translated by A. Maccioni, Bologna, Pendragon, 2019, p. 44 – my translation from the Italian edition.

[46]A. Artaud, 'Letter to Gaston Ferdière: 12 July 1943', in A. Artaud, *Scritti di Rodez*, edited and translated by R. Damiani, Milan, Adelphi, 2017, p. 44 – my translation from the Italian edition.

universal consent, nor with tradition, nor with authority. It seeks the support of its apparent enemy, reason.[47]

It was thanks to this stereoscopic attitude, that the visionary archaeologist Heinrich Schliemann was able to recognize the prophetic quality in the works of 'divine' Homer.[48] Moving across metaphysical and epistemological boundaries that seemed insurmountable to his contemporaries, Schliemann gained prophecy's assistance in bringing back to light the historical ruins of the city of Troy.

The ridicule with which Heinrich Schliemann's ambitions were initially addressed by his colleagues is a frequent companion to any attempt to engage with prophetic forms of culture – and not undeservedly.

A transcending character must be given to the words we use about God. They must not be given the human sense. [...] Therefore let us supremely praise this foolish 'Wisdom,' which has neither reason nor intelligence and let us describe it as the Cause of all intelligence and reason, of all wisdom and understanding.[49]

The grotesque quality of prophetic culture – and the attitude that it demands from those who wish to savour it[50] – is indeed

---

[47]Miguel de Unamuno, *Tragic Sense of Life*, translated by J.E. Crawford Flitch, New York, NY, Dover Publications, 1954, p. 75.

[48]'The divine poet' is Schlieman's definition of Homer in the first page of his publication on the archaeological finds on the site of Troy. See H. Schliemann, *Troja: Results of the latest researches and discoveries on the site of Homer's Troy*, Chicheley, Paul B. Minet, 1972, p. 1.

[49]Pseudo-Dionysius, *The Divine Names*, 865D-868A – in Pseudo-Dionysius, *The Complete Works*, translated by C. Luibheid, New York, NY, Paulist Press, 1987, p. 106.

[50]The metaphor of tasting or savouring is a frequent mystical trope to describe a subject's relationship with what is beyond linguistic representation. This is particularly the case in the tradition of Islamic mysticism: 'Al-Qushairi [in his book *Risala*,] says that *shauq* (taste) and *shrub* (drinking) are terms used by mystics with reference to the fruits of divine revelations. Mystic practices give them taste of the realities (*shauq al-ma'ani*), and when they develop further, they attain to *shrub*.' H. Mashita (ed.), *Theology, Ethics and Metaphysics: Royal Asiatic Society Classics of Islam*, Abingdon, Routledge, 2003, p. 71, f.6.

ridiculous and monstrous.[51] To host both facts and non-facts, both the linguistic and the ineffable dimensions of reality, prophetic language has to sacrifice the perfection of form,[52] falling short of the requirements of each of its fields, considered on their own. The figures populating prophetic culture are monstrous mysteries, capable of hosting within language the manifestation (*monstrare*, to manifest) of a dimension that is irreducible to it. They sketch an impossibly large cosmological picture through an extensive use of symbols drawn from high and low – much like the cosmic landscape seen by Neoplatonic philosopher Porphyry in Homer's description the Cave of the Nymphs.[53] And they do so, by partially 'closing their eyes' (*muein*, the etymological root of 'mystery')[54] to the strict grammatical norms of the world of linguistic factuality.

Inevitably, the finished work of prophetic culture appears always unfinished. It is imperfect, incomplete, lacking or excessive – not because of insufficient skill, or due to a mannerist posturing, but precisely to point to a particular way of reading a prophetic work, which might ignite a transformation in a subject's fundamental mode of worlding.

---

[51]'Eroticisim as seen by the objective intelligence is something monstrous, just like religion. Eroticism and religion are closed books to us if we do not locate them firmly in the realm of inner experience.' G. Bataille, *Eroticism*, translated by M. Dalwood, London, Penguin, 2001, p. 37.

[52]For an interesting examination of this notion across philosophy and the arts, see J. Biles, *Ecce Monstrum: Georges Bataille and the Sacrifice of Form*, New York, NY, Fordham University Press, 2007.

[53]Porphyry dedicated an astoundingly original and creative interpretation to verses 102–12 of the 13th book of the *Odyssey*, where Odysseus leaves inside a cave in Ithaca the gifts that he had received from the Phaeacians. According to Porphyry's interpretation, that cave, sacred to the nymphs, can be understood as a complete symbol, almost a hieroglyph, of the entire universe. See Porphyry, *On the Cave of the Nymphs in the Thirteenth Book of the Odyssey*, translated by T. Taylor, London, Watkins, 1917.

[54]In the vocabulary of the Pseudo-Dionysius, the term 'mystagogue' – literally, the guide into a mystery – has a similar ring to the term 'prophet' as it is used in the present volume. For the Pseudo-Dionysius, 'mystery' refers to ineffable conceptions regarding divine things in general (*Mystical Theology*, 1 997A 12) and the incarnation in particular (*The Celestial Hierarchy* 4 181B 13 and 21; *The Divine Names* 2 640C 34), as well as certain sacred ceremonies (*The Ecclesiastical Hierarchy* 3 429C 27, and 5 505B 17), particularly the Eucharist (*The Ecclesiastic Hierarchy* 3 445A 1–3, and 6 533C 29 and 563C 33).

Since the way of negation appears more suitable to the realm of the divine and since positive affirmations are always unfitting to the hiddenness of the inexpressible, a manifestation through dissimilar shapes is more correctly to be applied to the invisible [...] It was to avoid any misunderstanding among those incapable of rising above visible beauty that the pious theologians so wisely and upliftingly stopped to incongruous dissimilarities. [...] Indeed, the sheer crassness of the signs is a goad so that even the materially inclined cannot accept that it could be permitted or true that the celestial and divine sights could be conveyed by such shameful things.[55]

Perhaps, one image above all is capable of capturing the epistemological and metaphysical depth of the grotesque style of prophetic culture: Michelangelo's statue of *Il Giorno* (the Day), in the Medici Chapel in Florence. Placed next to the perfectly polished statue of *La Notte* (the Night), *Il Giorno* strikes the viewer for its odd state of unfinishedness; the face of the marble giant is almost unrecognizable, barely sketched out with a few chisel strokes. What is too obscure needs to be made visible through a luminous style, while the diurnal brightness of reality – understood in its totality – needs to be counterbalanced by an artful use of obscurity.

La Notte and Il Giorno *are not merely two allegorical personifications; they are two mysteries. To interpret them, it is not sufficient to observe their attributes (the owl, the mask ...) or to read Michelangelo's poems. [...] La Notte is silent: her strength lies in her silence, that is in her holding within herself a wealth of content that cannot be made explicit. La Notte is a conceptual labyrinth; it is the most accomplished emblem of Michelangelo as a sculptor. [...] [On the contrary,] whenever the image risks to convey too explicitly its religious or literary meaning – and thus to become too clear, devoid of allusiveness*

---

[55]Pseudo Dyonisius, *The Celestial Hierarchy*, 2 141A-B, in Pseudo-Dionysius, *The Complete Works*, translated by C. Luibheid, New York, NY, Paulist Press, 1987, p. 150.

and unknowns – Michelangelo resorts to the expedient of leaving it unfinished. When, on the other hand, he comes to invent such an intense, spiritualized and summarizing iconology of conflicting possibilities, as to be indistinct, uninterpretable with precision, and therefore not finished conceptually, Michelangelo then completes the chisel work. [...] The unfinished is the magical halo that triggers associations and emotions that belong to a sphere superior to reason. This unfinished can be both material and iconographical. It is a technique, not so much of execution, as of expression.[56]

---

[56]E. Battisti, *Magia e Non Finito*, in E. Battisti (ed.), *Michelangelo Scultore*, Rome, Curcio Editore, 1964, pp. 96–7 – my translation. It is interesting to compare Eugenio Battisti's reading of Michelangelo's statues in the Medici's Chapel with that suggested by Erwin Panofsky in his article 'The Mouse That Michelangelo Failed to Carve', in L. Freeman Sandler (ed.), *Essays in Memory of Karl Lehmann*, Institute of Fine Arts, New York University, 1964, pp. 242–51; and with his Neoplatonic reading in E. Panofsky, *Studies in Iconology: Humanistic Themes in the Art of the Renaissance*, New York, NY, Harper, 1962, pp. 201–10. On the prophetic potency of Michelangelo's art, the most succinct judgement has been issued by Pavel Florensky, with typical eloquence: 'Although he lived in the Baroque era, Michelangelo belonged to a Middle Ages that was neither entirely of the past nor of the future.' P. Florensky, *Beyond Vision: Essays on the Perception of Art, Reverse Perspective*, edited by N. Misler, translated by W. Salmond, London, Reaktion Books, 2002, pp. 197–272: 242.

THE PROPHET
AS A POSITION

FIGURE 3.5 *Jami*, The Miraj of the Prophet, *double folio from the* Haftawrang *(Seven Thrones), fifteenth century.* © *The Smithsonian Institution, National Museum of Asian Art.*

If you asked me to define it, I would say
that irony is a gesture of language
that achieves an effect of suspension or reality.[57]

Prophets speak grotesquely about a multidimensional picture of reality, which they summon to the furthermost limits of our imagination. But their language seldom lacks the lightness of a joke. Their monstrosity has the same lightness as anything that is touched by the Divine.

A prophetic understanding of comedy runs through the history of thought; from the obscene jokes that made Demetra laugh, to the humour of Taoist sages, to the Christian monk Fra Ginepro, one of St Franscis's first disciples, known as 'the Jester of the Lord' (*il giullare di Dio*). The importance of comedy for the expression of the ineffable elements of reality shouldn't be understated, and its relevance also to prophetic culture is sharply put by Rene Daumal:

Art and religion degenerated as soon as they lost that comic element (like the Festa de' Pazzi *in Catholicism), which preserved us from believing that 'it happened'.*[58]

The lightness of comedy, like a suspended atmosphere, gives malleability to the metaphysical structures of a world-form, and it enables its cultural figures to express more than their supposedly 'natural' traits would permit.

To create is not just to reproduce the truth. Talking about comedians, to incarnate, to interpret a comic type doesn't mean to create it. What the hell! ... Not even its author created it ...

---

[57]*Se proprio mi chiedete di definirla, direi che l'ironia è un gesto di linguaggio che sortisce un effetto di sospensione della realtà.* F. Berardi 'Bifo', *Come Finirà* – my translation from the unpublished manuscript.

[58]R. Daumal, 'L'origine du Théâtre de Bharata', *Mesures*, IV, 5 October 1935; in R. Daumal, *Lanciato dal Pensiero*, translated by C. Rugafiori and L. Simini, Milan, Adelphi, 2019 p. 48 – my translation from the Italian edition. For a description of the *Festa de' Pazzi* (Festival of Fools), a raunchy theatrical inversion of Catholic liturgy, akin to Roman *Saturnalia*, see M. Gioia, *Idee Sulle Opinioni Religiose e Sul Clero Cattolico*, Lugano, 1841, pp. 130–3.

Creating is something else: it means bringing into the world something that didn't previously exist. The rest, rather than 'creation', should be called 'imitation'. Imitating, however, is not art. [...] Art consists in deforming.[59]

Such lightness allows prophecy to emerge through a narrative mesh of linguistic and non-linguistic elements. Impalpable yet pervasive like an atmosphere, the mood produced by the grotesque style of prophetic culture creates a *situation* where the adoption of a different form of worlding becomes possible.[60]

Prophetic culture aims to create, not single works, but entire landscapes where the cosmogonic imagination of a subject can fully unfold. All imaginable dimensions of reality are included within the monstrous body of a grotesque narration, so that their syncretic combination might produce a new setting, where the reader's own world-creation can take place.

This atmospheric mode of cultural production finds an important echo in ancient Indian theories of aesthetics, as canonically set in the treaty on dramaturgy *Dasharupaka* by tenth-century poet-scholar Dhanamjaya, in the eleventh-century *Agnipurana*, and in the fifteenth-century study of aesthetics *Sāhityadarpaṇa* by Viśvanātha Kavirāja. Coherently with the Hindu focus on strengthening and purifying one's own awareness in view of liberation (*moksha*), art forms like poetry and theatre were analysed in reference to their contribution to a person's epistemological abilities.

The aim of public art forms, according to the Hindu tradition, is not simply to create individual connections in the mind of the reader, but to produce *rasa*: literally, 'taste'.[61]

---

[59]*Creare – in generale, non è fare la riproduzione del vero. E, riferendomi ai comici, incarnare, interpretare un tipo non significa crearlo. E, diavolo! ... Se non l'ha creato neanche l'autore ... Creare è un'altra cosa: è mettere al mondo ciò che non esisteva prima. Il resto più che creare si chiama imitare. Ma imitare non è arte perché se così fosse ci sarebbe arte anche nella scimmia e nel pappagallo. L'arte sta nel deformare.* E. Petrolini, *Al Mio Pubblico*, Milan, Casa Editrice Ceschina, 1937 – my translation.

[60]A 'situation' is here understood as 'a moment of life, concretely and deliberately constructed by the collective organisation of a unitary environment and a game of events' – the definition provided in the first issue of the journal of the Situationist International, *Internationale Situationniste* 1, June 1958.

[61]On the origin of the term *rasa*: 'Krishna is defined as *Ras* – nectar of emotions ... The Acharyas used the same words while defining the Krishan principle – He is

*The name Taste [rasa] is given to the immediate perception, from within, of a moment or of a certain state of existence, which is provoked by means of artistic expression. It is neither an object, nor a feeling nor a concept: it is an immediate evidence, the act of tasting life itself … Taste varies, according to the states or modes of existence (*bhava*) of which it is the 'supernatural' and disinterested perception.*[62]

As undefinable as the physical experience of taste, the *rasa* of an artwork provides its audience with an underlying aesthetic emotion, subtending all other forms of perception and rationality.

The rasa *in which poetry is fully accomplished escapes any possible definition. […] According to Abhinivagupta, it is akin to* the dominant emotive state *of an artwork (*sthayibhava*), whether love or pain, as illuminated by the light of divine consciousness – which under that condition is freed from those impairments that would otherwise obfuscate it, as it often happens in our everyday life, and that would make it appear circumscribed and limited. According to others, like Jagannatha,* rasa *is the very intelligence that shines within us, but in a state in which it is finally unbound from the obfuscation caused by empirical consciousness, while remaining temporarily delimited within the dominant emotive state of a particular artwork.*[63]

The notion of *rasa* as an all-encompassing mental atmosphere is crucial to Hindu theories of theatre, where it defines both the

---

Ras, joyous essence or juice. To attain Krishna means to *taste* this joyous essence, nectar and reach the state of perpetual or eternal bliss … This "Ras" is fully manifest in the Rasa dance performed by Krishna with his *shaktis*, the cowherd girls as we know them in colloquial language … Thus, Rasa dance is totality of essence. Hence, experiencing this Rasa dance is like experiencing in totality the essence of Krishna principle.' M. L. Varadpande, *History of Indian Theatre: Loka Ranga: Panorama of Indian Folk Theatre*, New Delhi, Abhinav Publications, 1992, pp. 37–8.
[62]R. Daumal, 'L'origine du Théâtre de Bharata', *Mesures*, IV, 5 October 1935; in R. Daumal, *Lanciato dal Pensiero*, translated by C. Rugafiori and L. Simini, Milan, Adelphi, 2019, p. 20 – my translation from the Italian edition.

types of performance (epic, erotic, comic, etc.) and the very object of any theatre piece. According to the treaty on performing arts, *Nāṭya Śāstra*, attributed to Bharata Muni – intended as the fifth Veda, through which all other Vedas might be made accessible – the origin of theatre itself is divine. It was Brahma, the Great Father, the ineffable above the Gods, who created theatre as a way to render His own unintelligibility manifest to the senses.

> *The Knowledge of Theatre was emanated by the Blessed, by Brahma, the all-knowing. Having produced the Knowledge of Theatre, the Great Father asked Indra: 'This Myth that I have emitted out of myself has to be transmitted to the Gods. You shall communicate this sacred Knowledge called Theatre to those expert beings, tempered by fire and by understanding, who proceed daringly and who can overcome great labours.'*
>
> *As these words were pronounced by Brahma, Indra bowed with folded hands and replied to the Great Father: 'Oh Blessed, oh Being that is more real than any other! The Gods are not able to grasp, remember and understand this science; I cannot entrust the duties of Theatre to them. However, there are the Prophets (ṛṣi) who know the mysteries of Knowledge and who have accomplished their vows; they can understand this teaching, they can apply it and remember it.'[64]*

Theatre is a job for prophets, because prophecy itself has the attitude of theatre. A work of prophetic culture stands as a vantage point from which reality can be seen under a particular, all-pervasive atmosphere – where the very settings of what we might understand

---

[63]G. Tucci, *Storia della Filosofia Indiana*, Bari, Laterza, 2005, p. 417 – my translation.
[64]Bharata Muni, *Nāṭya Śāstra*, 18–23, in R. Daumal, 'L'origine du Théâtre de Bharata', *Mesures*, IV, 5 October 1935; in R. Daumal, *Lanciato dal Pensiero*, translated by C. Rugafiori and L. Simini, Milan, Adelphi, 2019 p. 25 – my translation from the Italian edition. On the use of the term 'prophet' to translate the Sanskrit *ṛṣi*, see Daumal's commentary to paragraph 23, 'A *ṛṣi* (I approximate this term by saying "Prophet", in a biblical sense) is the one who "sees the hymns", who has the intellectual vision of the meaning of sacred words, and who transmits them to posterity.' Ibid., p. 41 – my translation from the Italian edition.

as 'reality' might be challenged and recomposed. Steeped in the *rasa* of prophecy, reality emerges as a field that is always in excess to itself, while the world and each object inside it are pierced from within by an excess of existence standing beyond logic.

But if this is the scope of prophecy – as it is of art – what kind of character is that prophetic artist who might be able to accomplish it?

Traditionally, and especially in ancient Jewish society, prophets are rebellious figures who live in contrast with the secular and religious authority of their age.[65] Their ability to bring about a certain *rasa* through their cultural work mirrors their inner adherence to a different metaphysics, and a different 'world', from the one on which their livelihood depends.[66]

> *Prophecy could not and cannot be controlled, and it is by its very nature disturbing. It takes as its point of reference something other than the status quo. The Deuteronomists never sorted out what they thought about prophecy, because they were first and foremost organizers and lawyers; prophecy was a problem to them.*[67]

An example of this attitude can be found in a famous story told in the Gospels. Interrogated on whether people should pay taxes to the Roman state, Jesus asked the enquirer to show him a coin.

---

[65]'But, ladies and gentlemen, had the youthful Moses listened to and accepted that view of life, had he bowed his head and bowed his will and bowed his spirit before that arrogant admonition he would never have led the chosen people out of their house of bondage nor followed the pillar of the cloud by day. He would never have spoken with the Eternal amid lightnings on Sinai's mountaintop nor even have come down with the light of inspiration shining in his countenance and bearing in his arms the tables of the law, graven in the language of the outlaw.' J. Joyce, *Ulysses*, Oxford, Oxford University Press, 2008, p. 137. On the political function and social context of Jewish prophecy, see D. Aune, *Prophecy in Early Christianity and the Ancient Mediterranean World*, Grand Rapids, MI, Wm. B. Eerdmans, 1991, pp. 81–152.

[66]I have discussed this aspect in the section of *kitman* and *taqiyya* in my book *Technic and Magic*.

[67]M. Barker, *The Lost Prophet: The Book of Enoch and Its Influence on Christianity*, Sheffield, Phoenix Press University of Sheffield, 2005, p. 68.

And He said to them, 'Whose image and inscription is this?'
They said to Him, 'Caesar's.'
And He said to them, 'Render therefore to Caesar the things that
are Caesar's, and to God the things that are God's.'⁶⁸

Jesus was facing an insinuation, by the Pharisees, that his teachings encouraged people to disobey the emperor and to re-direct their obedience to himself as the only legitimate ruler. As it had happened with Satan – who had tempted him with the offer of dominion over all kingdoms[69] – he was being tested in his relationship to worldly power. Jesus replied by disavowing the very notion of kingdom or empire: there is nothing in the catalogue of the world that can claim to itself an absolute dominion, because the world itself is nothing more than a dimension of the Whole. Asking 'whose image and inscription is this?' in front of the effigy of the most powerful emperor on the planet meant declaring from the onset his prophetic disengagement from the hegemonic 'facts' and 'truths' that were broadcast by his historical time.[70]

A prophet's ability to contemplate the multiple dimensions of reality derives, in part, from their everyday practice of breaking down their immediate surroundings into multiple layers, to which

---

[68]Matthew 22:20–1 (*New Oxford Annotated Bible*).

[69]Matthew 4:10.

[70]It is possible to read Christ's dismissal of the emperor, in parallel to the reluctance with which prophet Samuel anointed Saul, the first king of Israel. 'Then all the elders of Israel ... came to Samuel at Ramah and said to him ... "Appoint for us a king to govern us, like other nations." But the thing displeased Samuel ... And the Lord said to Samuel, "Listen to the voice of the people in all that they say to you; for they have not rejected you, but they have rejected me from being their king ... Only, you shall solemnly warn them, and show them the ways of the king ...." So Samuel Said [to them] "[A king] will take your sons and appoint them to his chariots and to be his horsemen ... he will take your daughters to be perfumers and cooks and bakers ... he will take the best of your fields and vineyards and olive orchards and give them to his courtiers ... he will take one-tenth of your flocks, and you shall be his slaves. And in that day, you will cry out because of your king, whom you have chosen for yourselves; but the Lord will not answer you in that day. [...] Today you have rejected your God, who saves you from all your calamities and your distresses; and you have said, 'No! but set a king over us.'"' 1 Samuel 8:4–18, 10:19 (*New Oxford*

they assign varying degrees of (non)allegiance. Their identification
with the hegemonic form of worlding in their own society, and with
the rhythm of its time-segment, is always very limited: a prophet is
never fully 'of the world', and certainly they are never 'contemporary'
to their age. Indeed, a prophet is not fully themselves either: they
can see within themselves more than they could possibly identify
with in the manner of an identity or of a belonging.

This existential position towards one's own social context
and socially constructed self is a starting point for producers of
prophetic culture – but, paradoxically, it is also the endpoint of their
work. Becoming-not-contemporary and becoming-not-oneself are
simultaneously the pre-conditions for creating prophetic culture,
and the results of a profound personal engagement with it.

It is possible to observe this mechanism at play in the exemplary
life of a young orphan from Mecca, who was to become Allah's last
rasul (messenger) and *nabi* (prophet). A rebel and a revolutionary
in his own time, Mohammed developed his prophetic work through
an intense combination of an existential detachment from himself
(as during his frequent retreats in the mountain cave of Hira), and
of a metaphysical readjustment of his own perspective towards
worlding.

Although fully real in historical terms, Mohammed was both
more and less than a person: he was *al insan al kamil* (the perfect
man),[71] not just a man but a *possibility* for the fundamental

---

Annotated Bible). As noted by Roberto Calasso: 'The king [Saul] was appointed only
because Samuel had anointed him ... [but] Samuel wanted to remind [the people of
Israel] that a king is an evil in itself. Wishing a king for oneself means wishing evil ...
From that day onward, the history of Israel would be marked by a series of kings,
like the history of all the other peoples around them. But somebody would always
remain to bring back the words of Samuel, who had judged kingship in itself to be a
form of degradation, although he had established it with his own hands.' R. Calasso,
Il Libro Di Tutti I Libri, Milan, Adelphi, 2019, pp. 28–9 – my translation.
[71]An exposition of this notion can be found in the book *Al Insan Al Kamil* by
fourteenth-century Sufi philosopher Al-Jili – who expanded Ibn Arabi's examination
in *Fusus al-Hikam*. See A. A.-K. Al-Jili, *Universal Man*, translated and commented
by T. Burkhardt, Lahore: Suhail Academy, 1965; and I. Arabi, *The Ringstones of
Wisdom (Fusus Al-Hikam)*, translated by C.K. Dagli, Chicago, Kazi Publications,
2000.

imagination and for the modes of worlding of every subject, regardless of the world and of the time-segment in which they might live. Becoming worthy of a prophetic mission is, first and foremost, a metaphysical task: before any ethical or behavioural transformations, it means refashioning one's own perspective towards the raw avalanche of perceptions investing us at any moment. In this sense, it is possible to interpret the process of initiation as a work of inner, metaphysical and epistemological architecture. To hear Allah's revelation, Mohammed had to build 'a temple deep inside [his own] hearing'[72] – better, he had to build *himself* as a locus where Allah's voice might become audible. Indeed, far from claiming to himself the authorship of the Quran, Mohammed repeatedly declared to have received it from the angel Gabriel, who was sent to him by Allah.

Long before twentieth-century debates about the death of the author, prophetic culture has always implied the withering away of authorship. A prophet is not an author: it is a position towards worlding. It is a certain metaphysics, filtered through lived existence and projected as a narrative atmosphere.[73] Prophecy declares its true origin to be irreducible to the historical person who utters it: it is the Holy Spirit that speaks 'like the sound of many waters'[74] through the prophets of ancient Judaism, just as Apollo speaks through the Pythia, or Allah, via Gabriel, through Mohammed. As pointed out by the Russian theologian Vladimir Lossky:

> Does not the author of the Epistle to the Hebrews say in quoting a psalm of David: 'But one in a certain place testified ... '?

---

[72]'You built a temple deep inside their hearing.' R.M. Rilke, 'Sonnets to Orpheus', I, in *Duino Elegies & the Sonnets to Orpheus*, translated by S. Mitchell, New York, NY, Vintage, 2010.
[73]'Precisely with great art (which is all we are concerned with here) the artist remains something inconsequential in comparison with the work – almost like a passageway which, in the creative process, destroys itself for the sake of the coming forth of the work.' M. Heidegger, *Off the Beaten Track*, edited and translated by J. Young and K. Haynes, Cambridge, Cambridge University Press, 2002, p. 19.
[74]Ezekiel 1:24; Ezekiel 43:2; Revelation 14:2; 2 Esdras 6:17.

[Heb. ii,6] thus showing to what extent the question of authorship is of secondary importance in the case of a text inspired by the Holy Spirit.[75]

Prophetic language doesn't have a historical author, because its origin exceeds the linguistic map over which we can draw causal connections – it exceeds the world and its history. The voice of prophecy is *bat qol*, a 'daughter of a voice', or 'echo of a voice', as defined in Rabbinic literature.[76] The supposed conveyor of prophecy – the prophet as the furthermost point in the causal chain behind its utterance – is in fact its first audience and its first reader.[77]

A prophet is a *place* where prophecy can make itself manifest. And, since the position of the prophet is just a particular articulation of the world, its application is not limited to human beings. Any portion of the world that can host the manifestation of the ineffable – that is, any form of existence, from a speck of sand to a mushroom to a political institution – can be considered potentially as a prophetic mirror.

---

[75]V. Lossky, *The Mystical Theology of the Eastern Church*, translated by a group of members of the Fellowship of St Alban and St Sergius, Cambridge, James Clarke & Co., 2005, p. 25.

[76]Josephus, *Antiquities of the Jews*, i.85 (cf. Gen. 15:13); ii.267–69 (cf. Exod. 3:2–4:23); iii.88–90 (cf. Exod. 19:16–20:01); viii.352 (cf. 1 Kgs. 19:9) – in Josephus, F., *Antiquities of the Jews*, translated by W. Whiston, Radford, VA, Wilder Publications, 2018.

[77]As noted by Jacques Derrida, when commenting on the *Book of Revelation* (commonly known as the Apocalypse) by John of Patmos: '[It is] necessary ... to unfold a detailed analysis of the narrative voice in the Apocalypse. I use the expression "narrative voice" in order to distinguish it, as Blanchot does, from the narrating voice, that of the identifiable subject, of the narrator or determinable sender in a narrative, a *récit* ... Jesus is the one who says "Stay awake ... I shall come upon you." But John is the one speaking, citing Jesus, or rather writing, appearing to transcribe what he says in recounting that he cites Jesus the moment Jesus dictates to him to write ... Jesus is cited as the one who dictates without himself writing and says, "write, *grapson*." But even before John writes, saying presently that he writes, he hears as a dictation the great voice of Jesus.' J. Derrida, 'Of an Apocalyptic Tone Newly Adopted in Philosophy', in H. Coward and T. Foshay (eds.), *Derrida and Negative Theology: With a Conclusion by Jacques Derrida*, Albany, NY, SUNY Press, 1992, p. 55.

Anything that becomes a place for the manifestation of the ineffable is a prophetic entity – where its prophetic quality doesn't consist in propagating a command or a certain message, but in functioning as a place that one can inhabit prophetically. The space of the sacred, in its essential form, is already the position of the prophet.[78]

> *Remember that there is nothing which lacks its own share of beauty, for as scripture rightly says, 'Everything is good.' [Genesis 1:31] Everything, then, can be a help to contemplation. [...] Forms, even those drawn from the lowliest matter, can be used, not unfittingly, with regard to heavenly beings. Matter, after all, owes its subsistence to absolute beauty and keeps, throughout its earthly ranks, some echo of intelligible beauty. Using matter, one may be lifted up to the immaterial archetypes.[79]*

For this reason, approaching a prophetic *opera* as one would approach the work of an 'author' impedes any real access to the architecture of their message. If one was to read the Quran like an authored text, all that they would take from it would be a complex catalogue of literal statements and allegorical connections. To be able to properly read a prophetic text, and thus to penetrate its symbolic meaning, it is necessary to occupy the same position that was taken by the (non)author while they were composing – or arranging – it.[80]

Together with the abolition of the author, prophetic culture proceeds to abolish the position of the audience. This is not a

---

[78]A definitive account of the 'space of the sacred', and of the temple as a 'cut' (*temenos*, from *temnein*, 'to cut') in the space of the profane, can be found in M. Eliade, *The Sacred and the Profane*, translated by W. Ropes Trask, New York, NY, Harcourt, Brace & World, 1959.

[79]Pseudo Dionysius, 'The Celestial Hierarchy', 2 141C and 144B, in *The Complete Works*, translated by C. Luibheid, New York, NY, Paulist Press, 1987, pp. 150–2.

[80]This mode relates, in part, to the 'anagogical' mode of approaching sacred scripture – which Hugh of Saint Victor, in *De Scripturis et scriptoribus sacris*, III, defines as the main among four different ways of approaching the sacred scriptures: literal (leading to information), moral (leading to behavioural changes), allegorical (leading to knowledge), anagogical (leading to direct contemplation).

form of participation of the audience to the work of the author, as it has been championed by cultural theorists in the twentieth and twenty-first centuries.[81] Rather, it is closer to the process of existential transformation defined in Orthodox Christianity as *theosis* (becoming-divine, as a return of the subject's awareness to the otherworldly realm).[82]

As they first approach the message of a work of prophetic culture, the audience shouldn't take it at a literal level or as a plainly decodable allegory. No prophetic entity – whether a text or an object – should be considered as a semiotic device pointing to yet another linguistic entity. Differently from an allegory,[83] the object of prophecy's symbolic language is not contained within language – and differently from a semiotic sign, it is not contained within its abstract conceptual content either. Even when it presents itself as 'divine law' (*shariat*), prophecy should not be considered in the same way as a secular code of laws. In the words of the late ancient pseudonym theologian Pseudo-Dionysius (which could have easily featured in a text by a Shia scholar of *tawil*, the art of interpreting the Quranic Revelation):

---

[81]For a poignant critique of the notion of audience 'participation' in contemporary culture, see C. Bishop, *Artificial Hells: Participatory Art and the Politics of Spectatorship*, London/New York, Verso, 2012.

[82]A powerful and inspiring explanation of the doctrine of *theosis* can be found in V. Lossky, *The Mystical Theology of the Eastern Church*, translated by a group of members of the Fellowship of St Alban and St Sergius, Cambridge, James Clarke, 1991.

[83]Allegory, from the Greek *allos agorein*, 'speaking of something else', indicates a horizontal movement within language. 'Allegory consists of an infinite network of meanings and correlations in which everything can become a representation of everything else, but all within the limits of language and expression. To that extent it is possible to speak of allegorical immanence ... The symbol [on the contrary, is] a form of expression which radically transcends the sphere of allegory. In the mystical symbol a reality which in itself has, for us, no form or shape becomes transparent and, as it were, visible, through the medium of another reality which clothes its content with visible and expressible meaning ... The symbol is an expressible representation of something which lies beyond the sphere of expression and communication, something which comes from a sphere whose face is, as it were, turned inward and away from us ... If the symbol is thus also a sign or representation it is nevertheless more than that.' G. Scholem, *Major Trends in Jewish Mysticism*, New York, NY, Schocken Books, 1995, pp. 26–7.

It would be unreasonable and silly to look at words rather than at the power of the meanings. Anyone seeking to understand the divine things should never do this, for this is the procedure followed by those who do not allow empty sounds to pass beyond their ears. [...] People like this are concerned with meaningless letters and lines with syllables and phrases which they do not understand, which do not get as far as the thinking part of their souls, and which make empty sounds on their lips and in their heart.[84]

As in the apse of a Byzantine church – where the size of the Christ *Pantokrator* is an allegory of his power, while the golden background surrounding him is a symbol of the ineffable divine essence – prophetic language 'throws together' (*syn-ballein*, the etymology of 'symbol') alien and irreducible elements.[85] It points towards the ineffable, inviting it to reflect itself on the mirror of language – and to do so, prophecy contorts itself in a shape that no longer fits the criteria of language, while also falling short of ineffability.

By recognizing the symbolic nature of prophetic language, the audience begins to move towards the prophet's own position as the 'first reader' of prophecy.

As [a Byzantine faithful] entered the nartex or stood in the nave [of a church], the participant in the services did not simply learn something about the great truths of Christian teaching, but he could realise that he himself was actually present in both seen and unseen worlds.[86]

---

[84]Pseudo-Dionysius, 'The Divine Names', 708C, in *The Complete Works*, translated by C. Luibheid, New York, NY, Paulist Press, 1987, p. 80.

[85]It is interesting to note how, etymologically, the contrary term to 'symbol' (*syn-ballein*, 'throwing together'; where *syn* derives from the Proto-IndoEuropean root **sem-*, 'one') is 'devil' (*dia-ballein*, 'to throw between', 'to cause quarrel between'; where *dia* derives from the Proto-Indo-European root **dwís*, 'two'). In prophetic terms, evil is represented by a figure which incarnates the act of severing and pulling apart the dimensions of reality that the symbol had managed to connect.

[86]J.M. Hussey, 'The Byzantine Empire in the Eleventh Century: Some Different Interpretations', *Transactions of the Royal Historical Society*, vol. 4 s., XXXII, 1950.

If Mohammed is *al insan al kamil* (the perfect man), then, to be able to read the Quran in the same way as Mohammed first received it, the reader has to become themselves a 'perfect'[87] person: they have to relocate their perspective towards reality to a point where what is non-factual and ineffable also becomes visible.

The challenge facing the prophet and their audience is substantially the same: they both have to extinguish themselves as author and reader, respectively, and to move as close as possible to that all-encompassing gaze over the irreducible complexity of reality, which is an attribute of the Divinity.[88]

Author and audience begin to merge into one position, thus rendering inoperative the geometry which is at the heart of communication. As a transfer of information, communication implies a traceable movement between nodes, which can be mapped linguistically. On the contrary, prophecy states that its ineffable object and its mysterious source coincide, and that both of them lie beyond the realm of information. If prophecy is to work at all, it cannot rely on a passage within the realm of denominations.

As it does to the notions of author and audience, prophecy imprints its own bent also on its choice of conceptual contents. Whenever prophecy speaks, its sole aim is to manifest a certain

---

[87]'Perfect' is intended here in its etymology, as related to *perficere* (to fully conclude) – in the sense that their mode of worlding would be able to include within its perspective as complete a range of the dimensions composing reality as it is possible for the imagination. 'And if you greet only your brothers and sisters, what more are you doing than the others? Do not even Gentiles do the same? Be perfect, therefore, as your heavenly Father is perfect.' Matthew 5:47–8. Due to its grotesque character, prophetic perfection has elements of apparent absurdity, not unlike the 'mao-dadaist' insurrectionary motto of Autonomists in 1977 Bologna: 'Zut is becoming super-perfect, super-perfect is becoming Zut' (*Zut e' divenire perfettissimo, perfettissimo e' divenire Zut*).

[88]This double passage of prophetic culture (extinction of one's own existing position, re-establishment of a new position in the same line of perspective as the Divinity) resembles the two moments of *fana* (annihilation) and *baqa* (subsistence) in Sufism: in their journey towards God, the Sufi mystic has first to annihilate their selfhood as a separate and autonomous entity, and then to re-establish it in such a way as to remain mindful of the all-encompassing presence of the Divinity within and throughout reality. This process is beautifully described by twelfth-/thirteenth-century Persian Sufi poet Attar – see Attar, *The Conference of the Birds*, translated by S. Wolpe, New York/London, W. W. Norton, 2017.

cosmology and cosmogony.[89] Like Orthodox icons or Islamic architecture, prophecy's narrative is always and fundamentally a cosmological/cosmogonic tale, presenting a metaphysical landscape that reconfigures our notion of the world in the light of what exceeds the very notion of a world.

To engage with prophetic culture is an 'exercise' (askesis) involving a subject's fundamental imagination about the stuff that makes up reality.[90] It is an active work, in that it requires a modification of one's own cosmological parameters – but it is also an exercise of non-activity (wei wu wei, 'action-non-action' in Taoist literature),[91] where one observes the new reality that begins to surface in front of their own eyes.

---

[89]For a historical overview of the conceptual development of Orthodox Icons, see L. Ouspensky, *Theology of the Icon*, 2 Vols., translated by A. Gythiel, Crestwood, NY, St Vladimir's Seminary Press, 1992. For a theological interpretation, see P. Florensky, *Iconostasis*, translated by D. Sheehan and O. Andrejev, Crestwood, NY, St Vladimir's Seminary Press, 1996, while a profound philosophical analysis can be found in M. Cacciari, 'Sull'Icona', in *Icone della Legge*, Milan, Adelphi, 2002, pp. 181–311. For a theological interpretation of Islamic architecture, see T. Burkhardt, *Art of Islam: Language and Meaning*, translated by J.P. Hobson, London, World of Islam Festival Publishing Company, 1976; and S.H. Nasr, *Islamic Art and Spirituality*, Ipswich, Golgonooza Press, 1987. For a philosophical/theological of the use of patterns in Islamic architecture, see K. Critchlow, *Islamic Patterns: An Analytical and Cosmological Approach*, London, Thames and Hudson, 1976.

[90]My use of this terms draws directly from its understanding in ancient philosophy: '"Exercise" corresponds to the Greek terms askesis or melete. Let us be clear at the outset about the limits of the present inquiry: we shall not be discussing "asceticism" in the modern sense of the word, as it is defined, for instance, by Heussi: "Complete abstinence or restriction in the use of food, drink, sleep, dress, and property, and especially continence in sexual matters." Here, we must carefully distinguish between two different phenomena. On the one hand, there is the Christian – and subsequently modern – use of the word "asceticism", as we have just seen it defined. On the other, there is use of the word askesis in ancient philosophy. For ancient philosophers, the word askesis designated exclusively spiritual exercises, [that is,] inner activities of the thought and the will.' P. Hadot, *Philosophy as a Way of Life: Spiritual Exercises from Socrates to Foucault*, edited by A. Davidson, translated by M. Chase, Oxford: Wiley-Blackwell, 1995, p. 128.

[91]'The highest key term in the semantic field of Negativity is the wu wei, Non-Doing ... The most basic meaning of Non-Doing is the negation of all "intention", all artificial (or "unnatural") effort on the part of man. And the Perfect Man is able to maintain this principle constantly and consistently because he has no "ego", because he has nullified himself. But the "nullification" of the "ego" as the subject of all desires and all intentional actions implies at the same time the establishment of a new Ego – the Cosmic Ego – which is completely at one with the Way [i.e. the Tao] in its creative activity.' T. Izutsu, *Sufism and Taoism: A Comparative Study of Key Philosophical Concepts*, Berkeley, CA, University of California Press, 1984, p. 448.

For some, it can become again an activity: if they accept to take upon themselves the task of perpetuating the architecture of their vision by creating a prophetic narrative that others can inhabit. But, regardless of whether a prophetic subject might wish to embark in an active creation of cultural artefacts, their movement towards *theosis* has already started. The ability which they have developed to contemplate reality in a prophetic register – that is, of seeing synoptically the linguistic and ineffable dimensions within existence, and those dimensions that altogether exceed 'existence' as we understand it – has already turned them into a surface where this new metaphysics is reflected. It has turned them into 'testimonies' (*martyr*) of an alternative mode of worlding.

To appreciate the transformative effects engendered by prophetic culture, it is useful to consider the particular treatment that it reserves to a notion, which is as frequent in ancient theological texts as in our contemporary parlance: infinity.

Whenever we ask ourselves whether the universe is infinite, we tend to take this issue to concern the level of extension: Is there a further centimetre after the furthermost edge of the expanse of space? Is there a further second after the furthermost edge of the expanse of time? Put in these terms, the question begs for a tautological answer: there is always a further centimetre and a further second in the series of space and time, precisely because infinite proliferation is one of the fundamental traits of how a linguistic series works.

Space lends itself just to repeatable things.[92]

Seen through this angle, infinity resembles the endless marathon of a horizon – though 'good for walking',[93] it is just an aspect implicit to walking itself.

---

[92] Joseph Brodsky, 'Lullaby of Cape Cod', VII, in J. Brodsky (ed.), *A Part of Speech*, Oxford, Oxford University Press, 1997.

[93] 'Utopia is on the horizon. I move two steps closer; it moves two steps further away. I walk another ten steps and the horizon runs ten steps further away. As much as I may walk, I'll never reach it. So what's the point of utopia? The point is this: to keep walking.' E. Galeano, *Window on Utopia*, in E. Galeano, *Walking Words*, translated by M. Fried, London/New York, W. W. Norton, 1997, p. 326.

The land beyond you is not round.
It is merely long.[94]

Yet, this is not the only possible interpretation of the notion of infinity. Aside from an extensional understanding, there is also one that seeks infinity in intensive terms. Within this perspective, the quest for infinity is not to be pursued along horizontal lines, but vertically. The answer is again positive: there is indeed a realm of infinity. Yet, this realm cuts vertically across the horizontal expanse of the world, piercing every point in space and every instant in time. It is an irreducible dimension to any form of extensive measure, thus escaping the notions of space or time. This dimension doesn't outrun finitude, but it escapes the dichotomy between finitude and infinity. It is not just infinite: it is eternal.[95]

This eternalist notion of infinity is the symptom of a frame of sense (a reality-system) through which existence emerges as a criss-crossing of multiple dimensions, which are mutually compatible yet irreducible to each other. At every point and every instant, the world is traversed by a vertical dimension that is entirely alien to temporal or spatial measure. Considered in these terms, notions such as 'point' (the dimensionless building block of space) and 'instant' (the durationless building block of time) take on symbolic value: they are clues of the interpenetration between the world and a multitude of realms exceeding any world.

Such is, for example, the understanding of the figure of Christ suggested by the Pseudo-Dionysius – who described him as akin

---

[94]Joseph Brodsky, 'Lullaby of Cape Cod', XII, in J. Brodsky (ed.), *A Part of Speech*, Oxford, Oxford University Press, 1997.

[95]'Thou dost precede all past periods, in the sublimity of an ever-present eternity, and Thou dost extend beyond all future periods because they are yet to be, and, when they come, they will be past periods; "but Thou art always the Selfsame, and Thy years shall not fail." ... All Thy years stand together, for they stand still, nor are those going away cut off by those coming, for they do not pass away ... Thy years are but one day, and Thy day is not a daily recurrent, but to- day; Thy present day does not give place to tomorrow, nor, indeed, does it take the place of yesterday. Thy present day is eternity.' St, Augustine, *Confessions*, 11, 13:16, translated by V.J. Bourke, Washington, DC, The Catholic University of America Press, 2008, pp. 342–3. For an examination of the metaphysical relationship between time, infinity and eternity in different religious traditions see A.K. Coomaraswamy, *Time and Eternity*, New Delhi, Munshiram Manoharlal, 2014.

to a point or an instant, where multiple dimensions of existence traverse each other while preserving their uniqueness.

> In a fashion beyond words, the simplicity of Jesus became something complex, the timeless took on the duration of the temporal, and, with neither change nor confusion of what constitutes him, he came into our human nature, he who totally transcends the natural order of the world.[96]

A similar intuition was at the basis of metaphysical/religious movement *Imiaslavie* (glorification of the name), which flourished in Russia at the beginning of the twentieth century. According to the *Imiaslavie*, as per the teachings of monk Ilarion,[97] the name of God is God Himself. The metaphysical aspects of this seemingly extravagant claim are well summarized by Russian philosopher Fr. Sergius Bulgakov:

> The name of God is as it were a point of intersection between two worlds and is the transcendental in the immanent; hence imiaslavie, apart from its general theological significance is so to speak a transcendental condition of prayer, rendering religious experience possible. [...] God, as it were, confirms His name and recognizes it as His own, not merely answering to it, but being actually present in it.[98]

Within this alternative frame, the closed world of pure immanence is suddenly opened to the passage of a dimension exceeding it. This openness is reciprocal; the vertically penetrating dimension of transcendence is itself penetrated by the horizontality of the world. Gaping between them, the thresholds of the point and of the instant emerge as passages to yet another dimension, in turn exceeding both transcendence and immanence.

---

[96]Pseudo-Dionysius, 'The Divine Names', 592B, in *The Complete Works*, translated by C. Luibheid, New York, NY, Paulist Press, 1987, p. 52.
[97]Ilarion's claims were first made public in his 1907 book *Na Gorakh Kavkaza* (In the Mountains of the Caucasus).
[98]S. Bulgakov, *Unfading Light: Contemplations and Speculations*, translated by T.A. Smith, Grand Rapids, MI, William B. Eerdmans Publishers, 2012, p. 24.

To proceed in this exploration of the figure of the prophet and of their audience, let us bring into our discussion another notion – though one that isn't remotely as popular today as the idea of infinity: *angelos*, the figure of the angel.

Like the *rasul*, the angel is literally a messenger between the Divinity and the world – but, again like a *rasul*, their function is far more complex than the simple passage of messages between spheres of existence.[99]

> *Theologians give the name 'angel' ... to heavenly beings by virtue of the fact that they make known the enlightenment proceeding from the Deity.*[100]

Let us approach the question of angelology through its prophetic examination by theologians of the Ismaili faith – among the most sophisticated interpreters of the angelic figure and of the relationship between visibility and invisibility within reality.[101] Born out of intra-Shia disagreements over the rightful succession to the Imamate, Ismailism is characterized by a unique combination of intellectual traditions from the Mediterranean and Indian regions, and by the intense poetical imagination (possibly influenced by Neoplatonic sources) with which it conveys its philosophy.

According to the cosmology of Ismailism,[102] a prophetic[103] understanding of reality has to start with the utterly ineffable figure

---

[99]Conversely, for a contemporary philosophical interpretation of the figure of the angel as primarily connected to the realm of communication and to modern science, see M. Serres, *Angels: A Modern Myth*, translated by F. Cowper, Paris/New York, Flammarion, 1995.

[100]Pseudo-Dionysius, 'The Celestial Hierarchy', 5 196C, in *The Complete Works*, translated by C. Luibheid, New York, NY, Paulist Press, 1987, p. 159.

[101]Christian theologians have also produced a profound and fascinating examination of the figure of the angel. For an anthology and historical overview on Christian angelology, see S. Chase (ed. and trans.), *Angelic Spirituality: Medieval Perspectives on the Ways of the Angels*, New York, NY: Paulist Press, 2002.

[102]I am here borrowing Henry Corbin's interpretation – in H. Corbin, *Cyclical Time and Ismaili Gnosis*, translated by R. Manheim and J.W. Morris, Abingdon, Routledge, 2013.

[103]Although Islam declares the end of prophecy with Mohammed, I follow Henry Corbin's frequent suggestion that, within Shia doctrine of *ta'wil* (esoteric interpretation), and in the hermeneutic function of the Shia Imam, it is possible to trace the same prophetic spirit that animated the last *Rasul*.

of the Divinity (not dissimilar, in its incommensurability, to the supreme notion of *al Haqq*, the Absolute, proposed by Ibn Arabi).[104] With a narrative twist that is peculiar to Ismaili theology, their cosmology adds here a 'pathetic' element (from *pathos*, feeling): the Divinity, God in its state as pure essence and pure existence, is traversed since His origin by a profound sentiment. God feels the sadness of an abyssal loneliness: entirely coincident with existence as such, God has no one to whom He can relate – He doesn't even have an image of Himself that He can contemplate.

To escape His original state of non-relationality, God emanates the angelic figures out of Himself. Ismaili angels stand towards God as the image of something that is, in itself, beyond any possible figuration.[105] Their position is paradoxical and it can only be rendered, somehow, through a vague series of metaphors – such as, for example, the comparison in *Ishraqi* literature of the angelic figures with the colours that are projected by a colourless beam of light traversing a prism.[106]

---

[104]Ibn Arabi – a giant of theology and one of the greatest ever Mediterranean and 'European' intellectuals – developed his theory of God's utter ineffability as *al-Haqq* in his magnum opus *al-Futuhat al-makkiyya* ('The Meccan Openings'). A shorter account can be found in his *Fusus al-Hikam* ('The Ringstones of the Wisdoms'). See I. Arabi, *The Ringstones of Wisdom (Fusus al-Hikam)*, translated by C.K. Dagli, Chicago, IL, Kazi Publications, 2000.

[105]This notion is also present in Christianity, especially in its re-elaboration by Renaissance humanists. As fifteenth-/sixteenth-century German humanist Konrad Mutian (also known as Mutianus Rufus) once remarked to a friend: 'There is but one god and one goddess, but many are their powers and names: Jupiter, Sol, Apollo … But have a care in speaking these things. They should be hidden in silence as are the Eleusinian mysteries; sacred things must needs [sic] be wrapped in fable and enigma.' – quoted in J. Seznec, *The Survival of the Pagan Gods: The Mythological Thought and Its Place in Renaissance Humanism and Art*, Princeton, NJ, Princeton University Press, 1972, p. 99.

[106]The *Ishraqi* (Illuminationist) school of 'theosophy' (to borrow Henry Corbin's definition of their combination of theology and philosophy) was established in the twelfth century by Iranian Shahab al-Din Suhrawardi. Drawing from Islamic theology, from pre-Islamic Iranian thought and from Greek philosophy, the Ishraqi school developed a complex metaphysical system centred around the metaphor of God's power as 'light'. Western readers owe to Henry Corbin the rediscovery of this crucial intellectual, and the exegesis of his sophisticated angelology. For a general examination of Suhrawardi's thought and of the *Ishraqi* school, see H. Corbin, *En Islam Iranien: Aspects spirituels et philosophiques, Vol. 2, Sohrawardi et les Platoniciens de Perse,*

The angel is an image of God. He is a manifestation of the hidden light. He is a mirror, [...] purely enlightening within itself as far as possible the goodness of the silence in the inner sanctuaries.[107]

Acting as a mirror, the angel of the world offers to God the possibility to see a reflection of His own image, and thus to break the crushing loneliness that marred His original state of absolute non-relationality.

According to Ismaili prophetic philosophy, everything within the range of experience and of perception has to be interpreted as an angel of sorts – including the world, which is perhaps the largest angel in the host (in this, their account is somehow reminiscent of the Stoic attribution of a soul to the world itself).[108]

For the Ismailis, being able to see the world, as an angel and oneself as a microcosmic angelic particle, means proceeding towards the highest form of *theosis* (becoming-divine) – where a subject shifts their perspective towards reality as close as possible to that occupied by the Divinity.

The angel – as the *locus* where pure existence reflects and contemplates itself, while remaining aware of its own irreducibility to mere phenomenon or to any literal formula – resembles the position taken by producers of prophetic culture and by their (non) audience. They see the world itself as a cultural artefact, always containing the possibility of hosting within itself the paradoxical composition of existence in its totality.

Paris, Gallimard, 1991. For a hermeneutical study of the symbolism of colours in Islamic esotericism, see H. Corbin, *Realisme et symbolisme des couleurs en cosmologie shi'ite: d'apres le 'Livre du hyacinthe rouge' de Shaykh Moḥammad Karim-Khan Kermani* (ob. 1870), Leiden, Brill, 1974; and K. Ottmann (ed.), *Color Symbolism: The Eranos Lectures*, Thompson, CT, Spring Publications, 2005.

[107]Pseudo-Dionysius, 'The Divine Names', 724B, in *The Complete Works*, translated by C. Luibheid, New York, NY, Paulist Press, 1987, p. 89.

[108]For a scholarly discussion of how also the Old Testament presents Yahweh both as an ineffable and invisible High God, and as a manifest and phenomenal 'Great Angel', see M. Barker, *The Great Angel: A Study of Israel's Second God*, London: SPCK, 1992, especially pp. 31–7 and 70–96.

I see nothing wrong in the fact that the Word of God [i.e. the Bible] calls even our hierarch [i.e. Christ] an 'angel', for it is characteristic of him that, like the angels, he is, to the extent of which he is capable, a messenger and that he is raised up to imitate, so far as man may, the angelic power to bring revelation.[109]

---

[109]Pseudo-Dionysius, 'The Celestial Hierarchy', 12 293 A, in *The Complete Works*, translated by C. Luibheid, New York, NY, Paulist Press, 1987, p. 176.

APOCATASTASIS

FIGURE 3.6 Trinity, *miniature from folio 79r of the* Rothschild Canticles, *thirteenth/fourteenth century, [Beinecke MS 404 fol. 79r]. © Beinecke Rare Book and Manuscript Library, Yale University.*

God's production has been double; one within the essence of His divinity, and the other outside. His inner production, which is without an origin and, so to say, consubstantial and eternal, is the Verbum *[word,* logos] ... *His external production, on the contrary, is not consubstantial to Him, and it is made ... of nothing and of time. And this was that first matter ... out of which God then extracted the sky, the Earth and all things.*[110]

According to Christian and Muslim theology, an angel can fall in two ways, each relating to an extreme. They can fall for obliviousness to the Divinity or for obliviousness to the world. In the Christian lesson, Lucifer, the most beautiful in the angelic host, fell from grace due to his desire to overcome God's authority and to establish his own dominion over the world. Conversely, in the Muslim account, the angel Iblis was damned by Allah because of an excess of devotion: ordered to bow in front of the newly created Adam, Iblis preferred to disobey Allah's injunction rather than recognizing anything other than the absolutely ineffable Divinity.[111]

---

[110]*Due sono state le produttioni che Dio ha fatte, l'una dentro della essential della sua divinita', et l'altra di fuori. La produttione di dentro, che e' produttion senza principio et (per dir cosi') consustantiale, et eterna, e' quella del Verbo. [...] La produttione di fuori non e' coessentiale, che fu fatta ... di niente et di tempo. Et questa fu la materia prima ... della quale Dio poi trasse il cielo, la terra et tutte le cose.* My own translation. For further reading, see G. Camillo, *L'Idea del Theatro*, Palermo, Sellerio, 1991, pp. 63–4.

[111]Several Sufi scholars – especially Mansur Al-Hallaj and Al Ghazali – suggest this interpretation for a series of Quranic passages such as: 'And behold We said to the angels: "Bow down to Adam"; and they bowed down, not so Iblis he refused and was haughty he was of those who reject Faith.' Quran, 2:34; 'It is We who created you and gave you shape; then We bade the angels bow down to Adam and they bowed down; not so Iblis; he refused to be of those who bow down.' (God) said: 'what prevented thee from bowing down when I commanded thee?' He said: 'I am better than he: thou didst create me from fire and him from clay.' (God) said: 'Get thee down from this: it is not for thee to be arrogant here: get out for thou art of the meanest (of creatures).' He said: 'give me respite till the day they are raised up.' (God) said: 'be thou among those who have respite.' He said: 'because Thou hast thrown me out of the way lo! I will lie in wait for them on Thy straight way. "Then will I assault them from before them and behind them from their right and their left: nor wilt Thou find in most of them gratitude (for Thy mercies)."' Quran 7:11–17. All Quranic quotes are in Abdullah Yusuf Ali's translation. On the complex relationship between Iblis/Satan and Muslim mysticism, see P.J. Awan, 'Iblis: Model of the Mystic Man', in *Satan's Tragedy and Redemption: Iblis in Sufi Psychology*, Leiden, Brill, 1983, pp. 122–83.

Both fallen angels are sworn enemies to Adam's progeny: they attempt to destroy humanity's chance to flourish in the world, by pulling it either towards an absolute system of language, or into the paralysing grip of utter ineffability.

In its angelic function as the *locus* where reality can manifest itself most completely, the prophet strives to stand between these extremes. Neither Lucifer nor Iblis, a prophet is more modestly a place where irreducibly different dimensions of existence can enter in contact. Prophetic culture intervenes in the space between what the Orthodox theologian Gregory Palamas defined as God's *ousia* (i.e. His essence as pure, ineffable existence), and his *energeia* (i.e. the 'energy' through which what is invisible makes itself manifest).[112] Like a concave mirror stretching between them, prophecy allows each to reflect itself in the other, and to have its image caught in turn.[113]

This function of prophetic culture can be detected in the philosophical structure of the Christian mystery of the Trinity,

---

[112]A similar distinction can be found in the Pseudo-Dionysius: 'The author of the *Aeropagitica* contrasts the "unions" (*enoseis*) with the "distinctions" (*diakriseis*) in God. The "unions" are "the secret mansions which are but seldom thrown open", the superessential nature of God where He remains as if in absolute repose, without manifesting Himself in any way. The "distinctions", on the other hand, are the processions (*prodoi*) beyond Himself, His manifestations (*ekfanseis*), which Dionysius also calls virtues or forces (*dynameis*), in which everything that exists partakes, thus making God known in His creatures. The contrast between the two ways in the knowledge of God, between negative and positive theology, is for Dionysius founded upon this ineffable but real distinction between the unknowable essence and the self-revealing energies of the Divinity, between the "unions" and the "distinctions". Holy Scripture reveals God to us by formulating the divine names according to the energies in which God communicates Himself, while remaining inaccessible in His essence, distinguishes Himself while remaining simple, and becomes manifold without leaving His unity.' V. Lossky, *The Mystical Theology of the Eastern Church*, translated by a group of members of the Fellowship of St Alban and St Sergius, Cambridge, James Clarke & Co., 2005, p. 72.
[113]'I'll make a fortune overnight/thanks to a trick which will allow me to fix images/ either in a concave or convex mirror/I believe I shall be definitely successful/once I manage to invent a coffin with a double bottom/which will let the corpse take a peek at the other world.' N. Parra, 'Madrigal', in *Anti-Poems*, translated by J. Elliot, *The Pocket Poets Series N°12*, San Francisco, CA, City Lights Books, 1960.

composed of Father, Son and Holy Ghost.[114] Placed between God Father and his Son, the Holy Ghost acts as a bridge between immateriality and incarnation, between ineffability and language. The intermediate realm between the various dimensions of reality belongs to the Holy Ghost, which is often depicted, in medieval paintings, as a constellation of small flames burning over the head of those who are receiving a revelation. Like the faithful assembled at Pentecost, its language covers more than one world and more than one time-segment.

> *When the day of Pentecost had come, they were all together in one place. And suddenly from heaven there came a sound like the rush of a violent wind, and it filled the entire house where they were sitting. Divided tongues, as of fire, appeared among them, and a tongue rested on each of them. All of them were filled with the Holy Spirit and began to speak in other languages, as the spirit gave them ability.*[115]

The figure of the Holy Ghost is the element that allows for the simultaneous inclusion, within reality, of the three seemingly incompatible principles of (ineffable) obscurity, (incarnate) knowledge and (ghostly) mystery. God Father, who would otherwise remain entirely secret in His absoluteness, makes Himself manifest

---

[114]'The mystery of the Trinity only becomes accessible to that ignorance which rises above all that can be contained within the concepts of the philosophers. Yet this *ignorantia*, not only *docta* ["learned"] but charitable also, redescends again upon these concepts that it may mould them; that it may transform the expressions of human wisdom into the instruments of that Wisdom of God which is to the Greeks foolishness.' V. Lossky, *The Mystical Theology of the Eastern Church*, translated by a group of members of the Fellowship of St Alban and St Sergius, Cambridge, James Clarke & Co., 2005, pp. 49–50.

[115]Acts, 2:1–4 (*New Oxford Annotated Bible*). See also Saint Paul's assessment of the Pentecostal experience in the everyday life of Christians, and of its distinction from prophecy in an evangelical sense: 'Pursue love and strove for the spiritual gifts, and especially that you may prophesy. For those who speak in a tongue do not speak to other people but to God; for nobody understands them, since they are speaking mysteries in the Spirit. On the other hand, those who prophesy speak to other people for their upbuilding and encouragement and consolation ... Now I would like all of you to speak in tongues, but even more to prophesy.' 1 Corinthians, 14:1–3 (*New Oxford Annotated Bible*).

through His relationship with the full incarnation of His Son. The Son, in turn, owes his existence and the awareness of his own limits – that is, of the limits of meaning – to the path that stretches back to the Father.[116] The figure of the Holy Ghost, like a metaphysical Hermes, acts both as the road and as the message between them. It is, to a certain extent, the very essence of the angel.[117]

God has so far been spoken of only as the positive Nothing, transcending all form and content. [...] The Christian doctrine based upon revelation speaks of God as a person, as God the Father, God the Son, and God the Holy Ghost. [...] God as the Absolute is superpersonal, and for this very reason the realm of personal being is open to Him, though it does not limit Him. Entering it He still, on the one hand, transcends existence as the positive Nothing, while on the other He exists as three Persons which form a perfect unity. [Russian philosopher Vladimir] Soloviev bases his interpretation of the Three Hypostases upon the idea of the self-manifestation of the Absolute, which

---

[116]The reader well versed in theology will not miss the apparent contradiction between such a definition of the role of the Holy Ghost and the repeated use of Orthodox references in this chapter. Indeed, the controversy over the filiation of the Holy Ghost constituted one of the main points of disagreement that lead to the schism between the Catholic and the Orthodox Churches in 1053. According to the Orthodox, the Holy Ghost proceeds only from the Father, whose 'monarchy' is metaphysically absolute. Conversely, Catholics argue that the Holy Ghost proceeds both from the Father and from the Son (*filioque*) – namely from the Father through the Son. My description of the Holy Ghost – as the process through which each realm of reality manifests itself to the other – differs from both these perspectives and it should be understood in the context of a philosophical (specifically, phenomenological) enquiry, rather than as an article of dogmatic theology. It is in this 'philosophical' spirit that I have borrowed from the thought of thinkers such as Vladimir Lossky, while remaining aware that I might be contravening his express admonitions not to dilute Orthodox dogmas outside of their proper framework. *Mea culpa*. Perhaps, the great Sunni theologian Al Ghazali was right about the ruthlessness and dangerous 'incoherence' of the philosophers.

[117]It is possible to recognize a comparable trinitarian structure also in ancient Greek religion. The three sky-divinities Oranos, Zeus and Apollo (a Titan, an Olympian issued from a Titan, and an Olympian) embody three different dimensions and stages of manifestation of reality: the sky in its state of hiding as an infinite, invisible expanse (Ouranos, the Father); the process through which the sky manifests itself as lightning and thunder (Zeus; the Holy Ghost); and the sky in its full manifestation as the sun (Apollo; the Son).

necessarily involves the following three moments: (1) that which is manifested in and for itself; (2) manifestation as such; i.e. the positioning of oneself in and for another. The expression or determination of the manifesting essence, its Word or Logos; (3) the return of that which is manifested to itself, or its rediscovery of itself in the manifestation.[118]

The realm where the prophet operates is the same intermediate place between cosmological dimensions that is occupied by the Holy Ghost and by the angel.[119] All three figures lack an autonomous essence of their own, except as the inter-dimensional reflections that they can provide through their works of culture. The white dove painted on the ceiling of Christian churches, like the human-faced, flying steed Buraq, who carried Mohammed during his celestial Night Journey,[120] can be taken as the effigy of the Muse of prophecy. Neither of these two exceptional animals move out of their own whim, but an inaudible order directs their flight. Like them, the prophet also creates their works not only out of a sense of wonder,[121] but also out of responsibility.[122]

---

[118]N. Lossky, *History of Russian Philosophy*, London, Allen and Unwin, 1952, pp. 100–1.

[119]The position of these three figures is central to esotericism across religious denominations: 'The doctrine of the Holy Spirit (in contrast to the dazzling manifestation of the Son, which the Church proclaims to the farthest confines of the universe), has the character of a secret, a partially revealed tradition.' V. Lossky, *The Mystical Theology of the Eastern Church*, translated by a group of members of the Fellowship of St Alban and St Sergius, Cambridge, James Clarke & Co., 2005, p. 161.

[120]Quran, 7 and 53.

[121]'When the lightning bolt of wonder strikes us, mysterious amazement bursts open, for which everything familiar suddenly becomes unfamiliar and question worthy. When the philosophical question arises, the human being does not immediately become more knowing but rather more unknowing, is thrown back into a not-knowing that shocks and terrifies. And the uncanniness of this situation consists in his having to regard his earlier knowledge as nugatory and untenable, as ungrounded and delusional, as a not-knowing that took itself for knowing and labored under a delusional blindness, and it consists in the fact that he initially feels that he is plunged into a poverty that knows that it knows nothing.' E. Fink, *Play as Symbol of the World and Other Writings*, translated by I.A. Moore and C. Turner, Bloomington, IN, Indiana University Press, 2016.

[122]A playful responsibility, to be sure, but a responsibility nonetheless. 'As long as you catch self-thrown things/it's all dexterity and venial gain – ;/only when you've

From the position that they occupy, a prophet can recognize within the multiple faces of reality the same sadness that the Ismaili theologians attributed to a Divinity locked in solitary confinement. An 'infinite demand'[123] reaches the prophet from the face of each dimension of existence, and it is to these multiple sadnesses, innervating reality, that the prophet caters their work.[124]

In the compassionate attitude of this gesture, we can find one of the elements that the figure of the prophet offers to the *tetrapharmakon* – the combination of perspectives which might constitute a suitable legacy for the archaic adolescents, after the end of this future. Within the total picture of existence, the metaphysician brings the gift of language, the shaman that of metamorphosis and the mystic the intuition of an eternal bedrock beyond all changes

---

suddenly caught that ball/which she, one of the eternal players,/has tossed toward you, your center, with/a throw precisely judged, one of those arches/that exist in God's great bridge-system:/only then is catching a proficiency, – /not yours, a world's. And if you then had/strength and courage to return the throw,/no, more wonderful: forgot strength and courage/and had already thrown ... (as the year/ throws the birds, those migrating bird swarms,/which an older to a younger warmth sends/catapulting across oceans –) only/in that venture would you truly join in.' R.M. Rilke, *Uncollected Poems*, translated by E. Snow, New York, NY, North Point, 1966, p. 139.

[123]The notion of an 'infinite responsibility' issuing from the 'face' of the other – as the face of God – is a key concept in the work of Lithuanian-French, Jewish philosopher Emmanuel Levinas – see E. Levinas, *Totality and Infinity: An Essay on Exteriority*, translated by A. Lingis, Dordrecht: Kluwer, 1991. An interesting development of this notion towards (post)anarchist politics can be found in S. Critchley, *Infinitely Demanding: Ethics of Commitment, Politics of Resistance*, London/New York, Verso, 2007.

[124]In this regard, it is useful to consider Jacques Derrida's comment on the narrative of the prophetic book of Revelation (or Apocalypse) by John of Patmos: 'One does not know (for it is no longer of the order of knowing) to whom the apocalyptic sending returns; it leaps from one place of emission to the other (and a place is always determined starting from the presumed emission); it goes form one destination, one name, and one tone to the other; it always refers to the name and to the tone of the other that is there but as having been there and before yet coming, no longer being or not yet there in the present of the *récit*. And there is no certainty that man is the exchange [*le central*] of the telephone lines or the terminal of this endless computer. No longer is one very sure who loans its voice and its tone to the other in the Apocalypse; no longer is one very sure who addresses what to whom.' J. Derrida, 'Of an Apocalyptic Tone Newly Adopted in Philosophy', in H. Coward and T. Foshay (eds.), *Derrida and Negative Theology: With a Conclusion by Jacques Derrida*, Albany, NY, SUNY Press, 1992, p. 57.

and definitions. To this treasure, the prophet finally adds emotion as one of the constitutive blocks of the stuff of reality.

Pathos is a constant presence among the existentiating principles of prophetic cosmologies, where it often adopts the role assigned by Empedocles to Love (*Philotes*) and Strife (*Neikos*) as the fundamental emotional (*emovere*, 'to disloge') drives behind the movements of the dimensions of existence.[125] This emotion enlivens prophetic cosmology, presenting each dimension of reality as equally endowed with pure existence – and, thus, equally alive. In a multidimensional perspective, the attribute of 'being alive' can be assigned only on condition of intensifying its definition. To be alive, in a sense that breaks out of the specificity of the linguistic world, means to be 'there' in whichever possible dimension of reality.[126] *Dasein* ('being there', as the essential status of the human) is not

---

[125]'Double is the birth of mortal things and double their failing; for the one is brought to birth and destroyed by the coming together of all things, the other is nurtured and flies apart as they grow apart again. And these things never cease their continual interchange, now through Love all coming together into one, now again each carried apart by the hatred of Strife' Empedocles, frag. B26 (but see also frag. B35 for a description of the movements of Love and Strife) – in G.S. Kirk et al., *The Presocratic Philosophers: A Critical History with a Selection of Texts*, Cambridge, Cambridge University Press, 2005, pp. 287, 296–7.

[126]An enlightening interpretation of the notion of 'life' as an equivalent to that of 'existence' was provided by Pavel Florensky in his magnum opus *The Pillar and Ground of the Truth*. While working on the etymology of the Russian word *istina* (truth), Florenksy observed how it derives from the verb *est* (to be). '*Est*' [(to be), in turn] comes from the root *es*, which in Sanskrit gives *as* ... *Est*' can without difficulty be related to the Old Slavic *esmi*; the Greek *eimi* (*esmi*); the Latin (*e*)*sum*, *est*; the German *ist*; the Sanskrit *asmi*, *asti*, etc. But in accordance with certain hints in the Sanskrit, this root *es* signified – in its most ancient, concrete phase of development – *to breathe* ... [Georg] Curtius points to the Sanskrit words *as-u-s* (the breath of life), *asu-ras* (vital, *lebendig*); and, equivalent to the Latin *os*, mouth ..., the German *athmen* is also related to this. Thus, "*est*'" originally meant to breathe. Respiration, or breath, was always considered to be the main attribute and even the very essence of *life*. And even today, the usual answer to the question, "Is he alive?" is "He's breathing." Whence the second, more abstract meaning of "*est*'": he's alive, he has strength. Finally, "*est*'" acquires its most abstract meaning, that of the verb that expresses existence. To breathe, to live, to be – these are the three layers in the root *es* in the order of their decreasing concreteness, an order that, in the opinion of linguists, corresponds to their chronological order.' P. Florensky, *The Pillar and Ground of the Truth: An Essay in Orthodox Theodicy in Twelve Letters*, translated by B. Jakim, Princeton, NJ, Princeton University Press, 2004, p. 15.

only the definition of those who are 'there' in the world, but also of those dimensions of reality for which 'here' has a different location. Each of these dimensions is as alive as the world, as sad as the world in its own enclosure, and as endowed as the world with an agency of its own.

The yearning for eternity of the inhabitants of time is the same that makes eternity long for a vision of time.

The incompleteness of the world mirrors that of the Heavens. In the Heavens, Christ awaits his own definitive resurrection, which will be such only in the resurrection of the creature. [...] Origen, whom Meister Eckhart called 'the great Teacher,' adumbrates the idea of a double sacrifice: for human beings, Christ shed 'the very bodily matter of his blood, whilst for the celestial creatures ... he offered the vital strength of his body as some kind of spiritual sacrifice'. The passion of Christ takes place also in Heaven.[127]

A prophetic text like Giuseppe Ungaretti's First World War poem *Mattina* (Morning), for example, acts in both directions, depending on whether it's read in sequence or with its conceptual poles inverted.[128]

M'illumino
D'Immenso

[I illumine myself
With immensity][129]

---

[127]M. Cacciari, *The Necessary Angel*, translated by M.E. Vatter, Albany, NY, SUNY, 1994, pp. 72–3.

[128]This same procedure of reverse reading can be applied to the prophetic texts of traditional fables, as argued by Cristina Campo: 'The impossible is open to the hero of a fable. But how is it possible to reach the impossible if not, indeed, through the impossible? The impossible resembles a word that is to be read the first time from right to left, and the second time from left to right. Or a mountain with two slopes, of which one is as steep as the other is gentle.' C. Campo, 'Della Fiaba', in *Gli Imperdonabili*, Milan, Adelphi, 2019, pp. 29–42: 32 – my translation.

[129]G. Ungaretti, *Selected Poems*, edited and translated by A. Frisardi, Manchester: Carcanet, 2003. For a discussion of the different possible translations of his poem *Mattina*, see Matthew Reynold's article, M. Reynolds, *Nicely Combed*, London Review of Books, vol. 25 No. 23, 4 December 2003.

In the bomb-ravaged trenches on the Carso plateau, Ungaretti's morning respite redeemed its own fleetingness by glimpsing at the oceans beyond the anguish of time. Through the same passage, however, eternity could also look past its own isolation, towards a place where things can finally become and change. The world gained a sight of Heaven, and the un-worldly realms a vision of Paradise.

These two seemingly outdated terms, Heaven and Paradise, deserve careful consideration under the lens of a prophetic attitude. Instinctively, one would locate Heaven 'up' in the sky and Paradise 'down' on Earth; yet the distinction between up and down depends on the point from which they are observed.

> *The dream is a sign of the passage from one sphere to the other, and as such it is a symbol. A symbol of what? As seen from above, it is a symbol of down here; as seen from down here, it is a symbol of what is above ... The movement between the frontiers of the worlds is due either to the ascent from the bottom or to the descent from the top, which is a return downwards. The images of the ascent represent the stripping of the clothes of daily life, of the scales of the soul, for which there is no room in the other world ... The images of the descent are the crystallisation of the mystical life upon the border between worlds.*"[130]

Heaven is what happens when ineffability pierces through the constructions of language, undoing their apparent isolation and relativizing the rhythm of their time-segments. It is the state in which the world ceases to believe that its own infinity can exhaust the whole of existence, while beginning to see its own contours reflected against the body of an authentically 'other' dimension of reality. Heaven comes close to Chaos – which 'does not exist in nature ... belonging to the relation between the mind and the speed of events'[131] – but with the important difference that its speed is weighed down by the mesh of language, through which it passes, and that its disorder is tamed within aesthetic bounds.

---

[130]P. Florensky, *Le Porte Regali: saggio sull'icona*, translated by E. Zolla, Milan, Adelphi, 1977, pp. 33–5 – my translation from the Italian edition.
[131]F. Berardi 'Bifo', 'The End of Prophecy', *e-flux journal*, no. 95, November 2018.

Paradise serves the same function as Heaven, but in reference to – and observed from – the outside to the world. Eternity itself is redeemed, when it is capable of recognizing the becoming of the world and the flow of its narrative. By looking at the world of language, what is ineffable hears the same prophetic message that is at the heart of the Changdoya Upanishad: 'You are that' (*Tat Tvam Asi*).[132]

This is not merely a 're-enchantment' of the world (or of the unworldly realms of existence), but a transfiguration[133] of the world (and of the unworldly). As symbolically recounted in a favourite Sufi parable:

Jesus and his disciples come across a dead, half-decayed dog, lying with its mouth open. 'How horribly it stinks', say the disciples, turning aside in disgust. But Jesus says, 'See how splendidly its teeth shine!'[134]

When one dimension of reality grows to the point of totalizing the awareness of its inhabitants and to crush them into a state of

---

[132]This saying appears in the *Chandogya Upanishad*, in the course of a dialogue where Hindu sage Uddalaka educates his son Shvetaketu to recognize that one's own Self (*atman*) coincides with the ineffable Ultimate Reality (*Brahma*). I am here modifying the address of this statement, as if it was an admonishment directed to the eternal ineffable dimension of reality to recognize its own fundamental kinship with the world of language. See, *Chandogya Upanishad*, 6.8.7.

[133]I am borrowing the term and the notion of 'transfiguration' from the synoptic gospels (Matthew 17:1–6, Mark 9:1–8, Luke 9:28–36, John 1:14). Christ's transfiguration represented the peak of his public life, which was marked at the beginning by his baptism and at the end by the ascension. 'Six days afterwards Jesus took Peter and James and his brother John with him, and led them up on to a high mountain where they were alone. And he was transfigured in their presence, his face shining like the sun, and his garments becoming white as snow; and all at once they had sight of Moses and Elias conversing with him. Then Peter said aloud to Jesus, Lord, it is well that we should be here; if it pleases thee, let us make three arbours in this place, one for thee, one for Moses and one for Elias. Even before he had finished speaking, a shining cloud overshadowed them. And now, there was a voice which said to them out of the cloud, This is my beloved Son, in whom I am well pleased.' Matthew, 17:1–5.

[134]As recounted by Navid Kermani, in N. Kermani, *Wonder beyond Belief*, translated by T. Crawford, Cambridge, Polity Press, 2018, p. 14.

paralysis, then the prophetic vision of a metaphysical elsewhere can offer them some respite and a chance to evade its grip.[135]

Adopting a prophetic perspective towards reality does not launch social revolutions, it doesn't make deforested areas re-blossom, nor does it automatically change interpersonal politics. All it can do is to redeem each dimension of reality from the paranoia of its metaphysical isolation. By presenting the world as a finite realm and its excess as an overflowing abundance, it transforms a subject's own experience of historical events – declaring both their legitimacy and the limits of their relevance.

Heaven is throughout the whole world, and it is also outside of the world, everywhere that is, or that can even be imagined. It fills all; it is within all; it is outside of all; it encompasses all; without division, without place ... [it] is revealed being one and undivided in all ... Because heaven is nothing else but a manifestation or revelation of the eternal one, wherein all the

---

[135]Although far too briefly, I would like to mention a recent prophetic understanding of reality, which bears some similarities (as well as some important differences) with that presented in this book. In his volumes *La Gloria* (2001) and *Oltrepassare* (2007), the Italian philosopher Emanuele Severino developed his earlier intuitions about the eternity of all that exists (understood as the Totality of existence, along the guidelines posed by Parmenides), towards a confutation of the idea of 'death' as an authentic and final event. By demonstrating the eternity of each being (inasmuch as it is just a way in which the eternal existent manifests itself – and eternally so – within the 'limited circle of appearances'), Severino suggested that a heavenly reconciliation with the trauma of one's own becoming, and of one's own apparent fleetingness, is always-already possible, and that it can be obfuscated only by a metaphysical perspective towards reality that is incapable of recognizing it. 'We are the eternal circles of appearance of truth, in which eternity manifests itself; for this reason, we are destined to the Glory of the Earth [i.e. to the eternal movement of existence through the circle of the finite] and to welcome into the light of appearance the Glory of Joy [i.e. the endless coming into manifestation of the Totality of existence], which is what we truly already are in our being the very inexhaustibility of Joy.' E. Severino, *La Gloria: Risoluzione di 'Destino della necessità'*, Milan, Adelphi, 2001, p. 561 – my translation. 'We are truly and totally ourselves where the contradiction that originally constitutes us is finally overcome. [...] We are the Totality: the infinite destiny. That is, the infinite appearing of the infinite. We are that One – the eternal Totality – that each of us is, however differently from the others, where our contradictions, and thus our anguish and unhappiness and pain are eternally overcome.' E. Severino, *La Follia dell'Angelo: Conversazioni Intorno Alla Filosofia*, Milan, Mimesis, 2006, p. 206 – my translation.

working and willing is in quiet love. So in like manner hell also is through the whole world, and dwells ... in that which the foundation of hell is manifested, namely, in [the] self ... The visible world has both in it; and there is no place that heaven and hell may not be found or revealed in it.[136]

By creating a difference between reality and the world, it allows life to emerge as always-already saved, always-already partly elsewhere. And by opening a window in the walls of the world, prophecy not only reveals the presence of more than was previously thought, but it also offers a space from which it is possible to return to the world and to intervene on it.

One should uplift oneself by the Self;
One should not degrade oneself;
For the Self alone can be a friend to oneself,
And the Self alone can be an enemy of oneself.[137]

Rather than promoting apathy and fatalism, a prophetic gaze offers that reassurance against the anguish of loss and of becoming, which is by necessity the foundation of any meaningful action. Indeed, the suffering of the world comes nearest to the place occupied by the prophet. And there is a close proximity between the impulse towards suicide and the impulse to prophesize. Taking up a prophetic approach towards reality kills a part of the subject, making them somewhat dead to the world. Likewise, the suicidal epiphany of seeing oneself as an unnecessary convention of language is already a recognition of an other realm (even just 'non-being') where one is reintegrated, once they abandon the world.

Yet, this proximity to the utterly un-worldly doesn't make prophetic culture a hymn to self-annihilation. Prophecy and suicide share a similar cosmological outlook, but they have different programmes of action. They wish to soothe suffering in opposite ways. While suicide attempts to throw a person's body outside the world, prophecy reminds them that they are always-already part of

---

[136]J. Boehme, 'Heaven and Hell', in *The Way to Christ*, translated by P.C. Erb, Mahwah, NJ, Paulist Press, 1977, p. 185.
[137]*The Bhagavad Gītā*, VI, 5, translated by W. Sargeant, Albany, NY, SUNY, 2009, p. 276.

realms exceeding the world – that they have always-already fled, that they have already been saved.

Seen as one island surrounded by other spaces, the world itself turns, from a serious game, into a game that can be played seriously. It has its own unbreakable inner rules, and its lure and threats can often feel overwhelming, yet it is just a process taking place within a specific board. Even if one wished to end their act before its natural closure, they wouldn't have to do so with acrimony – rather, like players gracefully abandoning the table.[138]

Prophetic culture offers another room in the house, beyond the games room and a place from which it is possible to intervene on the world as if always returning to it. Prophetic action is the adventure of a returning migrant – and its outlook is not unlike how archaic fishermen in New Guinea replicated the original gesture of their Ancestor, when they threw their harpoons.[139] This

---

[138]'Play is essentially a separate occupation, carefully isolated from the rest of life, and generally is engaged in with precise limits of time and place. There is place for play: as needs dictate, the space for hopscotch, the board for checkers or chess, the stadium, the racetrack, the list, the ring, the stage, the arena, etc. Nothing that takes place outside this ideal frontier is relevant ... [Play] happens only when the players have a desire to play, and play the most absorbing, exhausting game in order to find diversion, escape from responsibility and routine. Finally, and above all, it is necessary that they be free to leave whenever they please, by saying: "I am not playing anymore."' R. Caillois, *Man, Play and Games*, translated by M. Barash, Chicago, IL, University of Chicago Press, 2001, p. 6.

[139]'For instance, in New Guinea, when a mariner sets out to sea, he is repeating the acts and the story of the mythical hero Aori. The mariner dresses like Aori – with the same facial colouring and costume – dances and spreads his wings like Aori, and embarks on the fish hunt with the same attitude that Aori once had. The mariner does not invoke the mythical hero. The mariner imitates him as closely as possible to insure that he becomes contemporary with Aori. In this way, the mariner repeats a sacred archetype, model, and makes the mythical time present, real. What would otherwise be a profane, ordinary, task is now given value and supernatural power.' D. Cave, *Mircea Eliade's Vision for a New Humanism*, Oxford, Oxford University Press, 1993, p. 51. 'By making this gesture, a fisherman doesn't beg the divinity for help; he imitates and identifies himself with the divinity ... What has to eb understood is the existential value of the myth. A myth placates anguish and endows humans with a sense of security. The Polynesian mariner can venture over the ocean without fear, since he has the certainty that, as long as he repeats exactly the gestures of the Ancestor or of the God, his journey is going to end well.' M. Eliade, *La Prova del Labirinto: intervista con Claude-Henri Rocquet*, translated by M. Giacometti, Milan, Jaca Book, 1990, p. 142 – my translation from the Italian edition.

new position towards the world, which is offered by a prophetic attitude, is not that of the king or of the boss. It is a place of loss: a stepping back from the world, which relativizes the world and its lure. A place of loss, but a terrain where the force of mourning is capable of relativizing any threats of annihilation that might be waged by worldly powers. The world is not nothing, nor is it just an illusion, but it is still only a world: whatever traverses it also relates and belongs to whatever exceeds it. No longer a win-all/lose-all ordeal in a boundless desert, worldly existence manifests itself as one layer in a larger event, exceeding for the most part our ability to catalogue it linguistically. And once worldly events and structures are seen by a subject in their partiality, the latter finally gains the ability to act within the world. Action will no longer put at stake one's whole existence, since nothing is ever lost entirely. No failure is absolute, no life is ever wasted.

Perhaps, it is possible to direct and to produce historical events only when one's own will is sustained by an awareness of the ineffable excess overflowing the maps of language. As noted by Dadaist poet Hugo Ball:

> It is impossible at the same time to be artists and to believe in history.[140]

This implicit tenet of prophetic culture is also exposed by the Pseudo-Dionysius, when he considers the relationship between worldly activity and the peace that belongs to the ineffable dimensions of existence:

> If all moving things wish never to be at rest, but aim always for their own appropriate movement, this too is because of a wish for that divine Peace of the universe, which keeps everything firmly in its own place and which ensures that the individuality and the stirring life of all moving things are kept safe from removal and

---

[140]H. Ball, *Die Flucht aus der Zeit*, Munchen: Duncker & Humblot, 1927 – my translation from the Italian edition, H. Ball, *Fuga dal Tempo: fuga saeculi*, translated by R. Caldura, Milan, Mimesis, 2016, p. 192.

*destruction. This happens as a result of the inward peace which
causes the things in movement to engage in the activity proper
to themselves.*[141]

A similar understanding can be found also in Native-American
Winnebago culture, where the possibility of acting in the world is
seen as conditional on a subject's acknowledgement of the realms
of spirits beyond the field of the visible.

*The acquisition of a guardian and protective spirit at puberty
was one of the fundamental traits of Winnebago culture as it was
that of numerous other American Indian tribes. According to
Winnebago ideas, without it a man was completely unanchored
and at the mercy of events, natural and societal, in their crudest
and most cruel forms. When they lost their belief in the efficacy
of fasting and the sprits no longer vouchsafed their visions,
Winnebago culture rapidly disintegrated.*[142]

Logic doesn't suffice to extract meaning out of nothingness, and
no success ever lasts enough to cover the abyss of meaninglessness
within every 'thing'. To be able to persist within change – as to be
able to persist within eternity – a subject needs a supplement to
their own instinct and will.

The mirror of prophetic culture, set at the crosspoint[143] between
the multiple gazes traversing reality, provides such an aid, by
allowing for an instant[144] of redemption and for a traumatic chance

---

[141]Pseudo-Dionysius, 'The Divine Names', 952D, in *The Complete Works*, translated
by C. Luibheid, New York, NY, Paulist Press, 1987, p. 123.

[142]P. Radin, *The Trickster: A Study in American Indian Mythology*, New York, NY,
Schocken Books, 1972, pp. 115–16.

[143]On the symbolic meaning of the cross as the *axis mundi*, see R. Guenon, *The
Symbolism of the Cross*, translated by A. Macnab, Hillsdale, NY, Sophia Perennis,
2004; and Rev. Geo. S. Tyack, *The Cross in Ritual Architecture and Art*, London,
William Andrews & Co., 1900.

[144]The 'instant' to which I am referring is very close to the Greek-Orthodox notion
of *Kairos* as the 'opportune moment' when eternity manifests itself within time (on
the basis of scriptural passages such as Mark 1:15, and John 7:6). In Orthodox
churches, before the Divine Liturgy begins, the Deacon exclaims to the Priest, *Kairos
tou poiesai to Kyrio*, 'It is time [*kairos*] for the Lord to act', indicating explicitly that
the time of the liturgy is to be understood as an intersection with eternity.

to reset one's own feet within reality. Its horizon isn't that of a promise that shall be fulfilled some distant day, depending on a person's action. The redemption of reality that animates prophetic culture takes place always-already, like the timeless point of the instant is always and already at the heart of the durational present.

At once a mirror of Heaven and of Paradise, the 'end of the world' presented by prophetic culture is, in fact, the end of the world's belief to exhaust within itself the whole of reality. In the eyes of prophecy, fear of apocalypse is transformed into the vision of what the Church Fathers called *apocatastasis*.

Deriving from the verb *apokathistemi*, (to restore), apocatastasis is conceptualized by thinkers like Origen and Gregory of Nissa as the instant when the world loses its own separatedness and is finally re-absorbed within the Totality of the Divinity.[145] Nothing remains excluded from this restoration, not even the figure of Satan, since nothing was ever entirely outside of the Divine dimension.

> *Satan is not a real and single Person, but a severally postulated personality, a 'Legion.' Each of these personalities is capable of redemption (apokatastasis), and can, if it will, become again what it was before it 'fell' – Lucifer, Phosphorus, Helel, Scintilla, the Morning Star, a Ray of the Supernal Sun; because the Spark, however it may seem to be smothered, is an Asbestos that cannot be extinguished, even in hell.*[146]

---

[145]The notion of apocatastasis was first launched at the time of Origen and has gained a strong following in the Orthodox world, but it has maintained vigour under the name of 'universalism' also in other Christian denominations. According to contemporary universalist thought, salvation always-and-already befalls everyone, including Satan. See H.U. von Balthasar, *Dare We Hope 'That All Men Be Saved?*, translated by D. Kipp and Rev. L. Krauth, San Francisco, CA, Ignatius Press, 1993; and D. Bentley Hart, *That All Shall Be Saved: Heaven, Hell, and Universal Salvation*, New Haven/London, Yale University Press, 2019. For an overview of the debate around this theological problem, see I. Ramelli, *The Christian Doctrine of Apokatastasis: A Critical Assessment from the New Testament to Eriugena*, Leiden, Brill, 2013.

[146]A. Coomaraswamy, *Who Is 'Satan' and Where Is 'Hell'?* – in A. Coomaraswamy, *Selected Papers: Volume 2, Metaphysics*, edited by R. Lipsey, Princeton, NJ, Princeton University Press, 1987, p. 33.

The notion of apocatastasis intervenes on that of the apocalypse, subverting its course and its cosmological implications. By declaring that a final judgement shall befall the universe, and that its outcome will be immutable, the apocalypse separates the eternally saved from those who shall be damned eternally. Conversely, the apocatastasis does without a final judgement at the tail end of time, suggesting instead that within time itself there is an eternal instant where everything, always and already, is rescued from both the threats of eternal damnation and of complete annihilation.

It is worth quoting at length Massimo Cacciari's explanation of the difference between apocalypse and apocatastasis – where the former is epitomized by Dante's notion of an eternal Hell, while the latter focuses on the Second Coming of Christ as an event that abolishes the law, sparking the ultimate reintegration of reality.

Dante's Inferno is truly a test bench, not just of the fallen Angel and its victims, but of the whole Christian angelological dimension. If the originary decision is unappealable, ... if the Judgment does not 'review' but essentially repeats the sentence and the absolute division between the heavenly rose and Hell (a veritable Hades, complete absence of light and vision), then Necessity is the last word in this theology, where the most perfect torment is associated with the most perfect blessedness. The eschatological dimension is, literally, its apocalypse, its final and complete manifestation ... The eschaton is also a dimension of Necessity, nothing other than its supreme moment. [...]

[Conversely, we] need to understand the grace of the Second Coming beyond every 'chronological' tie to the actual world, in the fullness of its redemptive word ... : the Sacrifice inaugurates an epoch that no longer obeys the Nomos, that is no longer the servant of Nomos, but is the epoch of Charis and Aletheia (Grace and Truth). The Nomos judges no longer; it is no longer left up to the Nomos to judge on the basis of works. If this were the case, Christ would have died in vain. The vision of the apocalypse that is fixated on the dimension of Judgment is essentially nomothetic. Instead, it is not the triumph of the Nomos, but the unveiling of the power of Grace that constitutes its promise. But this promise must be thought as addressed to all, and therefore also to iniquitous spirits. Not only human beings, heavenly Angels, and stars ... but also the demon itself, the fallen

Angel itself, will be transfigured in the Parousia, for it seems untenable that the eschaton will not re-create the originary unity, will not abolish the inhospitable separation of sin. The cosmic krisis that sin continuously reproduces cannot be negated by a new sanction, but by an act of Charis, by a supreme Gift that opens every isolation, every separation, every autonomy (and therefore opens the foundation itself of every autonomy, which is Nomos), that opens a new Age in which ripens the redemption of all heavenly, earthly and infernal creatures.[147]

The suffering of the world, born out of its conviction to be an autonomous and solitary fact surrounded by absolute *nihil*, is itself already Hell – an emotional Hell not dissimilar from the anguished isolation of the Ismaili God.

We are used to saying that Adam was lost and fell because he ate that apple. I say it was because of his presumption and because of his 'I' and his 'Mine', his 'Me' and the like. He could have eaten seven apples, yet had this not been connected with his presumption, he would not have fallen.[148]

It is there, in Hell, that worldly powers can threaten a subject with metaphysical annihilation, so to break and to submit them to the diktats of their own laws.

Conversely, Heaven consists in the realization of the unity that always subtends all facets and dimensions of reality. Rebels always depart from Heaven to launch their incursions into the world – ambushing and striking the parameters of 'objectivity' that worldly powers impose as natural laws.

---

[147]M. Cacciari, *The Necessary Angel*, translated by M.E. Vatter, Albany, NY, SUNY, 1994, pp. 70 and 73. It is interesting to place Cacciari's reading of the overcoming of necessity through the apocatastasis, in parallel with Cristina Campo's reading of the essential prophetic message of fables: 'Victory over the law of necessity, and a constant passage to a new order of relationships is the tireless, inexhaustible lesson of fables – it is this and nothing else, since there is absolutely nothing else to learn on this Earth.' C. Campo, 'Della fiaba', in *Gli Imperdonabili*, Milan, Adelphi, 2019, pp. 29–42: 34 – my translation.

[148]*The Theologia Germanica of Martin Luther*, chapter 3, translated and commented by B. Hoffman, New York, NY, Paulist Press, 1980, p. 62.

The shift from damnation to salvation, from the fear of apocalypse that haunts a world locked in solitary confinement to the joy of apocatastasis, is as dramatic as it is imperceptible. The universal transformation engendered by a shift of perspective towards reality is a cosmic redemption that carries little material trace.

The Hassidim tell a story about the world to come, that says everything there will be just as it is here. Just as our room is now, so it will be in the world to come; where our baby sleeps now, there too it will sleep in the other world. And the clothes we wear in this world, those too we will wear there. Everything will be as it is now, just a little different.[149]

---

[149]This quote, attributed to Walter Benjamin in conversation with Ernst Bloch, is cited by Giorgio Agamben in G. Agamben, *The Coming Community*, translated by M. Hardt, Minneapolis/London, University of Minnesota Press, 2007, p. 53.

THE MEMORY OF HAVING FORGOTTEN

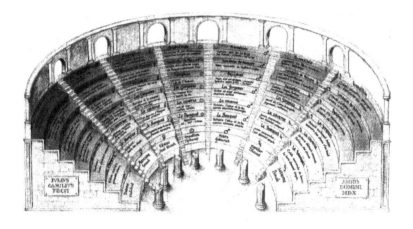

FIGURE 3.7 *Giulio Camillo Delminio,* Theatre of Memory, *visualization from* L'idea del theatro, *1550.*

The Hebrew letter aleph *cannot be pronounced, not because it is too complex but because it is too simple; because, unlike all others, it represents no sound at all ... Despite its phonetic poverty, however,* aleph *is a letter of prestige in the Jewish tradition ... [According to Hassidic rabbi Mendel of Rymanow, when God spoke to the tribe of Israel gathered at the foot of the mountain,] all that Israel heard was the* aleph *with which the first Commandment begins, the* aleph *of the word* anokhi, 'I' ... *All revelation is thus reduced to a letter whose sound none can recall ... Could God have shown to human beings in anything other than a letter that they had already forgotten? The sole material of divine speech, the silent letter marks the forgetting from which all language emerges.* Aleph *guards the place of oblivion at the interception of every alphabet.*[150]

When I close my eyes and I try to bring back the memory of a face or of a certain landscape, all I gain is a fleeting phantom. If I manage to summon it, its image persists for an instant before its contours blur beyond recognition. It makes no difference whether it is the face of someone dear to me, or if it was the landscape of an indelible moment of my life.

In our everyday experience, memory has little to do with the use that is made of this term by Information Technology. In the vocabulary of software, a 'memory' is an item that can be re-accessed at any time, as perfectly as when it was last 'saved'. But an actual memory, however fresh, is never a monolith that stands erect in front of our awareness. From the instant it emerges within us, it is a hare ready to flee an approaching eye.

Oblivion is the mode of existence of memories, and the ontological status of their presence. The spring of Mnemosyne, goddess of memory – so we are taught by the Orphic mysteries of ancient Greece – flows near that of Lethe, the water of oblivion.

How would you like me to call you? [– Hesiod asks Mnemosyne –] Every time we have to call you using a different word. You are like a mother whose name fades in time.[151]

---

[150]D. Heller-Roazen, *Echolalias: On the Forgetting of Language*, New York, NY, Zone Books, 2005, pp. 19–25.
[151]C. Pavese, 'Le Muse', in *Dialoghi con Leuco'*, Turin, Einaudi, 2014, p. 163 – my translation.

The constitutive fleetingness of memory also subtends every attempt at making sense, through the use of language, out of the avalanche of raw perceptions that invests us. Whatever cosmos we might be able to create around ourselves, its form remains always precarious and evanescent, in need of constant rebuilding. The tireless repetition of the name of God, typical of the highest forms of prayer across religions, manifests the awareness that any construction of language needs to be constantly repeated, if it is to evoke the presence of what it is meant to signify.

The intuition of religious prayer resounds with those visions of Heaven and Paradise discussed in the previous chapter, which constitute the essential content of a prophetic message. When a prophetic gaze reveals a synoptic view of reality, the image which it presents to a subject is but an ungraspable phantom; the memory of something metaphysically alien, whose vision vanishes just as it appears. Like a memory, the landscape of a world redeemed by *apocatastasis* comes forward in waves – it remains for the time of one breath, and flows back.

> *But the flame which kindles desire and illuminates thought never burned for more than a few seconds at a stretch. The rest of the time we tried to remember it.*[152]

Unable to possess and to store the reflection of the elsewhere that glares from the mirror of a prophetic world, a subject can only *theorize* (*theorein*, to contemplate) Heaven or Paradise. They can assimilate their vision only as a memory, upon whose quicksand they can build the stage of a metaphysical landscape – a world – where their own existence might unfold, free from servitude to worldly order or to eternal disorder.

The reality-settings of a world frame the lived experience of the subject as if within a set of theatre curtains. The vision appearing inside their embrace is of a moving landscape – at once the protagonist and the keeper of all destinies in the play. Reality is a theatre for one subject, whether this might be an individual or a synchronized collective.

---

[152]R. Daumal, *Mount Analogue: An Authentic Narrative*, translated by R. Shattuck, San Francisco, CA, City Lights Books, 1971, p. 62.

Prophetic culture, as a traumatic work on the limits of a subject's geography of existence, intervenes on the architecture of the theatre of memories where the world is recreated and infused with meaning at every instant.

It is worth looking in further detail at this stylistic trait of prophetic culture, which had its greatest developments in the tradition of the *Ars Memoriae* (Art of Memory).[153] Since its foundation, attributed to fifth-century BC Greek poet Simonides of Ceos, and through the work of practitioners like Ramon Lull, Robert Fludd, Giordano Bruno and Matteo Ricci, this art-form has specialized in composing mental landscapes where memories might take root and flourish. Extant treaties on the *ars memoriae* resemble handbooks of architecture, with clear indications on how to build, within one's own awareness, an abode that memories might wish to visit. Their instructions are as detailed as the design of the tabernacle in the *Exodus*, and as intricate as the rules of sacrificial rituals in the *Satapatha Brahmana*.

To create the conditions in which memories might wish to retain their contours a little longer, the memory-artist needs to handle their image-bodies with the touch of a scenographer. Among those who dared taking up this challenge, the sixteenth-century Venetian philosopher Giulio Camillo offers a poignant example to producers of prophetic culture.[154]

An eclectic intellectual of great ambitions, Camillo produced a detailed design for a Memory Theatre where all possible knowledge about reality could be accessed – not like records stored in a library, but through a form of mnemonic evocation. Thanks to funding from Francis I, king of France, Camillo built a material prototype in the form of a large wooden amphitheatre, where the observer would occupy the stage, while the memories-of-knowledge would occupy the rings that are usually assigned to spectators. Each memory corresponded to an item in Camillo's cosmology, and the unique statue that symbolized it in the theatre was designed to evoke each

---

[153]Frances Yates's work on this tradition remains an as-yet unsurpassed point of reference. See F. Yates, *The Art of Memory*, London, The Bodley Head, 2014.

[154]As well as the analysis of Giulio Camillo's thought and work offered by Frances Yates in *The Art of Memory*, see the scholarly investigation by K. Robinson, *A Search for the Whirlpool of Artifice: The Cosmology of Giulio Camillo*, Edinburgh, Dunedin Academic Press, 2006.

in its fullness – including those dimensions that cannot be grasped directly, neither through the senses nor through dialectic rationality.

> *This image, located in this place, will signify intelligible things that cannot fall under the grasp of our senses, but that we can only imagine and understand if we are illuminated by the active intellect.*[155]

By walking through his Memory Theatre – Camillo suggested – it would be possible to explore a materialized landscape, corresponding at the same time to a complete epistemology and to a complete metaphysics of reality.[156]

In a similar fashion to Giulio Camillo, and with his same grotesque ambition, prophetic culture weaves its narration, not out of concepts, but through figures that act as memory-igniters, capable of offering a fleeting vision of what exceeds the reach of any form of language. But this relationship with the reproduction of memory is

---

[155]*Questa imagine in questo luogo ci significhera' cose intelliggibili, et che non possono cader sotto il senso, ma solamente le possiamo immaginare et intendere illuminati dallo intelletto agente.* My own translation. For further reading, see G. Camillo, *L'Idea del Theatro*, Palermo, Sellerio, 1991, p. 62.

[156]It is possible to compare the use of palatial architecture by memory artists, to its employment in the prophetic narrations of Jewish Throne-Mystics: 'Most of [Throne-Mystic] tracts are called "Hekhaloth Books," i.e. descriptions of the *hekhaloth*, the heavenly halls or palaces through which the visionary passes and in the seventh and last of which there rises the throne of divine glory ... These texts are not Midrashim, i.e. expositions of Biblical passages, but a literature sui generis with a purpose of is own. They are essentially descriptions of a genuine religious experience for which no sanction is sought in the Bible.' In the case of Jewish Throne-Mysticism, however, mystical ascent is always preceded by ascetic practices: an account of these practices was given about 1000 AD by Hai ben Sherira, the head of a Babylonian academy. According to him, 'Many scholars were of the belief that one who is distinguished by many qualities described in the books and who is desirous of beholding the Merkabah and the palaces of the angels on high, must follow a certain procedure. He must fast a number of days and lay his head between his knees and whisper many hymns and songs whose texts are known from tradition. Then he perceives the interior and the chambers, as if he saw the seven palaces with his own eyes, and it is as though he entered one palace after the other and saw what is there'. See G. Scholem, *Major Trends in Jewish Mysticism*, New York, NY, Schocken Books, 1995, pp. 45–6 and 49.

not an exclusive prerogative of prophecy. More generally, all forms of culture create their own *cosmos* by installing memory-igniters with a subject.

It is not an accident that modern studies on the tradition of the *Ars Memoriae* were relaunched by affiliates of the Institute created by German art historian Aby Warburg. Drawing from the studies of zoologist Richard Semon,[157] Aby Warburg suggested that humans' primordial experiences of the overpowering forces of reality had been bridled artistically into particular forms. These forms were retained throughout the history of art as a series of 'engrams', and the sum of their metamorphoses progressively created the social memory of each age. Each cultural engram – such as the flowing dress and dishevelled hair of a Nymph,[158] or the symbolic representations of the Zodiac[159] – remains permanently active, and at each moment it can either keep bridling the chaotic force of reality, or it can open up and liberate it once again. An engram can always bring to the fore a memory of that particular experience of reality, and thus it

---

[157]'Put in a nutshell, Semon's theory amounts to this: memory is not a property of consciousness but the one quality which distinguishes living from dead matter. It is the capacity to react to an event over a period of time; that is, a form of preserving and transmitting energy not known to the physical world. Any event affecting living matter leaves a trace which Semen calls an "engram". The potential energy conserved in this "engram" may, under suitable conditions, be reactivated and discharged – we then say the organism acts in a specific way because it *remembers* the previous event. This goes for the individual no less than for the species. It was this concept of mnemic energy, preserved in "engrams", but obeying laws comparable to those of physics which attracted Warburg when he took up the theories of his youth on the nature of the symbol and its function in the social organism.' E.H. Gombrich, *Aby Warburg: An Intellectual Biography*, London, The Warburg Institute, 1970, p. 242. See R. Semon, *The Mneme*, translated by L. Simon, London, George Allen & Unwin, 1921.

[158]The theme of the nymph recurs throughout Warburg's *oeuvre*. See in particular his essays 'Sandro Botticelli', and 'Theatrical Costumes for the Intermedi of 1589' – both in A. Warburg, *The Renewal of Pagan Antiquity*, edited by K.W. Foster, translated by D. Britt, Los Angeles, CA, Getty Research Institute, 1999, especially pp. 159–60 and 379–82.

[159]Research on the iconology of the Zodiac occupied a good part of Warburg's mature years. See, in particular, his essays 'Italian Art and International Astrology in the Palazzo Schifanoia, Ferrara', and 'Astrology under Oriental Influence' – both in A. Warburg, *The Renewal of Pagan Antiquity*, edited by K.W. Foster, translated by D. Britt, Los Angeles, CA, Getty Research Institute, 1999, respectively pp. 563–92 and pp. 699–702.

can inaugurate a *krisis* (moment of judgement) when a subject is called to decide whether to confirm or to challenge the parameters of their own fundamental frame of meaning.

A similar quality belongs to the material on which prophetic culture operates. The stuff of a prophetic world-story is a body of memories, which are deployed on the scene clothed in the guise of symbolic language. Like the mysterious composition of Giorgione's painting *La Tempesta*,[160] a work of prophetic culture communicates not just by offering a series of more or less obscure references, but by summoning an overall atmosphere, a poetic *rasa*, where words, sounds and images might acquire the ability to open a vision of the *cosmos* in its entirety.

Yet, this doesn't explain exactly what kind of memories it might be possible to bring about through in a prophetic Memory Theatres. The problem, in responding to this question, is that a clear and distinct answer remains impossible. Although prophetic culture deals with images in the form of memories, these are never memories of 'something' specific. They are memories without an object – although not without an effect.

To shed some light on these odd memories without a content, let us return for a moment to an element of the activity of worlding that was discussed earlier in this book. As the reader might recall, the process of worlding corresponds to the establishment of a particular perspective towards the raw avalanche of perceptions investing a subject's awareness at each instant. Like all artifices of vision, also the cosmological perspective provided by one's own activity of worlding brings some elements to light, while leaving others outside of the range of the visible. An important factor in defining such a range of visibility is the location chosen by the subject as their point of self-identification – that is, the specific realm of existence where a subject accepts to take the question 'is this you?', by replying 'yes, this is me'.

---

[160]For a thorough analysis of the symbolism of Giorgione's painting *La Tempesta* (The Tempest) in the light of Aby Warburg's work on the imaginal landscape of the Italian Renaissance, see E. Wind, *Giorgione's 'Tempesta' with Comments on Giorgione's Poetic Allegories*, Oxford, Oxford University Press, 1969.

For example, a subject might wish to locate their 'true self' within the dimension of linguistic factuality – as it is the case with the figure of the metaphysician in the *tetrapharmakon*. In doing so, they would develop a perspective towards reality which would leave large parts of the ineffable realms of existence outside of visibility. Conversely, a subject might choose to position their own point of awareness within a realm that lies beyond the borders of what can be described through any form of language. To a subject whose perspective towards reality is outside of time, and inside eternity – as it happens with the figure of the mystic – the world, as such, remains for the most part excluded from the horizon of what is visible, and thus also from the range of what counts as possible and understandable.

In the context of these different dynamics of worlding, prophecy's ambition to reveal all dimensions of reality in one sole narrative encounters a seemingly insurmountable obstacle. To apprehend and to make sense of reality, every point of awareness can count only on the particular epistemological angle allowed by their location. Whenever a certain dimension encounters traces that belong to another one, the inevitable result is an obfuscation of visibility, akin to the aporia and paradoxes that accompany the emergence of ineffability within the formulations of mathematical language.

Regardless of a subject's position and of their self-identification with one or the other dimensions of reality, their grasp of what takes place within prophecy's memory theatre will be confined within the limits of their own epistemological stance. The inter-dimensional memory brought about through prophetic culture will inevitably remain a *memory of nothing* – that is, a memory whose content is indecipherable from a point of perspective that is outside of its own original realm.

Presented this way, the work of prophetic culture might finally appear as a flamboyant and ultimately worthless exercise – much evoking about nothing. But despite the fact that prophetic culture doesn't blend together all the different epistemologies that belong to the various dimensions of reality, and despite its inability to evoke 'some-thing', prophecy's ambition to create a bridge of solidarity between them remains intact.

A memory of nothing is not the same as no memory, and even memories without any possible object can play an important part in affecting the way in which a process of worlding is structured and performed.[161] This is, after all, the very essence of *apophatic* (negative) theology – which applies this epistemological tenet to the very essence of God, considered in its utter incomprehensibility:

> *We know nothing about God. But this not-knowing is a not-knowing of God. As such, it is the beginning of our knowledge of Him. The beginning, not the end.*[162]

Aside from theological speculations, however, most of us have also had prosaic and common experience of that particular form of knowledge, which a memory without an object is capable of bringing about. It might have happened also to my reader to have left their home one morning, shut the door behind themselves, and after a few steps along the pavement to have the clear feeling of having forgotten something. What I might have forgotten, I couldn't say at that point – but I know for certain, with paradoxical clarity, that there is something that I have forgotten. In fact, of that mysterious thing I cannot say anything else, but that I have forgotten it.

Although it is usually discarded as a frustrating anecdote from our everyday life, this form of a 'memory-of-having-forgotten' provides an interesting model for the epistemological relationship evoked by prophetic works of culture. Despite lacking an object, it is a form of knowledge endowed with a crystal-clear feeling of certainty. One is certain to have forgotten something, that is, one is certain that there is more, beyond what they can recollect in the total sum of the information that they have available. A memory-of-having-forgotten concerns an epistemological item, which shares with all the other elements of knowledge only the quality of existing somehow, without any further specification.

Such a memory-of-having-forgotten is the only authentic content of any prophetic utterance, yet it suffices to accomplish prophecy's narrative: it tells a tale about a reality populated by memories in the

---

[161]Let us recall that 'the symbol "signifies" nothing and communicates nothing, but makes something transparent which is beyond all expression.' – G. Scholem, *Major Trends in Jewish Mysticism*, New York, NY, Schocken Books, 1995, p. 27.

[162]F. Rosenzweig, *Der Stern der Erlösung*, Frankfurt a.M., J. Kauffmann, 1921 – my translation from the Italian edition, F. Rosenzweig, *La Stella della Redenzione*, translated by G. Bonola, Milan, Vita e Pensiero, 2017, p. 25.

shape of things, and by multiple dimensions of existence that are separated from each other by their reciprocal oblivion.

In the cosmology offered by prophetic culture, all dimensions of reality begin their separate existence through acts of forgetting. The world of language originates from the ineffable's decision to forget about it – from a God who became absent and *otiosus*, fleeing and forgetful of the world. Equally, the ineffable realm of existence moves its first steps only after being ejected from the world of language – a worldly forgetfulness of God, standing as God's cradle.[163] What from one side appears like the sinful severing of the 'Fall', from the other side takes the shape of a new beginning.

This aspect can be detected in theologies and mythologies from all over the world. Even when divine intervention consists in bringing culture and civilization to the world, this seemingly unilateral act of divine benevolence harbours an element of reciprocal co-creation between humans and gods.[164]

---

[163]'Parting is all we know of heaven/and all we need of hell.' E. Dickinson, *Complete Poems*, edited by T.H. Johnson, Boston, MA, Little Brown, 1960, p. 703.

[164]'We turn to [Heraclitus'] Fragment 30 in Diels's collection of the *Fragments of the Presocratics*. "This world-order, the same for every multiplicity, neither one of the gods nor humans have brought forth, but rather it always was and is and will eternally be living fire, lighting up in measures, going out in measures." ... An order and a beautiful radiance prevail through everything that is. But neither one of the gods nor a human being brought forth this beautiful dispensation of the whole. ... What is ultimately productive is the world-light of fire [*pyr*]. ... Fire does not mean that out of which all things exist, but rather the arranging power that strikes all individuated beings with the character of a beautiful, gleaming total dispensation. ... The world-fire is the course of the world itself. ... And of this course of the world he says in Fragment 52: "The course of the world is a child playing, who moves the pieces on the board here and there, is a child's kingdom." ... The most primordial production has the character of play ... Gods and human beings ... are not closed in on themselves like other things in the world; they are in an irrupted, ecstatic relation to *pyr*. ... [They] are essentially players. [...] Heraclitus ... refers us to a world-relation of gods and human beings, from which alone they are what they are ... Then the human ... would have to be conceived ... as such a thing that is first and above all a relation – one which ... would exist as an ecstatic openness. The relation of the human being to something that is no being and nevertheless is not nothing, that embraces, pervades and plays throughout all things and never itself appears in a finite shape ... – this relation characterizes and comprises the world-position of the human being. That means: the relation between the human being and the world can never be fixed

Why should a deity wish to bring culture to mankind? I think the answer must be that if he does so, this is not his primary purpose. It is incidental to his desire to express and develop himself. He cannot attain development in a void, and he consequently first attempts to bring some differentiation into this void. It is at this point that man intervenes. The latter cannot, quite correctly from his viewpoint, permit a deity to attain differentiation unless the possibility for man's differentiation is also provided. Thus man is more or less forcibly injected into the picture. He becomes merged with the gods and the gods with him, and the differentiation and education of the gods becomes as much the education of man as it does that of the gods. Since man begins as a completely instinctual being, non-social and undomesticated ... so also the gods must begin or, better, so the gods are forced to begin.[165]

Like the ineffable withdraws to leave room for the world, so the world 'de-creates' itself so that the ineffable may shine through.[166] As the child detaches themselves from their mother, they no longer know her as part of themselves: they 'forget' her. In doing so, they create not only a child, but also a mother – birth is reciprocal and continuous over time. Likewise, in theology, God had to be forgotten by the world in order to become an autonomous entity, just as much as the world had to be forgotten by God *ab origine* to be able to begin its own existence.[167] Forgetting is the primeval '*fiat!*' sung in unison by the dimensions of existence, as they separate from each other.

---

from without in any objective sort of determination. The human being, living *in* the world-relation, must determine this relation through thinking. According to Heraclitus this also holds for the gods.' E. Fink, *Play as Symbol of the World and Other Writings*, translated by I.A. Moore and C. Turner, Bloomington, IN, Indiana University Press, 2016, pp. 49–52, and 60–1.

[165]P. Radin, *The Trickster: A Study in American Indian Mythology*, New York, NY, Schocken Books, 1972, p. 126.

[166]I am referring to a process resembling Simone Weil's notion of 'decreation': the act through which each dimensions of reality 'makes room' within and beyond itself for an 'otherness' surpassing its own metaphysical bounds.

[167]The perspective suggested in this volume runs contrary to that proposed by Ludwig Feuerbach in 'The Essence of Religion Considered Generally', in *The Essence of Christianity*, translated by G. Eliot, Mineola, NY, Dover, 2008, pp. 10–28, especially pp. 10–11. While Feuerbach identified the birth of God with man's alienation of his

Forgetting, however, is a slippery word. Doesn't 'forgetting' always imply reversibility? Isn't it implicit in the very term that what has been forgotten could possibly be remembered again?

The act of forgetting, however, is not just the origin, but the foundation of the separate dimensions of existence. If they were ever to remember each other, they would again dissolve into one another. As long as the world remains a 'world', the furthest possible knowledge that it can attain of what lies beyond language is as a memory-of-having-forgotten. Likewise, as long as it remains separate in itself, the ineffable dimension of existence can perceive the world (the realm of language) only through the acknowledgement of a memory-of-having-forgotten.

Hence the prophetic nature of the miracle of the Incarnation in Christian theology, symbolizing the brief moment when the ineffable and the world remember each other and suddenly merge into one another – only to leave each other again, like a dream that awakens into a trauma.

But even though forgetting cannot be turned back into a stable memory, it might still suggest the presence of an earlier memory before it – a knowledge that was once, but that has been lost. After all, one can only forget something that they once knew.

This notion of a lost memory dating to the beginning of time is at the heart of the philosophical and theological trope of a primordial covenant between God and the world. It is represented in the Muslim genealogy of prophets, dating back to Adam, the first man and first prophet who reflected the moment of the initial spark, when the realms of God and the world were still united.[168] It can be found in Nietzsche's fascination with those pre-Socratic 'superhuman philosophers'[169] who saw the ineffable before it was

---

own powers, which were objectified and moved to an abstract hyperuranion, my perspective sees the origin of God, as such, in the very moment when worldly beings forget about Him. God becomes an entity, only once it becomes excluded from the storage of memories of the world. By the same token, also the 'world' (both that of linguistic factuality and that of the imaginal) originates from God's primeval act of forgetting it. Creation is seen prophetically as sparking at the same time in opposite directions: a synchronous, mutual and paradoxical co-creation between language and ineffability, between the world and God.

[168]Quran 7:172.
[169]I am borrowing Giorgio Colli's definition – see G. Colli, *Filosofi Sovrumani*, Milan, Adelphi, 2009.

veiled by concepts. Equally, it can be detected in Plato's notion of knowledge as *anamnesis*, a cognitive return to a state of original cosmic unity.[170]

The possibility of this primitive unity of all realms of existence is ultimately symbolized by the figure of the Golden Age: an original state when God and the world were together. A state that precedes and supervenes the very notions of 'God' and 'world', and that is lost forever as soon as a conceptual approach to existence is established. This new approach, defining and separating the dimensions of reality, is the original sin breaking the original unity of ineffability and language. It is the Fall. Yet, it is God's sin, and God's Fall, as much as it is that of the world.

Islamic theology adds an even earlier moment in the genealogy of encounters between God and the world, preceding the creation of Adam. Before the beginning of both time and eternity, in what is known as the 'pre-eternal covenant' (*mithaq*), God summoned the human creatures that He was about to create together with the world. 'Am I not your God?' He asked. 'Indeed, we bear witness' was their reply. The fanfare of these words – perhaps, *the* original prophetic words – announced the light of creation.[171]

But where is such pre-eternal realm, within the cosmology drawn by prophecy? So far, prophecy has talked only about the realms of ineffability and of language, while here we encounter words pronounced before the creation of either of these two dimensions. So far, prophecy has manifested only the interpenetration of time and eternity, while the dimension of pre-eternity precedes and exceeds both.

The original, lost knowledge of pre-eternity lies beyond the notions of ineffability and language, sameness and otherness, unity

---

[170]'Socrates: I have heard wise men and women talk about divine matters ... They say that the human soul is immortal; at times it comes to an end, which they call dying; at times it is reborn, but it is never destroyed ... As the soul is immortal, has been born often, and has seen all things here and in the underworld, there is nothing which it has not learned; so it is in no way surprising that it can recollect the things it knew before ... Nothing prevents a man, after recalling one thing only – a process men call learning – discovering everything else for himself, if he is brave and does not tire of the search, for searching and learning are, as a whole, recollection.' Plato, 'Meno', 81 a-d, in *Complete Works*, edited by J.M. Cooper, translated by D.J. Zeyl, Indianapolis/Cambridge, Hackett, 1997, p. 880.

[171]Quran 7:172.

and multiplicity. The image of pre-eternity suggests that there is another memory, behind the memory-of-having-forgotten. But this further memory, in turn, refers to an object which lies beyond direct apprehension. It is, itself, another memory-of-having-forgotten – only more evanescent and distant, more rapidly floating than the one cast towards each other by ineffability and language. This second memory-of-having-forgotten signals to yet another dimension beyond that which encompasses both God and the world, ineffability and language.

This further movement towards new cosmological horizons unveils the extent of prophetic cosmology. It is not just a metaphysics of two worlds, like that commonly attributed to Plato, but rather a metaphysics of multiple dimensions of existence.[172] Against any reality-system that might claim legitimacy only for one particular realm of reality – such as the absolute exclusiveness granted to the world by the cosmology of Westernized Modernity – prophecy signals to a superabundance of dimensions, stretching far beyond the dichotomy between language and ineffability.

A similar passage beyond God, so to say, can be found in the prophetic culture of the Gnostic tradition, particularly in Valentinianus and, more darkly so, in Marcion.[173] According to Gnostic cosmology, what the world calls 'God' is in fact an evil

---

[172]What Rene Guenon called *Les États multiples de l'être* (The multiple states of the Being) – see R. Guenon, *The Multiple States of the Being*, translated by S.D. Fohr, Hillsdale, NY, Sophia Perennis, 2004.

[173]Gnosticism (from *gnosis*, 'knowledge') was a theological and philosophical movement that originated around the first century AD in the Middle East. Its conception of the divinity and of the world has traversed virtually all religions of the Mediterranean basin, giving rise to similar 'gnostic' currents across religion denominations. Several gnostic thinkers, many of whom remain anonymous, have contributed to shaping this movement. Among them, Marcion of Sinope stands out due to his strong anti-natalist position, which he deduced from his notion of the world as the 'prison-industrial system' – so to say – of a malign Demiurge who's keeping souls from re-uniting with the superior realms of reality. See Tertullianus, *Ante-Nicene Christian Library: Translations of the Writings of the Fathers*, vol. 7, *Tertullianus Against Marcion*, edited and translated by A. Roberts, Edinburgh, T&T Clark, 1868. For a comprehensive examination of both Valentinianus and Marcion, see H. Jonas, *The Gnostic Religion: The Message of the Alien God and the Beginnings of Christianity*, Boston, MA, Beacon Press, 1963. For an analysis of Gnostic philosophy and of its influence on late ancient culture, see H.C. Puech, *En Quête de la Gnose*, 2 Vols., Paris, Gallimard, 1978.

Demiurge who has entrapped the world and who's shielding from it the view of its original, long-forgotten Divinity. Through initiation and purification, the Gnostics wish to break out of the veil that entraps the world in the grip of the Demiurge, moving towards a rediscovery and a reunion with the original Godhead. For the Gnostics, beyond 'God' there is the true, ineffable Godhead, standing as the very horizon of reality. In a prophetic fashion, Gnosticism attempts to save simultaneously the human – who can escape the captivity of the Demiurge – and also the Godhead, who can be saved by the return and reintegration of those souls who manage to liberate themselves.

Gnostic cosmology, however, ends there: beyond the illusion of the Demiurge there is the true, ineffable Godhead, who constitutes the final limit of reality. But the ineffable unity of the Godhead is not the last possible dimension that prophecy can pursue. Reflected in the mirror of prophecy, we can find more than the dichotomy between language and ineffability, that is, between becoming and eternity.

Against Parmenide's injunction, also Non-Being can find its place within a prophetic vision of reality. The supposed impossibility of Non-Being derives from the coincidence between the realm of existence and the horizon of human experience (linguistic or ineffable as it may be). No direct experience of Non-Being is ever achievable, but this impossibility simply delimits the field of 'existence' and of 'Being', while at the same time shaping the contours of a new terrain beyond it. A prophetic vision includes Non-Being within reality, precisely as that which is beyond both experience and existence, while remaining bound to a relationship with them.

The bond of *relationship* stands as the ultimate horizon to which a prophetic gaze can stretch. Whenever we think, experience, deduce or invent anything – including the notion of an ineffable absolute unity – we are able to bring it within the range of our imagination only by pulling the threads of relations which innervate it. Whatever dimension, within each fragment of reality, does not enter into any kind of relation remains beyond the range of what we can even faintly imagine. The narrative limits of prophecy coincide with those of the imagination.

The excess of reality that refuses any form of relationality is apprehensible only in its refusal, as the forgetting-of-having-forgotten that sends back in loop the enquiry of imagination. Yet, again, this speaks only about the geography of reality that falls under the surveying eye of imagination, while saying nothing about the limits of reality as such. The rest of reality – which we cannot know, experience, remember or forget – transcends even the horizon of mystery.

Considered prophetically, each fragment of reality emerges as a map traversed by several intersections across dimensions. Prophetic awareness moves across these interstices like a bird would jump between tree-branches. From each of them, it observes reality from a unique angle, where different dimensions become variably near or far, and where the definition of what an awareness reclaims as its own 'body' varies according to its own cosmological position. No longer confined within the worldly location of 'consciousness', a prophetic awareness can inhabit also those positions which are usually assigned to other-dimensional beings, like divinities and angels, or to abstract processes like grammar and death.[174] By moving across these different cosmological locations, a prophetic awareness engages in a constant journey within each fragment of reality. During its travel to the limits of imagination, like the protagonist of a *Bildungsroman*, awareness learns the different breath and limits of each vision of reality, and the taste of their specific sadness. All the way to the limits of non-relationality, and back home to consciousness. And then again *da capo*, ever dislodging (*emovens*) itself out of itself, following the paths of compassion (*cum-pati*, 'enduring together') that traverse and bind together the imagination of reality. In this consists the emotional work of the prophet, and the substance of their cultural legacy.

---

[174]See the reverse journey of awareness in the section *Cosmography*, later in this book.

PROPHECY AS THERAPY OF WORLDING

FIGURE 3.8 *Franco Berardi 'Bifo'*, L'apocalisse (quadro primo), 2020. *Courtesy of the artist.*

What do you mean by the bombastic word 'reality'?
The dynamic projection of individual trajectories of meaning
converging towards meaninglessness. This is reality indeed.[175]

Prophecy is many things: it is the political edge of a mystical experience, a possibility for worlding, a style of cultural production. But all in all, prophetically speaking, prophecy is only a term. The 'orthodox' approach to prophetic culture doesn't consist in a blind adherence to the letter of often contradictory rules, but it resides in the faithfulness to the ambition that animates them.

Like the Jewish prophets of antiquity, those who apply a prophetic lens to their own age subvert at the core any hegemonic narration about 'the world as it is'. The passage performed by prophetic culture shares a similar tension with the 'Copernican revolution' announced in the 1960s by Workerist philosopher Mario Tronti.[176] Whereas Tronti recognized the ability of the workers, 'within but against' their present conditions, to further the techno-evolution of their own emancipation, a prophetic approach to culture sees the possibility for a subject, through their activity of worlding, to escape from their captivity in pre-established frames of sense.

As the Workerist approach was revolutionary, so the prophetic approach is insurrectionary. The inner desire driving prophetic culture is not towards the establishment of any specific New World Order, but towards the invention of a mode of worlding that might be capable of freeing its subject from a paralysing anguish – which leads them to the negative resistance of depression, as often as to the pit of societal conformism.

Although most of the references which I have used in this chapter were drawn from the realms of theology, the interpretation of prophetic culture which I have suggested finds one of its closest relatives in the political imaginary of Autonomist philosopher Franco Berardi Bifo. In the course of his long career as a theorist and agitator, Berardi has deployed a sophisticated array of conceptual tools to decode, subvert and envisage an exit from the hegemonic system of reality imposed by contemporary capitalist imagination.

---

[175]F. Berardi 'Bifo', 'The End of Prophecy', *e-flux journal*, no. 95, November 2018.
[176]See M. Tronti, *Workers and Capital*, translated by D. Broder, London/New York, Verso, 2019.

Through a materialist vocabulary that often breaks open to ineffable depths, Berardi has followed the ghost of a different way of taking control of the seemingly irresistible force of language, and to direct it towards an alternative form of world-making.

Despite the different relationship towards materialism informing Berardi's work and the present volume, the tension that has animated my attempt to lay down the sketch of a theory of prophetic culture seeks and draws from similar existential sources.

The world is not all, neither in its present form nor in any form that it might take, and an outside to its imaginary boundaries and constraints is always present. Berardi calls this method 'communism as a therapy of singularisation',[177] while I call it prophetic culture, but both our suggestions are rooted in a similar acknowledgement of existential suffering as the ground-zero of theory, of work on language as a crucial realm of intervention and of the infinite malleability of what is called 'reality'.

If prophetic culture is just a form of literature, such is also the work of any political agent and thinker who remains mindful to the primacy of experience over the grammar of conceptual frameworks. Prophetic culture reclaims the ability to intervene underneath the logic of politics, and thus to be pre-political – since a political project runs on nothing, if it is deprived of a suitable metaphysical substratum.

Although these two approaches are separated at their origin, their shared faithfulness to the existential anguish of actually living subjects reveals their common endpoint. An endpoint that is as fleeting as an insurrection, rather than a revolution, and that is equally in need of constant re-evaluation and re-addressing.

The political valence of prophetic culture doesn't consist in its immediate effect on the social structures of a *politieia* (community), but in the establishment of a *pre-political* position from which it might be possible to move once again towards a transformation of the material conditions of life.

In the context of this book, prophetic culture should be understood in its relationship with the three forms of worlding that make up the core of its message: metaphysics, shamanism and

---

[177]F. Berardi 'Bifo', *Communism Is Back but We Should Call It the Therapy of Singularisation*, 2009, online at http://www.generation-online.org/p/fp_bifo6.htm

mysticism. By combining their modes of worlding, prophecy wishes to lay down an imaginal bridge that might allow a subject, stuck in a state of anguished powerlessness (whether political, social or existential), to approach again the project of worlding with enough confidence to be able to create a new landscape of sense where they can live – collectively, or individually as 'one sole multitude'.[178]

Depression can't be reduced to the psychological field. It questions the very foundation of being. Melancholic depression can be understood in relation to the circulation of sense. Faced with the abyss of nonsense, friends talk to friends, and together they build a bridge across the abyss. Depression questions the reliability of this bridge. Depression doesn't see the bridge. It's not on its radar. Or maybe it sees that the bridge doesn't exist.[179]

At the end of the time-segment of a civilization, when the future fades away from the field of possibilities, it becomes increasingly difficult for a subject to project that bridge of sense which, alone, can transform the onslaught of raw perceptions into a liveable world.

Confronted by the difficult task of learning how to die well, subjects standing at the tail end of a future often feel that their world-building aesthetic machine is beginning to jam. Meaning becomes scarce, fragile and rapidly eroding – and the inability to envisage how to close well their own aesthetic creation is immediately translated into the implosion of the very structures that they would need to be able to make-world around themselves.

Chaos is defined not so much by its disorder as by the infinite speed with which every form taking shape in it vanishes. [...] Chaos is an infinite speed of birth and disappearance. [...] Nothing is more distressing than a thought that escapes itself, than ideas that fly off, that disappear hardly formed, already eroded by the forgetfulness or precipitated into others that we

---

[178]*Una Sola Moltitudine* was the title chosen by Antonio Tabucchi for his collection of the poems of Fernando Pessoa – who, through the stuttering of his heteronyms, was himself a creator of prophetic culture. See F. Pessoa, *Una Sola Moltitudine*, 2 Vols., edited and translated by A. Tabucchi, Milan, Adelphi, 1979.

[179]F. Berardi 'Bifo', *After the Future*, Edinburgh, AK Press, 2011, p. 63.

*no longer master. [...] These are infinite speeds that blend into
the immobility of the colourless.*[180]

Prophetic culture combines grotesquely the worlding methods of
the metaphysician, of the shaman and of the mystic, precisely to
equip a subject sinking into chaos with the ability to imagine a
place from which to restart their activity of worlding – even if this
ability might coincide, as for those living at the end of a civilization,
with the task of creating fertile ruins over which new worlds can
emerge.

By adopting three contradictory modes of worlding at once,
prophetic culture wishes to provide enough different excesses to
any possible world that a subject might envisage – so that they
will always have an outside to which they can withdraw, and from
which they can return to their creation to transform it, or to close it,
or to use it as a trampoline for new forms of world-making.

In the context of the declining reality-system of Westernized
Modernity, the reactivation of a fundamental aesthetic process of
worlding aims to produce both a better past for those who shall
come after the end of its future and a possible present for those who
are living in the current age. In either case, it is a reminder that any
mode of worlding which a subject might adopt as their own is, in
fact, only one point of perspective towards existence and never a
total picture of 'reality as it is'.

The permanent insurrection promoted by prophetic culture
fights against two adversaries: the tyrannical injunctions of a world
that wishes to lock its inhabitants within the borders of its own
grammar and the terrifying presence of an abyss of meaninglessness
lying beneath any possible world-form.

Although it remains proudly alien to the contemporary notion of
entertainment, and despite falling short of the typical demands of
the cultural industry, prophetic culture is in fact the quintessential
kind of culture created for, and most importantly by, adolescents.
Not yet as idiotic as that of their adult counterparts, an adolescent's
idea of fun is an ambitious combination of self-care, insurrectionary

---

[180]G. Deleuze and F. Guattari, *What Is Philosophy?*, translated by H. Tomlinson and
G. Burchell, New York, NY, Columbia University Press, 1994, pp. 118 and 201.

adventure and autonomous creation of a new world. As paradoxical as it may sound, there is much more of that in texts written millennia ago in Aramaic and Sanskrit, than in most recent songs coming from major record labels.

If this might sound like a baffling statement today, its plausibility will become more evident once the libidinal push of contemporary capitalism will have faded away, together with the world that has produced it. By that point, in the eye of post-future subjects, each of the works of culture that will have survived the assault of this apocalypse will remain naked in their ability to actually offer something to the existential sensibility and the metaphysical ambitions of archaic adolescents. Everything that is new today will then appear just as dead, and as naked in its quality, as anything that we call 'old'.

For those who are living today within the last bars of this declining world-song, the *tetrapharmakon* of prophetic culture might seem an imaginary ground, where the wheel of our sense-making activity might be able to run in some direction. But it is more than that.

The *tetrapharmakon* of prophetic culture is not to be seen as a final result, to congeal and preserve in its definitive form. Rather, it is a *helpful comrade* (*teraps*, from which 'therapy') coming to mend the aesthetic machine on which the world itself depends. It is the agent of a new horizon of familiarity across worlds and time-segments, bound by the destiny of living as the past of a new present, which is yet to come.

> *An Epicurean saying puts it clearly: 'Vain is the word of that philosopher which does not heal any suffering of man.' Philosophical theories are in the service of the philosophical life.*[181]

For all its ridiculous grotesqueness, for all its untimeliness and its incongruousness with immediate political aims, prophetic culture

---

[181]P. Hadot, *Philosophy as a Way of Life: Spiritual Exercises from Socrates to Foucault*, edited by A. Davidson, translated by M. Chase, Oxford, Wiley-Blackwell, 1995, p. 267.

offers a possible way to transfigure, to redeem, and ultimately to save the foundations of that landscape where life can unfold. Only in a world that perceives itself as always-already saved, and only in the hands of a subject who is at once saved by their creation and its saviour, the lines of political and social action can become something more than vain flights of fantasy.

CHAPTER FOUR
COSMOGRAPHY

FIGURE 4.1 *Giovanni Domenico Tiepolo,* Punchinello Carried Off by an Eagle (Pulcinella rapito da un'aquila), c. *1800.*

Even as champions and wrestlers and such as practise the strength and agility of body are not only careful to retain a sound constitution of health, and to hold on their ordinary course of exercise, but sometimes also to recreate themselves with seasonable intermission, and esteem it as a main point of their practice; so I think it necessary for scholars and such as addict themselves to the study of learning, after they have travelled long in the perusal of serious authors, to relax a little the intention of their thoughts, that they may be more apt and able to endure a continued course of study.[1]

---

[1] Lucian of Samosata, *True Story*, translated by Francis Hikes, London, A. H. Bullen, 1902, p. 3.

0/15
SCHEINTÜR²

FIGURE 4.2 False Door of the Mastaba of Unis-Ankh, *plate L. from the Annual report of the Director to the Board of Trustees for the year 1906, 1906.* © *Field Museum of Natural History.*

---

²The *Scheintür* (false door) was a frequent architectural element in monumental tombs from ancient Egypt. It was the threshold between the underworld and the world of the living, and a passage through which spirits and divinities could enter the world. Yet, at the same time and conversely: 'For a mountain to play the role of Mount Analogue, I concluded, its summit must be inaccessible but its base accessible to human beings as nature has made them. It must be unique and it must exist geographically. The door to the invisible must be visible. [...] The area we seek must be able to exist in any region whatsoever of the earth's surface. Therefore, we must examine under what conditions it remains inaccessible not only to ships, airplanes, and other vehicles, but even to eyesight. I mean that it could perfectly well exist, theoretically, in the middle of this table, without our having the least suspicion it was there.' R. Daumal, *Mount Analogue: An Authentic Narrative*, translated by R. Shattuck, San Francisco, CA, City Lights Books, 1971, pp. 24 and 47.

The empty dishes on the kitchen table. A glass over the corner of a napkin. The liquid at its bottom, vibrating at the rhythm of my drumming.

There it was, in all its splendour: Reality. All the mysteries and any possible revelation were in that domestic glass, sleeping under a veil. Every possible adventure, already taking place at the point where a gaze encounters an object, or a mind a thought.

True, without error, certain and most true: that which is above is as that which is below, and that which is below is as that which is above, to perform the miracles of the One Thing.[3]

I looked at the shadow-lines that the table lamp cast on the napkin and followed their trajectory beyond their mark. I looked at the reflections on the glass and slid the back of my hand against its cold body. I wondered if it might feel me, the same as I felt it. If it was staring at me and receiving as silent an answer as the one I got from it.

Maybe I was doing it wrong. I should have proceeded with order: cataloguing what I could see and all its qualities, while looking for a gap where my reason could break in. Or maybe I should have done the opposite: becoming pure awareness, staring at my surroundings devoid of any intentions, with the clear eye of a hanging mirror.

The cigarette embers licked my fingers and I put it out in the ashtray. I had done that countless times already: looking and looking and finding nothing else than what I knew. I was surrounded by a library, encased within each speck of space and time, and yet I was blind to its words. I felt tired. The glass was still there. I closed my eyes to look for the image of it that I had impressed in my memory. I found it. I lost it. I found it again, and soon it faded. I stretched my legs under the table and I rested my head on the palm of my hands. The glass was still there in my memory. I found it. I lost it. I looked again.

---

[3]Hermes Trismegistus, *The Emerald Tablet*, translated by Sir I. Newton, CreateSpace, 2017.

1 – The island of facts[4]

We find ourselves on a sailboat, slim and fast over the turquoise sea. A confederation of souls sit silently across the deck.

'Hey,' says one of us, 'where … are we?'
Someone points beyond board. We're cutting waves in view of land.
'Who are you?' they insist.
'And who are you?'

Judging by the stares, no one has any recollection of how we got here. But there is a natural atmosphere of friendship between us. Somehow, we all feel that a vague mission binds us together. This is all that we know about ourselves. But we also know that that coast, with its line of rugged buildings, is the first solid object that we have encountered, since a fragment of reality became a sea.

One of us takes charge of the helm, the rest fumble with ropes and sails and our ship proceeds smoothly towards the harbour. The port is bustling with workers offloading transport boats, passengers moving in and out, officials directing the traffic. The nausea that hits us on land suggests that we have been at sea for a long time. The buildings, the trees, the noise from the streets nearby and even the weather have a familiar feel. The only thing to stand out is local fashion, so homogeneous that one sole tailor seems to have dressed this entire shore. Down to the pavement beneath us, every single thing here is covered by semi-transparent scales, tightly wrapped around their body. Whenever two things meet, their scales rhythmically rise accompanying their encounter.

---

[4]'The desert grows: woe to him who harbours deserts!/Stone grates on stone, the desert swallows down./And death that chews, whose life is chewing,/gazes upon it, monstrous, glowing brown … /Consumed by lust, O Man, do not forget:/you – are the stone, the desert, you are death … ' F. Nietzsche, *Dithyrambs of Dionysus, The Desert Grows: Woe to Him Who Harbours Deserts*, translated by R.J. Hollingdale, London, Anvil, 1984, p. 37.

We're still engrossed in this spectacle, when an officer walks out of the crowd. Their lips remain sealed, while a voice from its uniform orders to proceed to border control. Rearing their heads, their scales tilt in our direction until we make our way along the pathway.

All incoming passengers are converging into a large cluster, streaming towards the gates. A line of glass cubicles filters their exit from the port. Border agents interrogate them at the desks, peering through narrow gaps between the scales. Where were we born? What leads us here? What are our resources? How many of us, for how long? We make an effort to say something, out of courtesy. One of us believes to be the cartographer of the expedition; another the helmsman; one feels the youngest among the crew; another the oldest ... The border guard rewards each piece of information attaching a patch of film to our clothes or on our skin. The film immediately takes on the colour of the surface, only opaquer. As soon as the border guard carves a sign, we feel it growing heavier – and it takes to replying to questions in our stead. We are held at the desks until our scale armours are able to intercept and reply to every address in our direction. Finally, they let us through the gates.

The youngest one among us chuckles. Dressed like the locals, we look like our own, mediocre self-portrait. But these armours have endowed us with a new power of vision. We can see luminous lines traversing the space between people, objects, sounds, seconds of time. Whenever two entities exchange information, the air flashes with sparks. As they part ways, a glowing aura unrolls between them. We begin to notice the different luminosity of things. Some have their armour pierced by a forest of beams. They speed flexuously through the streets, with an orbit of satellites circling their aura. And there are others who bear armours that are hardly lit, with a handful of rays still binding them to the rest of the island. They shuffle around painfully, like rocks in the making.

Our youngest takes the lead of the exploration. They make some contact with the locals, mimicking their customs. They let their armour do the talking and exchange information with the other armours. Then they move on, even more resplendent, leaving the rest of us to trail behind.

Our eldest wails softly, before they collapse on the pavement, face down. We rush to remove their armour, but their darkened scales have grown so heavy that they are impossible to detach. We see their lips agape turn blueish. Nobody on the street seems to

take any notice. We must return to the ship before this island exacts
its victim from our midst.

'Destination?' ask the scales of a guard at the entrance to the
port.
'We're leaving immediately,' we reply with one voice.
'Leaving the island? Impossible.'
The helmsman raises our eldest, reverse in their arms.

'There is no exit from the Glass Dome,' say the scales, bending
towards a colourless rainbow across the sky. 'Beyond the Glass
Dome there is *nothing*: the desert that swallows. Only the dead
leave to the open sea.' The scales tilt towards the periphery of the
port, where processions of mourners are meandering through stacks
of wood and hay. A group has gathered at the limit of the waters to
set ablaze a small boat and they are pushing it offshore.
'Please, let us get back to our ship to bury our unlucky comrade,'
begs the helmsman.
'Unable,' quip the scales. 'Agreed. Come in. Just move to the
funeral quay and bury them at sea.'
We drag our eldest to the ship. Their armour has become so
heavy that we need ropes to lift them onboard. Some of us run to
the stacks, bringing back armfuls of combustible, until our vessel
has grown into a floating pyre. We rush on deck, pull the anchor
and set fire to the hay. The onlookers scream as we all lie down
amidst the flames. Groups of mourners push the horrific prodigy
away from the quay. Our ship gains speed over the waves, while
we lie still. The Glass Dome descends closer. Long lines of rain slide
off its outer surface. The sound of storming clouds announces the
frontier of this realm.
The gates slide open with a hiss. Meters of glass pass over us,
and immediately shut in our wake. The rain pours over our ship,
drowning the fire. Our armours fall to pieces as soon as we stand
up, with their semi-transparent scales dissolving in rivulets over the
deck-boards. We hear our eldest breathing convulsively.
Nightfall catches us off guard – some already sheltered under
deck, some still mid-way down the stairs. While we close our
eyes inexorably, glimpses of the island surface to our memory.
The geometrical perfection of its connections, the speed of its
recombinations, the neatness of its workings. Only beauty has
remained.

14 – Consciousness

I can see both shores, the buildings along the waterfront to one side, and the long, multi-coloured beach to the other. Here, between them, I'm home at last.

I'm no longer Death's pure awareness, no longer Grammar, or God, or Angel; I have returned to being Consciousness.

I'm tired of travelling through the nights of this large horizon of reality. I want belief, and the truths and definitions that come together with having a world. The bitter tranquillity and the thrill of living in a world.

My gaze has changed again. The optician that I am, and me alone, has tilted the angle of my eyes. Now I see dreams and facts, living and sleeping and running alongside each other. I see the contours of their geography, the dizzying patterns of 'these' and 'those' dancing together. I can't tell if I have been here before, but nostalgia has pulled me to this place since I began my journey.

I will sail again, back to the place where I was born; against the icy cliffs of non-being and the drop of what rejects any form of relation. One day. Not now. Now I feel myself shattering into each and all of them, separate and distinct as their names. I can feel myself becoming again the cartographer, the mute, the young one … And as I become them, I forget all that I've seen. Soon, a nostalgia without object will be all that remains, a memory of having forgotten. And that, too, will fade away, and all that I will have left will be an unexplainable desire to sail again within a fragment of reality. Soon. Not yet.

Now it's time for me to sleep and to forget. To believe again in this world, as if it was the whole world.

2 – Mundus Imaginalis[5]

The rattle of ropes swung by the wind awakens one of us. They adjust themselves on the steps, trying to recollect their thoughts. A comrade touches their shoulder.

---

[5]'Missions are stupid, Tereza. I have no mission. No one has. And it's a terrific relief to realize you're free, free of all missions.' M. Kundera, *The Unbearable Lightness of Being*, translated by M.H. Heim, London, Faber & Faber, 1995, p. 305.

'I can't … remember falling asleep.'

The sea is an unbroken circumference around us, except one dot in the distance. With some effort, the crew regains control of the ship and we head towards the only rest in this azure.

A new island begins to emerge, with a conical mountain towering at its centre. Its forested slopes are cut by gorges where birds assemble in flight. A thin, sandy coastline encircles it. It might be a fata morgana in the morning light, but the colours of this island refuse to stand still. Waves of blue, red, white, yellow, black and emerald green swash across the land as if through a sea. Between the scattered echoes brought by the wind, we can hear something like a winding melody.

We take down the sails and stall our ship at a distance. The helmsman is walking down from the quarterdeck, when a sudden jolt sends us all legs up. We don't seem to have hit a shallow and from the board the water appears as deep as ever. Something must have grabbed the hull from below, and it has started pulling our ship to the beach.

As we get closer, the spectacle of the island becomes ever more intense. The land seems to be caressed by an invisible brush, transforming trees, birds, water and rocks at the rhythm of the voices emerging everywhere.

A bank of sand seizes the bow of our ship. 'Keep steady for impact!' shouts the helmsman. 'Keep steady!' sings the echo. Rising from the beach, multiplicated by shells and seaweed, this undefinable music has grown deafening. Sometimes we can extract strings of words out of its avalanche, although their message remains impenetrable.

'Hey,' whispers the cartographer, gesturing to gather around them. They point up, where there used to be the sky. Its celestial valley has now rolled into a ring, cast against an abyss of darkness. A group of bright figures are promenading over this belvedere above the island. We see a lion and two youths, a woman carrying water and a crab, a bull, a centaur, and other monsters passing in slow procession over our heads.

'At this latitude,' says the cartographer in a low voice, 'that mill, up there, is time itself. It governs the tides of colours and sounds that surround us.' They pause for a moment. 'We're not the first to have arrived here. Travellers have written about this place and they've called it *Mundus Imaginalis*.' The cartographer draws a notebook out of their jacket. 'I found it this morning, among the papers downstairs. It contains the diaries of those who have preceded us on this route. But I swear that every time I open it, its contents change.'

'What do they say?' our youngest asks.

'I couldn't understand most of what they said. But their general advice, as I could gather it, was to explore inland.'

'We should go ... in there?'

'Their only warning is not to stay too long,' the cartographer concludes, unrolling the ladder offboard. They stare at the crew, then they step over the broadside.

'Why not,' rejoins the youngest.

The beach moves under the pressure of our feet. Some of us instinctively apologize when they touch the ground, as if they had stepped on somebody. Life blooms on the beach. Even the gusts of wind seem to have a life of their own, a voice, perhaps a name. It's hard to say if there's anything here that isn't somebody. We gather close. If this whole island is alive, wouldn't we provoke its anger by walking on it?

'What does the notebook say about this?' the helmsman anxiously asks.

Our youngest steps forward. 'No need to worry,' they say. 'The island is alive, but so are we. Our walking here is like fingers tapping their own shoulder. It won't mind us, fear not!' Then they head inland, without adding a word. In a few moments, we follow their lead.

There is an opening in the forest at the end of the beach, with marks of a passage through the foliage. The path winds through the vegetation. Trees and brambles change colour, sometimes shape. 'Fear not!' they sing in different tonalities. 'Hey,' whispers a jumble of roots, turning yellow. 'Where ... where are we?' asks a decomposing trunk on the forest floor. Tree branches sing out their calls, addressing each of us by name. At times they call 'cartographer' the helmsman, or vice versa. Or they call us 'drizzle', 'shipwreck', 'azure' ... 'Keep steady for impact!' they repeat, before morphing into another voice from another time. 'We should go back to the ship!' cries a whitening pebble, preceding by an instant our youngest. They have turned pale: the path from which we came is moving its spires. 'Before the way to the beach closes behind us!' chirps a nightingale. We turn as one person, hastening to trace back our steps. But our steps are gone. The path now curves in another direction, it's interrupted by a landslide, then it reappears a little further and finally opens onto a meadow, surrounded by a tight wall of trees.

There is one among us, whose silence so far has won them the appellative 'the mute'. They run to the front of the crew and stop us with open palms. They pick a stick off the ground, draw a spiral on the soil and then they trace a straight line cutting through its spires.

'The mute is right,' nods the cartographer. 'This path won't get us out of here. We must make our way through the foliage, beyond those trees.'

Animals move between the trees. Their size varies, with some reaching the tallest branches. Some of them sport symbols marked on their skin. We are emerging from a difficult tangle of brambles, when one of them stops in front of us. An ouroboros is marked on each of its three necks, raised in unison and crowned with heads of different animals. They look at us for a moment, as if judging whether it is worth attacking. We stand petrified. Then they turn towards the wall of trees, and its three heads begin vomiting flames against the trunks. The beast hisses, bleats and roars one last time, before running away to chase the new wave of colours that is sweeping through the forest. The fire left by the beast rapidly gnaws at the trees, opening the contours of a passage. We run and jump through the smoking embers, out of the edge of the forest, back on the shore.

The ship is still there, As we catch our breath, we notice its transformations. Whatever the waves have wetted, they have converted into a new piece of the beach orchestra. The ladder that we used to disembark is still hanging offboard, but its feet, washed over by the sea, have turned into paws that pace restlessly. The mute holds them steady for the rest of us to climb up.

Reaching the top of the ladder, the first in line stops shy of crossing on board.
'Did you see that?' they whisper, looking down.
'Those shadows?' says our eldest mid-way.

A group of them are moving across the deck. They don't seem to have noticed us. The features on their faces are too faint to see, but the shape of their bodies has something uncannily familiar.

The cartographer shudders, when they see one of them unrolling a ladder over the broadside, staring back for a moment and then climbing down the steps.

'Don't look,' says our eldest.
We wait for the shadows to disembark, before we say another word.
As soon as we are on deck, our youngest comrade walks to the cartographer.
'What's going on here? What is all this?'

The cartographer attempts a reassuring tone. 'No need to panic. Other travellers have been here before and most of them managed to leave safe and sound. Now, perhaps, I understand a little better the reports in their diaries. Let me explain. They wrote that this island is populated by images, allegories, archetypes and symbols. These are creatures of the same family, but they are also quite distinct from each other: "archetypes" are models that cast themselves over the land, imposing their form on whatever they touch. "Images" are what results from this casting. And "allegories" are the bonds of kinship between images. We have already encountered all these three kinds of creatures: those currents of colour and sound; those metamorphic creatures; that echo that endlessly revolves. It was them.'

The mute raises their arms in protest. Our youngest translates, 'You mentioned also symbols. Have we met them yet? Was it them who saved us from the forest, or were they the ones who moved the labyrinth to get us lost?'

'They're neither,' replies the cartographer. 'And nobody has saved us or has attempted on our lives. In this realm, it's irrelevant whether we're alive or dead, since nobody ever fully leaves these shores. Didn't you see those shadows that were disembarking from our ship, while we were climbing up, exactly with our same gestures from a little while ago? But "symbols" are something altogether different, and no, we haven't seen them yet. The reports say that they are like mirrors, conveying the light of an ineffable realm beyond space and time and, in a sense, beyond existence. But then they also add, paradoxically, that symbols reveal a spark of pure existence. I can't explain any better what they are, I'm afraid. It might be that we have already encountered them, and we didn't realize it.'

'So, do we have ... to go back inland to find them?' our youngest asks anxiously.

'Well, we have a mission to accomplish, after all. Or at least, some mission ... ' concedes the helmsman.

The rest of the crew falls silent.

Our eldest shakes their head, 'We don't really have a "mission". This is an adventure, not a job. At some point before this journey, I too must have read the tales of old travellers. And I remember them saying that symbols are not found, but that they are encountered. No matter how hard we'll look inland, we won't catch them unless they'll come to us. If they'll ever wish, symbols will show themselves. Let's move on forward, now, before we're swallowed by this island.'

A sigh of relief welcomes the words of our eldest. We push with the oars to free the bow of our ship from the bank of sand. The crew returns to their places; the helmsman at the steer, the cartographer on their papers. The paroxysm of colours and sounds is still sweeping through the waters off the shore. Shadows of our past selves are still traversing the deck, arguing, repeating themselves with tonal variations.

Our youngest is climbing up the mast, when they suddenly freeze.

'There!' they shout.

On the line of the horizon, a bank of mist is growing from the confluence between air and water. We see it galloping towards us, airborne, frictionless and phosphorescent against the dark sky. The crew tries to hasten our departure in any way they can, but to no avail. The mist has already swallowed us before we could leave the shallows.

In a matter of instants, an impalpable golden blanket seems to cover everything. The ring of the Zodiac high up and the forest inland glow with the same light, while we find ourselves floating on golden waters. The symphony has lowered to a monotonal humming, penetrating and deep throughout the body of the island.

The mute rests a hand on the shoulder of our youngest, turned golden.

'Yes ... I can see them. There they are,' they say. 'Even we ... We have become symbols.'

And while we stare, entranced, through this impenetrable light, our ship floats further off the coast.

3 – The world[6]

It's been hours since we left the island. All is still immersed in light. The helmsman is standing vigilant on the quarterdeck, while the rest of the crew has gone to rest in their bunk beds. Alone in the cavity of the hull, the cartographer is curved over a map across the surface of a desk. They are drawing a circle inside the shape of a square. *The Glass Dome*, they write next to it. Then they black out the immeasurable path of the night, until the tangled edges of the *Mundus Imaginalis*.

The cartographer is writing *The Night*, when the ship steers abruptly. They jump from the chair, drop the pen and rush upstairs. Over the deck, the air is so saturated with light that it might as well be ablaze. The cartographer can barely peer through a gap between their fingers, searching for the quarterdeck. Up there, the helmsman presses their weight against the bar. 'There's something … in the water … ' they growl.

The cartographer leans overboard, looking down through the crystalline water at the contours of massive crease bending the seabed upwards. The sea rises along its curve, like a piece of fabric over a body. Their eyes follow the curve, while the blinding light begins to reveal the volume of an enormous wall of water, fast approaching in front of the ship. It falls perpendicular against the sealine, as if two oceans were merging into one. Clouds of mist explode out of their point of confluence. The helmsman attempts again to steer; the cartographer crouches. There is no time to say anything. They both shut their eyes, when the ship enters the ascending angle of the waters.

---

[6]'The one pursues while him the other flies,/And with lament resounds the thicket gray./They issue in a spacious mead, on which/Appears a lofty mansion, rare and rich./Of various marbles, wrought with subtle care,/Is the proud palace. He who fast in hold/Bears off upon his arm the damsel fair,/Sore pricking, enters at a gate of gold./Nor Brigliador is far behind the pair,/Backed by Orlando, angry knight and bold./Entering, around Orlando turns his eyes,/Yet neither cavalier nor damsel spies.' L. Ariosto, *Orlando Furioso*, Canto XII, 7–8, translated by W.S. Rose, London, John Murray, 1823.

The ship's mast creaks frightfully, while our equipment smashes underdeck amidst bodies rolling off the bunk beds. The crew crawls along the stairway holding onto the edge of the steps. The ship stabilizes itself before they have reached the deck, sending them all crashing back down. The vertical and the horizontal planes have swapped places, it seems, like a passage between musical scales. The sea that we've left behind keeps roaring and flowing against this new one. From their mutual waterfall, the banks of mist begin their journey.

It takes us a while to adjust to the new plane of navigation. The crew gathers on the quarterdeck with uncertain steps. A wind keeps pushing our ship upwards, or forward, further away from the luminous mist. We watch this long non-day beginning to withdraw and a vanguard of abyssal darkness marching from the distance. The battle at twilight sees the Night triumphant, swiftly occupying every corner deserted by the mist.

The wind seems to be pacified by the arrival of darkness, settling on a steady stream that gently rocks the hull of our ship. And from somewhere, without or within, we feel an invisible caress disentangling our muscles and softening our knees.

'I'm feeling so tired, all of a sudden … I might … ' yawns a voice.

The mute begins to shuffle their feet towards the staircase. The rest of the crew follows them through the large embrace of the Night, like a line of sleepwalkers. The helmsman, too, has left the steer and lies curled at its feet. The deck remains as empty as the starless sky.

The cartographer stares through the darkness, exhilarated. Somehow, the Night has spared them. They stumble across the ship, stretching their arms forward. They are completely alone, except a nagging doubt in their mind. Who knows how long they have left, before they too will fall to slumber? As the only witness to the Night, they should remain there, feeling, observing, breathing it. They should abandon themselves to the experience. But they are also a writer, and their notes are still unfinished.

The cartographer bows their head to descend underdeck. They make their way down the stairs, groping for a light. Their papers are scattered on the floor amidst pieces of broken equipment. They pick up the notebook and flip through its pages. The notebook has become perfectly blank, with each page neatly ripped in half.

The cartographer leaves it aside, unrolls the map on the table, picks a pen and draws another circle around both islands. An atoll now weaves into one family the *Island of Facts* and the *Mundus Imaginalis*.

They catch themselves yawning. 'No, not yet … ' they mutter.

Then, near the rim of the circle, they write *The World* and, in brackets, *one sole climate over the nests of facts and archetypes.* They draw the ascending course of the mist with brief strokes, binding *The World* to the vertical sea.

The Night deals another blow. The cartographer sinks their teeth into their lip until they taste blood. They take the notebook, and on the remaining half of its first page they write with slow haste, in oblique calligraphy.

We have been travelling for two days across this sea. The reader won't need to know how our journey started. If they're wondering, they must be near where we departed. So far, we have encountered two islands. The first is a land contained by a dome so high that it is indistinguishable from the sky. This island is plagued by a parasite, which covers and rules all its inhabitants, people and objects alike. The parasite is transparent, almost volumeless; it feeds off information and its digestion takes place in the exchanges across creatures. Peculiarly, starvation makes this parasite heavier, not slimmer. Hence how it disciplines its hosts: with death-by-crushing. I doubt that anyone can rest there for long, without incurring great danger. But exiting the island is forbidden. The dome around it opens only for the funeral pyres heading to the open sea. We too had to perform our own funeral to be able to escape. The following day we met a land contorted over its own spires. It is a realm of great confusion, inhabited by creatures that indifferently take on friendly and terrifying masks. The place itself is one living monster. I recommend that the traveller doesn't go too far inland, lest they wish to remain among the ghosts that haunt it. But they shouldn't leave too soon, either. Banks of bright mist at times descend from afar, to polish its surface like a mirror, revealing the way to a second sea. The mist led us upwards into this other sea, which meets the first one perpendicularly. This is where we find ourselves at the moment, unsure whether we're hanging off it, or if we're sailing plainly. I believe that those two islands were part of one atoll, sitting on the first, horizontal plane. They both shared the same climate, in which things existed and developed in the manner of a story, whether made of facts or of figures. Only the mist and the Night could cut through the borders of that atoll.

The pen slips off their fingers. A drop of ink spreads over the last word. The cartographer stares at it expanding, until their eyes surrender to the incantations of the Night.

13 – Angel

I remember the moment I saw the first silhouette of an object. It was in the shape of an island, twisting in spirals. I burst into tears. The contours of that island were a bird announcing 'somewhere' – a promise of some rest, just a little stretch away. On the other side, I could still see the ineffable – an ocean of light soaring to the heights.

I learned the pleasure of playing with my own two bodies, moving them in and out of solitude. I projected myself onto the plane of the ineffable, melting my form into a shadow of light, then I moulded myself into a figure among the imaginal crowds. For the first time, I felt the tension between the dimensions that surrounded me. I contemplated their mutual desire and I suffered for their separation. Until I realized that I was the gap that separated them – but also the bridge over which their extremities might touch.

I tried to smoothen my own surface to the best of my abilities, I polished both my bodies and I polished them again. I relaxed them, until I was able to swing from one to the other like a tide that washes back and forth. Seen from one side, I must have looked like a flow of light; a stroke of colour, as seen from the other.

I made myself silent to hear the murmuring of the two dimensions, rubbing against each other.

I could have remained there indefinitely, contemplating that joy. But a part of me wanted that joy for itself. I wanted to feel that touch, to lose myself and to find again what extends beyond me. I left behind a shadow of my own body – an evanescent bridge between dimensions. The rest of me travelled on, over the curve of these two oceans that eternally merge into one another.

Home feels closer, now. Perhaps it's only a little stretch away.

4 – The point-island of the ineffable[7]

However long the Night has been, none of us feels rested. We have assembled on deck, while daylight begins to illuminate the featureless expanse of this vast sea.

Then, an island emerges.

Our eyes close in unison, as if under the same hand. Some of us sink to the floor; others stand on jittery legs. We sense the island approaching us at terrifying speed, and we feel the exact moment when it penetrates our flesh. We feel it tunnelling through our organs, pushing inside our breath. We hear it breaking inside the room where our inner sundial dwells, surrounded by the measures of time. It holds there for an instant, before exploding in a light without shadows. The marks of 'before' and 'after' grow paler, multiply, overlap, melt into invisibility.

That is when the body of the island comes crushing against us. We jolt at the bite of the passerelle that it lowers within us, but we remain paralysed before the coming onslaught. The people of the island descend calmly, at the pace of the master. We see the border guards in their transparent armour, the floating pyre, the choir of imaginal colours, returning all together within us. How strange it is to recognize them at once! Even the glass dome comes in, like an actor onto a stage. We can see also ourselves in the crowd; on the island of facts, on the ship, sleeping through the Night, running across the forest ... We look just as fragile and tender as the rest of the troupe of the World.

What a funny spectacle is the World, now that we can see its floorboards. Even the horrors and the terrors have returned with the thrill of a game. We feel exhilarated beyond words, while thoughts in our mind congeal into a stupor, ecstatically singing praise. How wonderful to know that a World exists beyond this vertical sea, and eternally within each thing! What an honour to have played there, and how reassuring to see now the curtains that

---

[7] 'God is communicable in what He imparts to us; but He is not communicable in the incommunicability of his essence,' Maximus the Confessor, quoted in Euthymius Zigabenus, *Panoplia Dogmatics*, III, P.G., CXXX, 132 A. – in V. Lossky, *The Mystical Theology of the Eastern Church*, translated by a group of members of the Fellowship of St Alban and St Sergius, Cambridge, James Clarke & Co., 2005, p. 73.

hang from its frame, the walls around its stage and an open door leading out of the theatre. As seen from here, this island within us looks enchanting.

But if we, too, are characters in this play, what has happened to our ship? What has happened to our bodies?

The mute timidly parts their eyelids. Birds are flying around the sails, as ever in the proximity of an island. When they intersect in flight, though, they no longer cast shadows on each other. They slide over one another, like sheets of paper. The mute widens their mouth in a perfect two-dimensional oval. Also the ship has become a figurine without volume, sliding across a shimmering sea that hangs flat off the sky. The sky too has changed. No more azure, mist or darkness: a golden monochrome fills every shadow.

All is silent, except a laughing tremor that irradiates through the golden distances. Another one of us opens their eyes, while a warm current begins to spread through our muscles. Standing against the mast with open arms, our youngest attempts to tightrope-walk across the deck. Sliding their tongue between their teeth, they move their paper-thin limbs in a few steps of dance. Warmer and warmer, the currents traversing us have latched to connect the whole crew. A wide grin draws the lips of the cartographer over their depthless face, the helmsman rolls their eyes and even our eldest partakes to the carnival of this *danse macabre*. The mute's laughter booms through an excited silence.

We must have hit a reef, or a mountain peak on this invisible island. We feel it cutting through our flesh, messily breaking us from within. We groan and close again our eyes, anxiously looking for the theatre of the World. Nothing has happened to the actors on our inner stage. It is only us, the bodies that provide a stage for their play, who have changed. Looking down, we can no longer feel the spinning of a beautiful game. We can only feel the print of our absence, our being confined to the exile of pure spectators. The dream of the World is sealed within its boundaries; we watch it from afar. The peak of this island has cut a distance within us that not even our longing can mend.

Another shot of pain, and we feel the island beginning to sink. The chandeliers collapse over the floor of the theatre, the boards are unscrewed off stage. Nothingness is eating away the walls of the building. The crew falls on their knees. It's getting cold, within us and outside. We hear a rumble coming from within. There is no inside anymore.

We feel our eyelids withdrawing within their sockets. The sky has turned the colour of embers. As it happened on the island of facts, now we can see the currents shooting between objects and latching them together. The same nerve-endings run through this landscape. As on the island of the imaginal, everything everywhere lives – but it lives in silence. And its silence surrounds us like a foreign land.

We begin to perceive the abomination of this eternal prison, where everything is condemned to existence, and us to loneliness. Round tears roll off our jaws, scintillating in three dimensions. They run across the deck-boards, ribbing the landscape. Their paths mix with the tears of the birds, of the sails, of the ropes piled on deck. It's not only us who have lost our own image in the mirror of the World. Everything around us has also become an orphan.

Merciful, silent Night unrolls its blanket over the golden sky. Its oblivion comes tepid. Our sadness, ecstasies and terrors fade together, while sleep descends upon the day of eternity.

5 – The dream[8]

Finally, Night loosens its grip. We're scattered on deck, wherever slumber caught us the previous day. Face-down on a pile of folded sails, the cartographer opens their eyes to a terse sky. Images from yesterday return confused and vivid in their memory.

'It's going to be a long day,' they mutter. And the sound of their own voice startles them. They get ready for the aches of having spent a night outdoors. But when they push themselves up on their arms, they almost fall backwards. They feel only a subtle numbness, without pain. Regaining balance, the cartographer rubs their eyes to the new day. The golden foil has vacated the horizon and the internal monologue of their consciousness is no longer the bustling

---

[8] 'Once Zhuang Zhou dreamed he was a butterfly, a fluttering butterfly. What fun he had, doing as he pleased! He did not know he was Zhou. Suddenly he woke up and found himself to be Zhou. He did not know whether Zhou had dreamed he was a butterfly or a butterfly had dreamed he was Zhou. Between Zhou and the butterfly there must be some distinction. This is what is meant by the transformation of things.' From Zhuangzi, *Zhuangzi*, translated by J. Legge – quoted in W. E. Soothill, *The Three Religions of China: Lectures Delivered at Oxford*, Oxford, Oxford University Press, 1929.

noise of a theatre. The landscape spreads again in three dimensions, although its surface looks somewhat crumpled.

The cartographer walks carefully between the sleeping bodies, stopping to examine a rope, a dent in the mast, the head of a nail. Almost automatically they head down to the cabin, lighting a candle on the stairs. They sit at their desk and remain still, wondering if it's worth annotating their observations when they're unsure if they're awake.

Then they raise the pen and let a drop of ink fall on the paper. A black dot now floats outside the atoll of *The World*, hanging off the vertical sea. Next to it they add, in minute calligraphy: *Point-Island of the Ineffable*. 'It's incorrect to call it an island, though,' they think. 'It resembled more closely a mood, or an experience … Yes, an experience. And the language of experience is not that of description. Ecstasy, nostalgia, laughter, terror were encased within us like currents in a wire … The only portion of yesterday's island to have emerged above the floating line of language was the residue of its symptoms.'

The cartographer holds the pen mid-air, staring vacantly at the cabin walls. 'But the place where we were yesterday … what was it? Perhaps I could say that … No, no I can't … But at least I can say that … it existed. No, actually … '

'That it exists!' they burst out. 'The part of reality that does the job of existing, that's what we met yesterday. The heart of existence, enlivening what is alive; a light bringing to the fore anything experienceable within reality.'

A noise from the deck announces that someone else has awakened. The oldest member of our crew descends the stairs to the cabin. 'The youth are still asleep', they say hoarsely. 'It seems that we are the first to have woken up.' The cartographer turns expectantly. 'Well, we're waking up, at last,' says our eldest.

'And what about the islands we've seen?' asks the cartographer. 'What about yesterday? I can't get my head around it.'

'Yesterday was amazing … and terrifying,' says our eldest, straightening their back. 'But it was a dream. All of it has been a dream. Until this morning. I don't think that we'll be dreaming from now on.'

Another rustling sound comes from the deck. Someone else is waking up. The old one smiles a brief salute and makes their way to the kitchen.

The cartographer remains alone at their desk. 'Everything so far has taken place within, not without us,' they think. '"The elder is right. We saw it yesterday. But everything seemed so perfectly, so objectively ... "real".' The cartographer stretches their arms. Little time remains before the daily routine of ship duties.

With one movement, they draw a second circle, crowning the upper edge of the vertical sea. It forms the profile of a well, with the World at its bottom. Next to it, they write *The Dream*.

They take out the notebook. Its pages have returned whole again, without any trace of yesterday's ripping. They feel heavier and coarser, and the mark of infinite cancellations shows through the sheets. The cartographer flips to the centrefold and begins to write.

'We have reached a new island. It didn't occupy any space, but it expanded immensely within us. Inversely to the *mundus imaginalis*, its mirror surface reflected not what was ahead of us, but the islands that we had left behind. Figures seen and unseen descended from its passerelle, reaching our innermost rooms from the depths of our memory. They roamed within us, pulling the curtains of our inner theatre, revealing the rows of seats, the hall, the corridors ... and beyond the doors, who knows, perhaps a street, or the wild.

We rose and sunk together with this island. Then the Night buried us again under its blanket. This morning, we found that the sea and the clouds had returned to their usual places. But this regained normality has a peculiar taste. Today, on our fourth day of navigation, I feel as if I had just awakened from a long dream. I have a sense that from now on, whatever we will encounter will be truly independent from us. I have no proof to substantiate this feeling, but I appeal to the cartographer that hides within each reader of maps, and to the trust that exists between colleagues.'

The cartographer stands up from their desk and salutes the arrival of another comrade, descending underdeck.

12 – God

Half and half. I realise for the first time what it means to exist in-between things. Half asleep and half awake, I can feel my dormant eye dreaming the other, and a waking gaze returning the attention.

I already had a body, but only now it has a flesh that can feel and suffer; a flesh with an agency of its own.

Sadness is a welcome energy in the midst of this impalpable atmosphere. The God that I have become is split within; it feels nostalgia for itself, and love. What a strange thing, being God. Part of me is still dissolved, and part of me is struggling to arrange a shape for itself. Which one is waking or sleeping, even for me it's hard to say. I can still tell my own origin, as pure awareness, only by remembering where I've come from. But this pull that I feel in the direction of the World remains beyond my understanding.

The further I travel towards becoming a consciousness in the World, the more I lose a clear idea of what I am. I remain aware that this body of mine is but a projection; a country that exists only in my imagination. Yet, my imagination has become so vivid that I have little reason to believe anything else. This is a dream, I am asleep, this isn't any more solid that the ethereal plane of Being which I have traversed so far – but so what? I am God, and I can choose to believe my own shadow. The God that I am, needs to choose between destinies – whether to head back to my origin, or back to the place where my desire pulls me. And I have made my decision.

6 – The sleeping gods[9]

'Land! Land!'

At the intersection of sky and water, a series of rolling hills rise slowly, crowned by a rugged beach. We keep the island at an arrow's throw, while we discuss what we should take onshore with us. Consensus converges on the suggestion of our eldest: we'll carry only weapons. We know that our makeshift spears could do very little against who knows what entities that we will meet. But our

---

[9]'A single garden, if the scenes to be eternalized are recorded at different moments, will obtain innumerable paradises, and each group of inhabitants, unaware of the others, will move about simultaneously, almost in the same places, without colliding. But unfortunately, these will be vulnerable paradises because the images will not be able to see men.' A. Bioy Casares, *The Invention of Morel*, translated by R.L.C. Simms, New York, NY, New York Review of Books, 2003, pp. 82–3.

weapons are not meant to offend. They might help us to charm and imprison our anxiety, if only for a moment, like talismans.

The low profile of the island is undulated by arid slopes, dotted with bushes. We descend from our ship and, cautiously, we make our way to the beach. There is something strange to this island. Every object that we grab is significantly heavier than we would have expected. Even the smooth surface of pebbles feels coarse to the touch. The oldest one among us rubs a pinch of sand between their fingers and looks at the cartographer. They agree silently. Indeed, we are awake.

The beach proceeds inland, mixed with the shrubs growing over the slopes of a nearby hill. At its top, a wooden hut basks in the daylight. We try to silence our steps and our rattling breath in this viscous air. The hut resembles the abode of a fisherman, with one window on each side and a curtain flowing through an open door. The single room that makes up its interior is shrouded in darkness. We can see only the silhouette of a bed, placed in the middle of the room. 'Please, come in!' a voice says from indoors, startling us. 'Come in, please!' it insists in a friendly tone. We look at each other for a moment, before depositing our weapons at the entrance. As our eyes get accustomed to the darkness of the room, we begin to see a body reclining over the mattress. Their eyes and lips remain sealed, while they invite us to make ourselves at home. We gather around the bed. In the manner of a ventriloquist, our host asks what brings us here. We are attempting a response, when they immediately interrupt us. 'Oh, I already know about your journey. About the two seas, the theatre of the World, the ineffable and all that you have seen. Please, take me with you,' they sigh. 'I'm ready. I've been ready for a long time.'

The crew falls silent. Who is this person? The mute steps forward, slowly approaching the bed. Just as they hunch over the body of our host, a gust of wind sweeps through the open door. The air pushes the windowpane off its stops and bangs it against the frame. We stare in horror at what happens next. Our host springs up mechanically and their torso cuts through our comrade, as if through air. The mute jolts, slipping back with their mouth agape.

Our host remains seated on the bed, scratching their chin. 'They came back to visit me last night,' they mutter. 'And I failed again to convince them. Why do I never get to see their ship?' Their voice has a slight delay compared to the movements of their lips. The windowpane bangs a second time. They stand up and traverse the room to close it, pacing through the cartographer along the way.

To each other, we feel as solid as we've ever been. We still oppose some resistance to objects, even though we seem to have grown weaker. But to our host, we have lost all substance. Have we truly ever landed on these shores? Are we present here at all?

'One of them is always the helmsman,' continues our host, picking their clothes and getting dressed against the window. 'This time I didn't hear them speak, though … '

'Well, at least they know who I am,' quips the helmsman, with a strained grin.

We have become less than we were – or that we thought we were. But we haven't quite faded into nothingness.

We walk out of the door. Some of us instinctively collect their weapons from the entrance, only to drop them again. Their talismanic power has faded: we are locked at an infinite distance from the inhabitants of this island. Above us, two seabirds hang perfectly still in the terse sky. The helmsman looks up. 'I bet they can't see us either. Maybe, only when they sleep … '

We can hear our host humming. The sound lingers inside the hut for a while, after they've come out to tend a tiny patch of garden around the corner. We could continue to watch our host going about their day, perhaps on occasion recollecting their dreams about us. We could wait here until the night, to tell our host to come onboard with us. We could give them the location of our ship, in the hope that they will remember it when they wake up. But would they even be able to see it? Wouldn't the wood vanish under their feet, if they ever walked over the deck?

From the top of the hill, we see an arid plateau stretching far inland, until the edges of a distant city.

'Shall we go?' asks our youngest.

The crew remains unmoved. Only the cartographer seems to have some desire to continue exploring, but they too can taste the dryness of this soil. Whatever we'll see, whoever we'll encounter here, they won't be able to encounter us. We are awake at last, but to no avail.

'Let's go back,' says the helmsman, turning in the opposite direction. They head down the slope and we follow them towards the beach, leaving our weapons behind as an invisible offering. None of us looks back to our former host, still humming out of sync while watering their plants.

The ship is moored where we left it, its sails are bright under the sun. The two sea birds are still hanging above us, almost motionless, while we re-embark without waiting for Night to fall.

7 – Being[10]

We have travelled far and wide. We have been the landscape of dreams, and the stuff of the dreams of others. Only the succession of days and nights allows us to keep some sense of time. The ruins of our inner sundial tell us that nightfall is due. But a bright day still reigns over the sea.

We indulge in ever-more minute repairs to our nautical equipment. The journey has taken its toll on the ropes and the sails, it has reshuffled our stock of supplies and has turned our once-neat cabin into a hovel. The youngest among us is singing a little refrain while they fix the hinges of a door. They have gained a new sense of defiance since we left that arid island. They keep singing, until the rest of the crew joins their *ritournelle*. We sing to celebrate the continuation of our journey, our being here now, in this indefinite azure. Tiredness, anxiety, melancholy seem to evaporate into the exhilaration of survivors.

The afternoon sees our celebrations ebb away, while we complete the last repairs. Everything is in its right place; there are no threats in sight. Only Night is overdue. And whenever silence falls, the soft sound of waves makes our skin crawl.

---

[10]'This Infinity implies Radiation, for the good tends to communicate itself, as St Augustine observed; the Infinity of the Real is none other than its power of Love. And the mystery of Radiation explains everything: by radiating, the Real as it were projects Itself "outside Itself", and in separating Itself from Itself, It becomes Relativity to the very extent of this separation. It is true that this "outside" is necessarily situated in the Real itself, but it none the less exists qua outwardness and in a symbolic fashion.' F. Schuon, *Esoterism as Principle and as Way*, translated by W. Stoddart and Pates Manor, Bedfont, Perennial Books, 1981, p. 48.

The helmsman stands up from a bench. 'You know what? There's one thing that I've been meaning to ask,' they roar jokingly, pointing to the cartographer. 'You haven't shown us any of your maps. What better time than now? Tell us where we've been so far, and perhaps we might guess where we're heading.'

The crew bursts in cheers, covering the silence of this interminable afternoon.

The cartographer savours the attention. 'I'll need my papers,' they say, rising from their seat. They head downstairs to collect their work, then they re-emerge on deck as if walking through stage curtains. Silence ensues again – this time untainted by anguish. The cartographer looks at us gravely while he opens the notebook. All the pages inside have disappeared. They show us the empty covers, then they cast the notebook aside with a dramatic gesture. They unroll on the floor the map over which they've laboured. Its paper is traversed by a few, sinuous lines, some closing in a circle and some giving a sense of three-dimensionality to the drawing. The cartographer looks again at the crew and begins their story: 'In the beginning, it was a glass of water on a table, or a spiderweb in the corner, or the echo of a thought ... I remember myself observing it, wondering what secrets it hid within. Then, it all became azure. There I was, with all of you on this ship. There we were – and that mysterious notebook confirms that we weren't the first to have been cast adrift within a fragment of reality. Certainly, we won't be the last to experience this. This is why I'm drawing this map. I don't want to say what expects the adventurers that will follow us. I want to reassure them that each adventure is in the wake of a long tradition. And that they, too, are a part of this tradition.'

The cartographer presses their finger on a small circle on the map, 'The *Island of Facts*. It was the first place which we encountered, so it might be the closest to where we were, before the beginning of this adventure. It was a familiar land, and not without beauty – recall its geometrical perfection, the velocity of its links ... But we almost lost you there,' they say, turning towards our eldest. 'Whatever doesn't take part to the frantic workings of that island is as good as dead. Under its glass dome, creatures survive in fear of being annihilated. When we fled on a flaming pyre, and we discovered that "annihilation" is only a movement forward, we experienced for the first time the incantations of the Night. I can't say much more about the Night: an invincible sleep hides its constellations.

I have marked it here with a trace of charcoal. Perhaps some other cartographer, on another expedition, will be able to chart its course.

On the second day, we encountered the Island of the Imaginal. A strange place indeed: everything, there, is alive – and it's alive as a person. I recognized it in the descriptions that old travellers left of a realm called *Mundus Imaginalis*. They said that it was peopled by images, allegories and ... symbols.' The cartographer looks at the mute, then at our youngest. 'You two were impatient to see them. And we didn't just meet them, we became symbols ourselves! Every speck on those shores turned into a silver surface, where a distant light reflected itself. Since that day, I've been asking myself whether that phosphorescent mist didn't simply reveal something that had been present all along ... But the mist pulled us forward, and, as Night began to fall, we made a discovery. You were the first to notice it,' they say, turning towards the helmsmen. 'When the ship steered upwards and we took to sailing vertically. We realised that the island of facts and that of the imaginal are part of one atoll, *The World*, which is surrounded by a perpendicular wall of water.' Their finger moves along an oblique line departing from a broader circle.

Our youngest instinctively raises their hand. 'Are you saying that what we saw in *The World* of words and images was just a bunch of muck at the bottom of a well? If that's closest to where we were, before we were thrown on this ship, then we too were stuck down there, before this journey.'

'Not quite,' responds the cartographer, turning the map at 180 degrees. '"Up" and "down" is like "here" or "there". If you look at it the other way, the well turns into a tower soaring from the sea where we find ourselves now. It's a matter of perspective. Which is precisely what we discovered on our next stop.' They catch their breath and look around. 'Come the next morning, a new island took shape within us. I find it impossible to describe it through words. But I'm sure that you remember it. Somehow, we became the sea and the sky and the land ... Something started to walk within us, as if through a landscape. Suddenly, it was revealed to us the true location of everything that we had seen until then. It had taken place within, not outside us. I have marked this island on the map with one dot, having no other means to account for its existence. I felt confused for a long time after we left its shores. I was struggling to make any sense of what had happened. Until you came to my aid,' says the cartographer, smiling to our eldest. 'You helped me realize, as I believe we all did, that we had been dreaming all along. Our dream had become lucid during the time when the *Ineffable* was traversing us. We could still see the phantoms within us, but at least we recognised them as such, and we acknowledged that we had always been the landscape for their play. It wasn't easy, especially when the dream of the World disintegrated and suddenly we were left void and orphans. And then, again, Night descended upon us. I drew this third Night on the map with a trace of charcoal. I drew it perpendicular to the ineffable stretch of the sea, because I couldn't find a better way to describe this new state of wakefulness than to make it again horizontal. The place where we are now, we must admit it, feels as plain and horizontal as was the sea of words and images. It didn't take us long to forget.' The cartographer stays silent for a little while, as if they were uncertain whether to continue the story. They move their finger across the map. In a low voice, they say: 'I have drawn our next stop in the shape of a square. It was a dry land, heavy and coarse like a bad awakening. The only person we met there, sleeping inside their hut, could talk to us only in their sleep. As soon as they woke up, we disappeared from their vision. All that we had woken up to, was the discovery that we had become dreams ourselves. I still feel the pain of that moment, and their absence still haunts me. I have named this place *The Island of the Sleeping Gods*. We left it before nightfall. And then, the Night,' says the cartographer, looking up. 'The fourth Night is late to come,' they conclude with a smile. 'All I know about where we are now, is that this place exists. It is a place, and we can sail through it. It is Being. It's not much, but this is all I'm able to say.'

11 – Grammar

What a funny thing it is, to have a body. I reclaim a part of reality, and I call it 'myself'. I play with the extensions of my awareness, and I can turn myself into something else. I expand and I shrink, drawing lines across being and non-being, tracing shapes that define my positions. And then I imagine sinews between them, and I let my gaze run along their course. I am still just a point of awareness, but now I am able to invent my own objects. I can furnish this barren landscape. And at last I can speak of something other than my surprise at resurrecting from the embrace of Death.

My body now surrounds me, as far as my attachments wish to extend themselves. Me and myself have become separate. But I can set the field with the pressure of my feet, and I can set the positions for the entire universe. I can draw the lines between them. I can shape myself and dissolve myself again. I can do everything, and then withdraw into nothingness.

But I want more of this, more of myself. However long it shall take, I will return to be the master of my own home.

8 – Non-being[11]

'There!'

A bright line has emerged from the water, rapidly occupying the length of the horizon. In an instant, the deck is swept by our frenzied activity. Some crawl up the mast to lower the sails, others are taking the oars, the helmsman rushes to the steer, our eldest prepares the anchor. Only the cartographer remains seated among their papers.

The wind that fills our sail has turned freezing, and it is pushing us towards this new land, at once revealed and hidden by the aura of daylight. As we get closer, passing through a light so intense to resemble darkness, we realize that the approaching land is in fact one sole icy cliff, stretching uninterrupted as far as our eyes can see. It is neatly cut at the top, like a frame between sea and sky. Beyond it, perhaps, lies a plateau whose depth we can't detect from down here.

The cartographer brandishes the notebook, exposing a new page that has suddenly appeared. 'Stay away! Stay away from that wall!' they scream. 'That's the Island of Non-Being. We ... must not reach it!'

'Shut up and help us already!' growls one of the crew. The ropes sizzle under the friction between wood and seawater. The helmsman is losing their struggle to control the steer. Our ship falls prey to the

---

[11]'And immediately resumes/the journey/as/after the shipwreck/a survivor/sea-Wolf.' *E subito riprende/il viaggio/come/dopo il naufragio/un superstite/lupo di mare.* Giuseppe Ungaretti, *Allegria di Naufragi (Joy of Shipwrecks)*, Vesta, 14 February 1917 – in G. Ungaretti, *Vita di un Uomo: 106 poesie 1914–60*, Milan, Mondadori, 1992, p. 43 – my translation.

winds and currents. We drop our anchors, one after the other, as a last resort. But we keep on sailing towards the cliff.

The mute looks at the icy wall, now a stone's throw away. A small, dark figure is standing at on its edge. Its almond shape seems a hole piercing ice and sky.

'It's finished,' whispers the mute, abandoning the ropes.

Ice growlers come crashing against the hull. Another push, and under the umpteenth strain the steer breaks in the helmsman's hands. Our ship creaks horribly. Like a drunkard, it bends its course, drawing a large curve amidst the floating ice.

Our eldest turns to our youngest comrade. 'Don't be afraid,' they say. Our youngest glimpses at the cliff through the sweat congealing on their eyelids. 'I'm not afraid. This is an adventure, I know.'

The end comes swiftly. One side of our ship crashes against the wall of ice, exploding in a flurry of splinters. The floorboards tilt sideways, shooting us against the rails. A second blow flings us to the other side. Our vessel disintegrates completely. If any of us screamed, no one heard us. We sink like dead objects in the freezing water.

High on the edge of the cliff, the dark figure steps forward. Its almond shape, descending upon us, is the last thing that we see before the sea seals our eyes. Our last feeling is its touch, when it fishes us one by one out of the water. We enter its embrace. Then, nothing more.

We are dead. We are safe.

Here, at last, our journey ends.

My return begins.

10 – Death

I was all of them. The cartographer, the mute, the young one, the eldest and the helmsman ... I was their tired arms and the floorboards on their ship.

But 'I' wasn't at all. They were – each by themselves. They lived, and they died. They dissolved and melted; and I was born.

I look around myself now.

I am nothing but this – a gaze that looks around and doesn't see anything. Pure awareness, homeless within reality. I can only see that there are the two parts to this deserted landscape: to one side, the prairies of pure negation; to the other side, an interruption, a negation that negates even itself.

To my north, reality drops into the abyss of non-relationality. To my south, the Night; and beyond the Night, the mystery of non-being. Somewhere further south, I remember, there should still be the World. I am now only the ray of a gaze, an awareness without a body. I know nothing, and yet I remember where my home was once.

I shall travel high above the ice, above the sea and the islands. Only by Night; until daybreak.

9 – Non-relationality

AFTERWORD: SENSUOUS PROPHECY

By Franco Berardi 'Bifo'

The phenomenon of prophecy has intrigued me for a very long time, but I've never dared to tackle it directly. Now that Federico Campagna has dedicated to this notion a delightfully erudite and philosophically innovative book, I can at last attempt to approach it – although still tentatively and with a certain trepidation. Perhaps, I am just afraid of revealing my cards and of exposing the secrets of my job.

Even though I share the central concept of this book – that the prophet doesn't fore-see or predict the future, but that they 'see' the present and, more importantly, what is inscribed within the present – my point of view differs from that exposed by Campagna. This doesn't imply a theoretical divergence between us, but rather a different focus. What interests me the most is not the relation between prophecy, metaphysics, mysticism and shamanism, but the relation between prophetic vision and the unconscious.

My focus is on the ability of the human mind (at least, of some human minds) to tune in to the collective unconscious or, more precisely, to the flows circulating in the collective psycho-sphere.

It's difficult to say exactly how this 'tuning in' might take place: you must smell the air, observe the faces crowding the subway trains in the early morning, listen to the voices of drinkers in a local pub and count the number of smiles that pucker the lips of passers-by. Multiply all this for the average salary of a precarious worker and … well, in the end you must interpret the signs that you are able to intercept among the whispering of cities.

What is commonly called 'reality' does not exist in itself. As Campagna explains very well, especially in the charmingly enigmatic chapter that closes this book, reality is the effect of the particular gaze that looks at it.

Reality is but the point of convergence of innumerable psycho-dynamic pathways, intersecting over the surface of daily life. Thus, interpreting the mesh of signs that make up the psycho-sphere of the present is also the best way to gain an intuitive vision of what might be the future of the world.

Following Henri Bergson's suggestion – in *La Pensée et le Movant*[1] and in *Matière and Mémoire*[2] – I argue that even though analytical reason might lead us to generalizations, analysis on its own doesn't allow us to grasp the singularity of objects and processes.

Intuition, on the contrary, arises from sym/pathy – from the sym/pathetic experience of each object and of each process. The term 'sym/pathetic' means here: conjunctive, and capable of sensitive tuning. The analytical mind can systematize, distinguish, connect, but only the sym/pathetic mind can perceive the singular becoming of the event. No analytical category can help you to attune to the absolutely new that emerges from the magma of Chaos. The analytical mind can retain what has happened, but it is unprepared to perceive what is inscribed in the 'now' – and thus it's even less ready to tune in to the flow of becoming.

That is the work (the travail, the torment, the suffering and the enjoyment) of the prophet.

Commenting on the visions of Ezekiel, Cardinal Carlo Ravasi writes:

> *Reading Ezekiel, we understand that he is using his body in its expressive-symbolic duplicity, which means as corporeality in itself … Communication has the function of being* dia-phanic, *(from the Greek: transparent, passing through), it has the function of transmitting the message, not of making it opaque like an impenetrable screen.*[3]

---

[1]H. Bergson, *The Creative Mind: An Introduction to Metaphysics*, translated by M. L. Andison, Mineola, NY, Dover Publications, 2007.

[2]H. Bergson, *Matter and Memory*, translated by N.M. Paul and W.S. Palmer, New York, NY, Zone Books, 1991.

[3]C. Ravasi,*Ezechiele e i Profeti Postesilici: Cinque conferenze tenute al Centro culturale S. Fedele di Milano*, Bologna, Edizioni Dehoniane, 2012 – F. Berardi's translation.

The 'transparency' mentioned by Ravasi to explain the prophetic potency of Ezekiel (the torment and the baroque excitement of Ezekiel) is the sign of an embodiment of the *verbum*, and of an embodiment of meaning. If Ezekiel is the prophet of hallucinatory baroque lightness, Jeremiah is the prophet of darkness and of suffering. But despite the different quality of their visions, both Jeremiah and Ezekiel recognize that the source of a prophetic word lies in the body, in the flesh, in sensibility – that these are the potencies enabling vision. Prophetic vision arises from the sensitive disturbance of the vibrating antenna at the receiving end of the cosmic vibration. Or, to say it more clearly, it arises from the sensitive reception of the stimuli issued by the collective psychical sphere, from which the *cosmos* emerges as a provisional and mutating projection.

I cannot conclude these meditations on the sensitive origin of prophetic vision without remembering Tiresias, if I may speak of him in a tone that isn't that of theoretical analysis. In the few extant fragments of a whimsical poet, Tiresias says:

> *As the time of my death approaches*
> *I'll speak of the fate that awaits*
> *the inhabitants of coastal cities.*
> *To sense the coming of catastrophic events –*
> *This has been my job, since the jealous Goddess*
> *deprived me of my eyesight*
> *and made me able to see*
> *what should remain unseen.*
>
> *Accept the offering of my dreams of agony*
> *This intimate, foreign land of euphoric desperation.*
>
> *Uncountable misfortunes punctuated*
> *This overlong life of mine.*
> *One day, while walking along the riverbank*
> *I saw the cruel nakedness of Athena,*
> *bathing intolerably gorgeous.*
> *Seeing her caressing her skin with wildflowers*
> *Mutilated my eyes and*
> *expanded the universe.*

Blinded, through the forest I wandered,
and lost I came upon two copulating snakes,
lustfully oblivious, of their pleasure mindful.
With my cane I killed them,
and Hera took revenge of my sacrilege.
She morphed my body into that of a female,
As if it was a scar that I had to carry.
I awoke from my sleep,
Sensibly female
I fell on my knees in the temple,
I was a high priestess
And I gave away my body
to powerful men in exchange for money.
I gave birth to Neuromantic, a daughter,
then, seven years later, I was male again.

At the Central Station in Milan
I was in the waiting room for the ten-to-seven train
when I heard my name pronounced by
the stentorian voice of loudspeakers.
Metallic, it ordered me to reach
the marble staircase at the entrance,
where Zeus and Hera expected me
to give them an explanation
for my prophetic words.

– The lady caressed the sex
of the man known for his wisdom,
while her mouth lasciviously kissed
the vigorous captain.
Then, with clever irony
she mocked my silly jealousy
(I was waiting for her in the cold). –

We ask you, Tiresias,
You who experienced both genders,
who takes more pleasure? I realised then
that my life was approaching its end
and I said, 'my strange illness,

that doctors cannot diagnose nor cure,
is prophetic insight; bitter, dark
premonitions of orgasmic departures from life.
The dreamer alone is the witness of their dreams
and rivulets of terror proliferate from the dream
of this sudden realisation:
there is no death
only an eternal flow
of interminable spirits prefiguring our future,
when, naked, we'll be pulled
into the whirlwind
of unimagined beginning.'[4]

Similarly, Anagarika Govinda talks about the distinction between *shabda* and *mantra*:

Shabda *is the ordinary word that is used to denote objects and concepts in the normal exchange of operational meanings.* Mantra, *on the contrary, triggers the creation of mental images and of sensible meanings ... In the word* mantra, *the Sanscrit root* man = *to think (in Greek:* menos, *Latin:* mens*) is combined with the element* tra, *which forms tool-words. Thus,* mantra *is a tool for thinking, a thing that creates a mental picture. With its sound, it calls forth its content into a state of immediate reality.* Mantra *is power, and not merely speech which the mind can contradict or evade. What* mantra *expresses by its sound exists, and it comes to pass. Here, if anywhere, words are deeds, acting immediately. It is the peculiarity of the true poet that his word creates actuality, calls forth and unveils something real. His word does not talk – it acts.*[5]

Mantra is a vocal emission that has the power to create mental states with no conventional signification. And prophecy is the vibration of the voice tuning in to the vibrating *cosmos*.

Jalāl ad-Dīn Muhammad Rūmī, the master of the swirling dervishes writes:

---

[4]Anonymous fragment, translated by F. Berardi, F. Campagna and F. Strocchi.
[5]A. Govinda, *Foundations of Tibetan Mysticism*, Newburyport, MA, Red Wheel/ Weiser, 1969, p. 19.

We prophets, o my Lord, we are lutes
but you are the fiddler.
You, who emits whispers
through us.
We are the flutes
but the blow comes from you, my Lord.
We are like mountains,
but the echo, the echo comes only from You.

And finally, we cannot forget of William Blake, who writes

...all things exist in human imagination...
all you behold, tho' it appears without, it is within
in your Imagination, of which this world of mortality is but a
shadow.[6]

And also:

Man has no Body distinct from his soul: for that call'd body is
a portion of soul discern'd by the five senses, the chief inlets of
soul in this age. Energy is the only life and is from the body; and
Reason is the bound or outward circumference of Energy.
                              Energy is eternal delight.[7]

This is the essential point: energy is delight and energy is the source of those poetic words, which contain within their rhythm, within their sound and their vibration all the possible meanings that correspond to the intentions of Chaos.

But Chaos has no intentions.

Those words read: 'Poetry is the pathway to the only order that counts: the order of the rhythm of breathing.' Prophecy of Inspiration.

---

[6]W. Blake, *The Complete Poems, Jerusalem*, edited by A. Ostriker, London, Penguin, 1977, p. 785.
[7]W. Blake, *The Complete Poems, The Marriage of Heaven and Hell*, edited by A. Ostriker, London, Penguin, 1977, p. 181.

BIBLIOGRAPHY

BOOKS

The Bhagavad Gītā, translated by W. Sargeant, Albany, NY, SUNY, 2009.

The Chaldean Oracles, edited and translated by R. Majercik, Leiden, E.J. Brill, 1989.

The Holy Qur'an: Transliteration in Roman Script with Arabic Text and English Translation, translated by Abdullah Yusuf Ali, Delhi, Kitab Bhavan, 2001.

The New Oxford Annotated Bible (4th edition), Oxford, Oxford University Press, 2001.

The Theologia Germanica of Martin Luther, translated and commented by B. Hoffman, New York, NY, Paulist Press, 1980.

Agamben, G., *The Coming Community*, translated by M. Hardt, Minneapolis/London, University of Minnesota Press, 2007.

Agamben, G., *Pulcinella: Or Entertainment for Children*, translated by K. Attell, Kolkata, Seagull Books, 2015.

Al-Jili, A. A-K, *Universal Man*, translated and commented by T. Burkhardt, Lahore, Suhail Academy, 1965.

Alexander, M. (ed.), *The Earliest English Poems*, London, Penguin, 1977.

Arabi, I., *The Ringstones of Wisdom (Fusus Al-Hikam)*, translated by C.K. Dagli, Chicago, IL, Kazi Publications, 2000.

Aristotle, *Physics*, translated by R. Hope, Lincoln, NE, University of Nebraska Press, 1961.

Aristotle, *Metaphysics*, Books 1–9, translated by H. Tredennick, Cambridge, MA, Loeb Classical Library, Harvard University Press, 1989.

Artaud, A., *Scritti di Rodez*, edited and translated by R. Damiani, Milan, Adelphi, 2017.

Astruc, R., *Le Renouveau du grotesque dans le roman du XXe siècle*, Paris, Classiques Garnier, 2010.

Athanassiadi, P. and M. Frede (eds.), *Pagan Monotheism in Late Antiquity*, Oxford, Oxford University Press, 1999.

Attar, *The Conference of the Birds*, translated by S. Wolpe, New York/London, W. W. Norton, 2017.

Attias, J.-C., *A Woman Called Moses*, translated by G. Elliott, London/ New York, Verso, 2020.

St, Augustine, *Confessions*, translated by V.J. Bourke, Washington, DC, The Catholic University of America Press, 2008.

Aune, D., *Prophecy in Early Christianity and the Ancient Mediterranean World*, Grand Rapids, MI, Wm. B. Eerdmans, 1991.

Awn, P. J., *Satan's Tragedy and Redemption: Iblis in Sufi Psychology*, Leiden, Brill, 1983.

Bachrach, B.S. (ed.), *Liber Historia Francorum*, Lawrence, KS., Coronado Press, 1973.

Ball, H., *Die Flucht aus der Zeit*, Munich, Duncker & Humblot, 1927.

Ball, H., *Fuga dal Tempo: fuga saeculi*, translated by R. Caldura, Milan, Mimesis, 2016.

Baltrušaitis, J., *Anamorphic Art*, translated by W.J. Strachan, New York, NY, Harry N. Abrams, 1977.

Barbero, A., *Costantino il Vincitore*, Rome, Salerno Editrice, 2016.

Barbero, A., *9 Agosto 378: Il Giorno dei Barbari*, Bari, Laterza, 2012.

Barker, M., *The Great Angel: A Study of Israel's Second God*, London, SPCK, 1992.

Barker, M., *The Lost Prophet: The Book of Enoch And Its Influence on Christianity*, Sheffield, Phoenix Press University of Sheffield, 2005.

Barocchi, P. (ed.), *Trattati d'arte del Cinquecento fra Manierismo e Controriforma*, 3 Vols., Bari, Laterza, 1960–2.

Bataille, G., *Eroticism*, translated by M. Dalwood, London, Penguin, 2001.

Battisti, E. (ed.), *Michelangelo Scultore*, Rome, Curcio Editore, 1964.

Benjamin, W., *One Way Street and Other Writings*, translated by E. Jephcott and K. Shorter, London, NLB, 1979.

Berardi 'Bifo', F., *After the Future*, Edinburgh, AK Press, 2011.

Berardi 'Bifo', F., *Futurability: The Age of Impotence and the Horizon of Possibility*, London/New York, Verso, 2017.

Bergman, I., *Script of The Seventh Seal*, translated by L. Malmstrom and D. Kushner, London, Lorrimer Publishing, 1972.

Bergson, H., *The Creative Mind: An Introduction to Metaphysics*, translated by M.L. Andison, Mineola, NY, Dover Publications, 2007.

Bergson, H., *Matter and Memory*, translated by N.M. Paul and W.S. Palmer, New York, NY, Zone Books, 1991.

Biles, J., *Ecce Monstrum: Georges Bataille and the Sacrifice of Form*, New York, NY, Fordham University Press, 2007.

Bishop, C., *Artificial Hells: Participatory Art and the Politics of Spectatorship*, London/New York, Verso, 2012.

Blake, W., *The Complete Poems*, edited by A. Ostriker, London, Penguin, 1977.

Bloch, E., *Heritage of Our Time*, translated by N. Plaice and S. Plaice, Cambridge, Polity, 1991.

Balthasar, H. U. von, *Dare We Hope That All Men Be Saved?* translated by D. Kipp and Rev. L. Krauth, San Francisco, CA, Ignatius Press, 1993.

Bentley Hart, D., *That All Shall Be Saved: Heaven, Hell, and Universal Salvation*, New Haven/London, Yale University Press, 2019.

Bioy Casares, A., *The Invention of Morel*, translated by R.L.C. Simms, New York, NY, New York Review of Books, 2003.

Blondel, F., *Cours d'Architecture Enseigne dans l'Academie Royale*, Paris, P. Aubouin & F. Clousier, 1675–83.

Blum, R., *Kallimachos: The Alexandrian Library and the Origins of Bibliography*, translated by H.H. Wellisch, Madison, WI, The University of Wisconsin Press, 1991.

Boehme, J., *The Way to Christ*, translated by P.C. Erb, Mahwah, NJ, Paulist Press, 1977.

Borges, J.L. and A.B. Casares, *Racconti Brevi e Straordinari*, Milan, Adelphi, 2020

Borges, J.L., *Labyrinths: Selected Stories and Other Writings*, edited and translated by D.A. Yates and J.E. Irby, London, Penguin, 2000.

Bradley, F.H., *Appearance and Reality*, Oxford, Clarendon Press, 1930.

Brodsky, J., *A Part of Speech*, Oxford, Oxford University Press, 1997.

Brown, P., *Society and the Holy in Late Antiquity*, Berkeley, CA, University of California Press, 1989.

Browne, Sir T., *Religio Medici and Urne-Burial*, New York, NY, NYRB, 2012.

Bulgakov, S., *Unfading Light: Contemplations and Speculations*, translated by T.A. Smith, Grand Rapids, MI, William B. Eerdmans Publishers, 2012.

Buonarroti, M., *The Complete Poems*, translated by J.F. Nims, Chicago/London, The University of Chicago Press, 1998.

Burkhardt, T., *Art of Islam: Language and Meaning*, translated by J.P. Hobson, London, World of Islam Festival Publishing Company, 1976.

Busi, G. and R. Ebgi, *Giovanni Pico della Mirandola: Mito, Magia, Qabbalah*, Turin, Einaudi, 2014.

Cacciari, M., *Icone della Legge*, Milan, Adelphi, 2002.

Cacciari, M., *The Necessary Angel*, translated by M.E. Vatter, Albany, NY, SUNY, 1994.

Cacciari, M., *Tre Icone*, Milan, Adelphi, 2007.

Cacciari, M. and P. Prodi, *Occidente Senza Utopie*, Bologna, Il Mulino, 2016.

Caillois, R., *Man, Play and Games*, translated by M. Barash, Chicago, IL, University of Chicago Press, 2001.

Calasso, R., *Ardor*, translated by R. Dixon, London, Penguin, 2015.

Calasso, R., *I Geroglifici di Sir Thomas Browne*, Milan, Adelphi, 2019a.

Calasso, R., *Il Libro Di Tutti I Libri*, Milan, Adelphi, 2019b.

Calasso, R., *The Unnamable Present*, translated by R. Dixon, London, Penguin, 2019c.

Camillo, G., *L'Idea del Theatro*, Palermo, Sellerio, 1991.

Campagna, F., *Technic and Magic: The Reconstruction of Reality*, London, Bloomsbury, 2018.

Campo, C., *Gli Imperdonabili*, Milan, Adelphi, 2019.

Carroll, L., *Alice's Adventures in Wonderland and through the Looking Glass*, London, Penguin, 2003.

Cave, D., *Mircea Eliade's Vision for a New Humanism*, Oxford, Oxford University Press, 1993.

Chase, S. (ed. and trans.), *Angelic Spirituality: Medieval Perspectives on the Ways of the Angels*, New York, NY, Paulist Press, 2002.

Chastel, A., *La Grottesca*, translated by S. Lega, Milan, Se, 2010.

Cellini, B., *Autobiography*, translated by J. Addington Symonds, New York, NY, Cosimo Classics, 2009.

Cline, E., *1177 B.C.: The Year Civilization Collapsed*, Princeton, NJ, Princeton University Press, 2015.

Colli, G., *Filosofi Sovrumani*, Milan, Adelphi, 2009.

Colli, G., *La Nascita della Filosofia*, Milan, Adelphi, 1975.

Colli, G., *La Ragione Errabonda: Quaderni Postumi*, edited by E. Colli, Milan, Adelphi, 1982.

Colli, G., *La Sapienza Greca*, 3 Vols., Milan, Adelphi, 1990–3.

Connelly, F. S., *The Grotesque in Western Art and Culture: The Image at Play*, Cambridge, Cambridge University Press, 2012.

Coomaraswamy, A., *Selected Papers: Volume 2, Metaphysics*, edited by R. Lipsey, Princeton, NJ, Princeton University Press, 1987.

Coomaraswamy, A. K., *Time and Eternity*, New Delhi, Munshiram Manoharlal, 2014.

Corbin, H., *Cyclical Time and Ismaili Gnosis*, translated by R. Manheim and J.W. Morris, Abingdon, Routledge, 2013.

Corbin, H., *En Islam Iranien: Aspects spirituels et philosophiques, Vol. 2, Sohrawardi et les Platoniciens de Perse*, Paris, Gallimard, 1991a.

Corbin, H., *En Islam Iranien: Aspects spirituels et philosophiques*, vol. 3, *Les Fideles d'Amour, Shi'isme et Soufisme*, Paris, Gallimard, 1991b.

Corbin, H., *History of Islamic Philosophy*, translated by L. Sherrard, Abingdon, Routledge, 2014.

Corbin, H., *L'Imam cache et la renovation de l'homme en theologie shi'ite*, Paris, L'Herne, 1960.

Corbin, H., *Realisme et symbolisme des couleurs en cosmologie shi'ite: d'apres le 'Livre du hyacinthe rouge' de Shaykh Moḥammad Karim-Khan Kermani* (ob. 1870), Leiden, Brill, 1974.

Coward, H. and T. Foshay (eds.), *Derrida and Negative Theology: With a Conclusion by Jacques Derrida*, Albany, NY, SUNY Press, 1992.

Critchley, S., *Infinitely Demanding: Ethics of Commitment, Politics of Resistance*, London/New York, Verso, 2007.

Critchlow, K., *Islamic Patterns: An Analytical and Cosmological Approach*, London, Thames and Hudson, 1976.

Dante, *Monarchy*, translated and edited by P. Shaw, Cambridge, Cambridge University Press, 1996.

Daumal, R., *Mount Analogue: An Authentic Narrative*, translated by R. Shattuck, San Francisco, CA, City Lights Books, 1971.

Daumal, R., *Lanciato dal Pensiero*, translated by C. Rugafiori and L. Simini, Milan, Adelphi, 2019.

Deleuze, G. and F. Guattari, *Anti-Oedipus*, translated by R. Hurley et al., London, Bloomsbury, 2013.

Deleuze, G. and F. Guattari, *What Is Philosophy?* translated by H.Tomlinson and G. Burchell, New York, NY, Columbia University Press, 1994.

De Martino, E., *La Fine del Mondo: contributo all'analisi delle apocalissi culturali*, Turin, Einaudi, 2002.

Dickinson, E., *Complete Poems*, edited by T.H. Johnson, Boston, MA, Little Brown, 1960.

Diogenes Laertius, *Lives and Opinions of Eminent Philosophers*, vol. 2, translated by R.D. Hicks, Cambridge, MA, Loeb Classical Library, 1989.

Dodds, R., *The Greeks and the Irrational*, Berkeley, CA, University of California Press, 2004.

Ebgi, R. (ed.), *Umanisti Italiani: Pensiero e Destino*, Turin, Einaudi, 2016.

Eliade, M., *Images and Symbols*, translated by P. Mairet, Princeton, NJ, Princeton University Press, 1991.

Eliade, M., *La Prova del Labirinto: intervista con Claude-Henri Rocquet*, translated by M. Giacometti, Mian, Jaca Book, 1990.

Eliade, M., *The Sacred and the Profane*, translated by W. Ropes Trask, New York, NY, Harcourt, Brace & World, 1959.

Feuerbach, L., *The Essence of Christianity*, translated by G. Eliot, Mineola, NY, Dover, 2008.

Fink, E., *Play as Symbol of the World and Other Writings*, translated by I.A. Moore and C. Turner, Bloomington, IN, Indiana University Press, 2016.

Finley, M.I., *The World of Odysseus*, New York, NY, New York Review of Books, 2002.

Fisher, M., *The Weird and the Eerie*, London, Repeater, 2016.

Florenskij, P., *La Concezione Cristiana del Mondo*, translated by A. Maccioni, Bologna, Pendragon, 2019.

Florenskij, P., *Le Porte Regali: saggio sull'icona*, translated by E. Zolla, Milan, Adelphi, 1977.

Florenskij, P., *L'Infinito nella Conoscenza*, translated by M. Di Salvo, Milan, Mimesis, 2014.

Florensky, P., *Beyond Vision: Essays on the Perception of Art*, edited by N. Misler, translated by W. Salmond, London, Reaktion Books, 2002.

Florensky, P., *Iconostasis*, translated by D. Sheehan and O. Andrejev, Crestwood, NY, St Vladimir's Seminary Press, 1996.

Florensky, P., *The Pillar and Ground of the Truth: An Essay In Orthodox Theodicy In Twelve Letters*, translated by B. Jakim, Princeton, NJ, Princeton University Press, 2004.

Foucault, M., *Discipline and Punish: The Birth of the Prison*, translated by A. Sheridan, London, Penguin, 1991.

Foucault, M., *Madness and Civilization: A History of Insanity in the Age of Reason*, translated by J. Murphy and J. Khalfa, New York, NY, Vintage Books, 2006.

Freeman Sandler, L. (ed.), *Essays in Memory of Karl Lehmann*, New York, NY, Institute of Fine Arts, New York University, 1964.

Galeano, E., *Walking Words*, translated by M. Fried, London/New York, W. W. Norton, 1997.

Galli, C., *Janus's Gaze: Essays on Carl Schmitt, Ch. 5: Schmitt and the Global Era*, translated by A. Minervini, Durham and London, Duke University Press, 2015.

Gerstinger, H., *Bestand und Überlieferung der Literaturwerke des griechisch-römischen Altertums*, Graz, Kienreich, 1948.

Gioia, M., *Idee Sulle Opinioni Religiose e Sul Clero Cattolico*, Lugano, 1841.

Girard, R., *Violence and the Sacred*, translated by P. Gregory, London, Bloomsbury, 2013.

Gombrich, E.H., *Aby Warburg: An Intellectual Biography*, London, The Warburg Institute, 1970.

Govinda, A., *Foundations of Tibetan Mysticism*, Newburyport, MA, Red Wheel/ Weiser, 1969.

Gracian, B., *The Pocket Oracle and the Art of Prudence*, translated by J. Robbins, London, Penguin, 2011.

Griffiths, J.G., *The Origins of Osiris and His Cult*, Leiden, Brill, 1980.

Groys, B., *Introduction to Antiphilosophy*, translated by D. Fernbach, London/New York, Verso, 2012.

Guenon, R., *Introduction to the Study of the Hindu Doctrines*, translated by M. Pallis, Hillsdale, NY, Sophia Perennis, 2004a.

Guenon, R., *The Lord of the World*, translated by A. Cheke et al., Moorcote, Coombe Springs Press, 1983.

Guenon, R., *The Multiple States of the Being*, translated by S.D. Fohr, Hillsdale, NY, Sophia Perennis, 2004c.

Guenon, R., *The Reign of Quantity and the Signs of the Times*, translated by Lord Northbourne, Hillsdale, NY, Sophia Perennis, 2002.

Guenon, R., *The Symbolism of the Cross*, translated by A. Macnab, Hillsdale, NY, Sophia Perennis, 2004d.

Guenon, R., *Symbols of Sacred Science*, translated by A. Moore, Hillsdale, NY, Sophia Perennis, 2004b.

Guthrie, K.S., *The Pythagorean Sourcebook and Library*, Grand Rapids, MI, Phanes Press, 1988.

Hadot, P., *Philosophy as a Way of Life: Spiritual Exercises from Socrates to Foucault*, edited by A. Davidson, translated by M. Chase, Oxford, Wiley-Blackwell, 1995.

Hakl, H.T., *Eranos: An Alternative Intellectual History of the Twentieth Century*, translated by C. McIntosh, Abingdon, Routledge, 2013.

Haskins, C.H., *The Renaissance of the Twelfth Century*, Cambridge, MA, Harvard University Press, 1971.

Hegel, G.W.F., *Elements of the Philosophy of Right*, edited by A.W. Wood, translated by H.B. Nisbet, Cambridge, Cambridge University Press, 2003.

Heidegger, *The Fundamental Concepts of Metaphysics: World, Finitude, Solitude*, translated by W. McNeill and N. Walker, Bloomington, IN, Indiana University Press, 2001.

Heidegger, M., *Being and Time*, translated J. Macquarrie and E. Robinson, New York, NY, HarperCollins, 2008.

Heidegger, M., *Off the Beaten Track*, edited and translated by J. Young and K. Haynes, Cambridge, Cambridge University Press, 2002.

Heidegger, H., *Poetry, Language, Thought*, translated by H. Hofstadter, New York, NY, Harper and Row, 1971.

Heller-Roazen, D., *Echolalias: On the forgetting of Language*, New York, NY, Zone Books, 2005.

Hesiod, *Works and Days*, translated by D. Wender, London, Penguin, 1973.

Hesse, H., *The Journey to the East*, translated by H. Rosner, London, Peter Owen, 2007.

Hoban, R., *Riddley Walker*, London, Bloomsbury, 1980.

Hodgson, M.G.S., *The Secret Order of Assassins: The Struggle of the Early Nizârî Ismâî'lîs against the Islamic World*, Philadelphia, PA, University of Pennsylvania Press, 2005.

Homer, *Iliad*, translated by M. Hamond, London, Penguin Classics, 1987.

Horace, *The Complete Odes and Epodes*, translated by D. West, Oxford, Oxford World Classics, 2008.

Horapollo Niliacus, *The Hieroglyphics of Horapollo*, translated by G. Boas, Princeton, NJ, Princeton University Press, 1993.

Hudson, W., *Modern Moral Philosophy*, London, Macmillan, 1970.

Hugh of Saint Victor, *Hugonis de S. Victore Operum Pars Prima, Exegetica, I, in Scripturam Sacram, De Scripturis et scriptoribus sacris*, vol. 175, edited by J.P. Migne, 1849–55.

Iamblichus, *The Theology of Arithmetic: On the Mystical, Mathematical and Cosmological Symbolism of the First Ten Numbers*, translated by R. Waterfield, Grand Rapids, MI, Phanes Press, 1986.

Izutsu, T., *Sufism and Taoism: A Comparative Study of Key Philosophical Concepts*, Berkeley/Los Angeles, CA, University of California Press, 1984.

Jacobson, R., *Child Language, Aphasia, and Phonological Universals*, The Hague, Mouton, 1968.

Jaeger, W., *Paideia: The Ideals of Greek Culture, Volume I: Archaic Greece*, translated by G. Highet, Oxford, Oxford University Press, 1965.

Jonas, H., *The Gnostic Religion: The Message of the Alien God and the Beginnings of Christianity*, Boston, MA, Beacon Press, 1963.

Josephus, F., *Antiquities of the Jews*, translated by W. Whiston, Radford, VA, Wilder Publications, 2018.

Joyce, J., *Ulysses*, Oxford, Oxford University Press, 2008.

Jung, C.G., *The Archetypes and The Collective Unconscious, Collected Works*, 9, translated by R.F.C. Hull, Princeton, NJ, Princeton University Press, 1981.

Jung, C.G. and C. Kerenyi, *The Science of Mythology*, translated by R.F.C. Hull, Abingdon, Routledge, 2001.

Jünger, E., *On The Marble Cliffs*, Harmondsworth, Penguin, 1970.

Jünger, E., *The Adventurous Heart: Figures and Capriccios*, translated by T. Friese, Candor, NY, Telos Press, 2012.

Kant, I., *Critique of Pure Reason*, translated by M. Weigelt, London, Penguin, 2007.

Kantorowiwcz, E., *The King's Two Bodies: A Study in Mediaeval Political Theology*, Princeton, NJ, Princeton University Press, 1957.

Kermani, N., *Wonder beyond Belief*, translated by T. Crawford, Cambridge, Polity Press, 2018.

Kircher, A., *Ars Magna*, Rome, 1646.

Kirk, G.S. et al., *The Presocratic Philosophers: A Critical History with a Selection of Texts*, Cambridge, Cambridge University Press, 2005.

Lacan, J., *The Seminar of Jacques Lacan: The Formations of the Unconscious 1957–1958*, Book V, edited and translated by J.A. Miller, Cambridge, Polity, 2017.

Lacan, J., *The Seminar of Jacques Lacan: The Ethics of Psychoanalysis 1959–1960*, Book VII, edited and translated by J.A. Miller, Cambridge, Polity, 1997.

Lacan, J., *The Seminar of Jacques Lacan: Transference*, Book VIII, edited and translated by J.A. Miller, Cambridge, Polity, 2015.

Lacan, J., *The Seminar of Jacques Lacan: Anxiety*, Book X, edited and translated by J.A. Miller, Cambridge, Polity, 2016.

Lacan, J., *The Seminar of Jacques Lacan: The Other Side of Psychoanalysis*, Book XVII, edited and translated by R. Grigg, New York, NY, W. W. Norton, 2007.

Laude, P., *Pathways to an Inner Islam: Massignon, Corbin, Guenon, and Schuon*, Albany, NY, SUNY Press, 2010.

Leonardo da Vinci, *Trattato della Pittura*, Catania, Brancato, 1990.

Levinas, E., *Totality and Infinity: An Essay on Exteriority*, translated by A. Lingis, Dordrecht, Kluwer, 1991.

Lewis, D., *Counterfactuals*, Oxford, Blackwell, 2001.

Lewis, D., *On the Plurality of Worlds*, Oxford, Blackwell, 1986.

Lewis, C.S., *Miracles*, London, HarperCollins, 2002.

Lossky, N., *History of Russian Philosophy*, London, Allen and Unwin, 1952.

Lossky, V., *The Mystical Theology of the Eastern Church*, translated by a group of members of the Fellowship of St Alban and St Sergius, Cambridge, James Clarke & Co., 2005.

Loux, M.J. (ed.), *The Possible and the Actual: Readings in the Metaphysics of Modality*, Ithaca, NY, Cornell University Press, 1979.

Lucian of Samosata, *True Story*, translated by F. Hikes, London, A. H. Bullen, 1902

Mashita, H. (ed.), *Theology, Ethics and Metaphysics: Royal Asiatic Society Classics of Islam*, Abingdon, Routledge, 2003.

McTaggart, J., *The Unreality of Time*, The Perfect Library, 2015.

Mercer, L., *Speculative Emblematics: An Environmental Iconology*, Royal Holloway, London, University of London, 2020 (PhD thesis).

Miller, A., *Contemporary Metaethics*, Cambridge, Polity, 2017.

Morton, T., *Ecology without Nature*, Cambridge, MA, Harvard University Press, 2007.

Morton, T., *Humanknd: Solidarity with Non-Human People*, London and New York, Verso, 2017.

Nabokov, V., *Ada, or Ardor: A Family Chronicle*, London, Penguin Classics, 2011.

Namaziano, R., *Il Ritorno* (dual language edition), Torino, Einaudi, 1992.

Nappo, F., *Poesie 1979–2007*, Macerata, Quodlibet, 2007.

Nasr, S.H., *Islamic Art and Spirituality*, Ipswich, Golgonooza Press, 1987.

Neher, A., *L'Essenza del Profetismo*, translated by E. Piattelli, Genova, Casa Editrice Marietti, 1984.

Neocleous, M., *A Critical Theory of Police Power: The Fabrication of the Social Order*, London/New York, Verso, 2020.

Niceron, J.F., *La Perspective Curieuse*, Paris, 1638.

Nietzsche, F., *The Birth of Tragedy*, translated by S. Whiteside, London, Penguin, 1993.

Nilsson, P., *The Mycenaean Origin of Greek Mythology*, Berkeley, CA, University of California Press, 1972.

Origen of Alexandria, *Contra Celsum*, translated by H. Chadwick, Cambridge, Cambridge University Press, 1980.

Ottmann, K. (ed.), *Color Symbolism: The Eranos Lectures*, Thompson, CT, Spring Publications, 2005.

Otto, R., *The Idea of the Holy*, translated by J.W. Harvey, Oxford, Oxford University Press, 1958.

Ouspensky, L., *Theology of the Icon*, 2 Vols., translated by A. Gythiel, Crestwood, NY, St Vladimir's Seminary Press, 1992.

Paleotti, G., *Discorso Intorno alle Immagini Sacre e Profane, diviso In cinque libri*, Bologna, 1582.

Panofsky, E., *Studies in Iconology: Humanistic Themes in the Art of the Renaissance*, New York, NY, Harper, 1962.

Parra, N., *Anti-Poems*, translated by J. Elliot, *The Pocket Poets Series N°12*, San Francisco, CA, City Lights Books, 1960.

Pavese, C., *Dialoghi con Leuco'*, Turin, Einaudi, 2014.

Pavese, C., *Dialogues with Leuco'*, translated by W. Arrowsmith, London, Peter Owen Publishers, 1965.

Pavić, M., *Dictionary of the Khazars: A Lexicon Novel*, translated by C. Pribićević-Zorić, New York, NY, Vintage, 1989.

Paz, O., *The Labyrinth of Solitude and Other Writings*, New York, NY, Grove Press, 1994.

Perler, D. and U. Rudolph, *Occasionalismus: Theorien der Kausalität im arabisch-islamischen und im europäischen Denken*, Göttingen, Vandenhoeck & Ruprecht, 2000.

Pessoa, F., *Selected Poems*, edited and translated by J. Griffin, London, Penguin, 2000.

Pessoa, F., *Una Sola Moltitudine*, 2 Vols., edited and translated by A. Tabucchi, Milan, Adelphi, 1979.

Petrolini, E., *Al Mio Pubblico*, Milan, Casa Editrice Ceschina, 1937.

Piron, S., *Dialectique du Monstre*, Brussels, Editions Zones Sensibiles, 2015.

Piron, S., *Dialettica del Mostro: Indagine su Opicinus de Canistris*, translated by A.G. Nissim, Milan, Adelphi, 2019.

Plantinga, A., *The Nature of Necessity*, Oxford, Oxford University Press, 1982.

Plato, *Complete Works*, translated by D.J. Zeyl, edited by J.M. Cooper, Indianapolis/Cambridge, Hackett, 1997.

Pliny the Younger, *Letters*, vol. 1, translated by W. Melmoth and W.M.L. Hutchinson, London, William Heinemann, 1931.

Plutarch, *Moralia*, vol. XII, translated by H. Cherniss and W. C. Helmbold, Cambridge, MA, Loeb Classical Library, Harvard University Press, 1986.

Plutarch, *Plutarch's Lives*, translated by J. Dryden, New York, NY, The Modern Library, 2001.

Poincaré, H., *The Foundations of Science*, translated by G.B. Halsted, Washington, DC, University Press of America, 1982.

Porphyry, *On the Cave of the Nymphs*, translated by T. Taylor, London, Watkins, 1917.

Praz, M., *Studi Sul Concettismo*, Milan, Abscondita, 2014.

Pseudo-Dionysius, *The Complete Works*, translated by C. Luibheid, New York, NY, Paulist Press, 1987.

Puech, H.C., *En Quête de la Gnose*, 2 Vols., Paris, Gallimard, 1978.

Radin, P., *The Trickster: A Study in American Indian Mythology*, New York, NY, Schocken Books, 1972.

Ramelli, I., *The Christian Doctrine of Apokatastasis: A Critical Assessment from the New Testament to Eriugena*, Leiden, Brill, 2013.

Ravasi, Cardinal C., *Ezechiele e i Profeti Postesilici: Cinque conferenze tenute al Centro culturale S. Fedele di Milano*, Bologna, Edizioni Dehoniane, 2012.

Rilke, R.M., *Duino Elegies & the Sonnets to Orpheus*, translated by S. Mitchell, New York, NY, Vintage, 2010.

Rilke, R.M., *Uncollected Poems*, translated by E. Snow, New York, NY, North Point, 1966.

Robinson, K., *A Search for the Whirlpool of Artifice: The Cosmology of Giulio Camillo*, Edinburgh, Dunedin Academic Press, 2006.

Rosenzweig, F., *Der Stern der Erlösung*, Frankfurt am Main, J. Kauffmann, 1921.

Rosenzweig, F., *La Stella della Redenzione*, translated by G. Bonola, Milan, Vita e Pensiero, 2017.

Rovelli, C., *The Order of Time*, translated by S. Carnell and E. Segre, London, Penguin, 2018.

Said, E. and D. Barenboim, *Parallels and Paradoxes: Explorations in Music and Society*, London, Bloomsbury, 2004.

Salvemini, G. and E. Gencarelli (ed.), *Carteggi, I, 1895–1911*, Milano, Feltrinelli, 1968.

Scheffer-Boichorst, P. (ed.), *Chronica Albrici Monachi Trium Fontium*, in *Monumenta Germaniae Historica: Scriptorum*, vol. 23, Leipzig, Verlag Karl W. Hiersemann, 1925.

Schilpp, P.A. (ed.), *Albert Einstein: Philosopher-Scientist*, New York, NY, MJF Books, 1970.

Schimmel, A., *Mystical Dimensions of Islam, The Rose and the Nightingale: Persian and Turkish Mystical Poetry*, Chapel Hill, NC, The University of North Carolina Press, 1975.

Schliemann, H., *Troja: Results of the Latest Researches and Discoveries on the Site of Homer's Troy*, Chicheley, Paul B. Minet, 1972.

Schmitt, C., *The Nomos of the Earth: In the International Law of the Jus Publicum Europaeum*, translated by G.L. Ulmen, New York, NY, Telos Press, 2006.

Scholem, G., *Major Trends in Jewish Mysticism*, New York, NY, Schocken Books, 1995.

Schuon, F., *Esoterism as Principle and as Way*, translated by W. Stoddart and Pates Manor, Bedfont, Perennial Books, 1981.

Schuon, F., *Understanding Islam*, Bloomington, IN, World Wisdom, 1998.

Semon, R.W., *The Mneme*, translated by L. Simon, London, George Allen & Unwin, 1921.

Serres, M., *Angels: A Modern Myth*, translated by F. Cowper, Paris/New York, Flammarion, 1995.

Severino, E., *Immortalità e Destino*, Milano, Rizzoli, 2008a.

Severino, E., *La Filosofia dai Greci al Nostro Tempo: La filosofia antica e medioevale*, Milano, Rizzoli, 2004.

Severino, E., *La Follia dell'Angelo: Conversazioni Intorno Alla Filosofia*, Milan, Mimesis, 2006.

Severino, E., *La Gloria: Risoluzione di 'Destino della necessità'*, Milan, Adelphi, 2001.

Severino, E., *La strada: La follia e la gioia*, Milan, Rizzoli, 2008b.

Severino, E., *Nihilism and Destiny*, edited by N. Cusano, translated by K.W. Molin, Milan, Mimesis International, 2016.

Severino, E., *Oltrepassare*, Milan, Adelphi, 2007.

Seznec, J., *The Survival of the Pagan Gods: The Mythological Thought and Its Place in Renaissance Humanism and Art*, Princeton, NJ, Princeton University Press, 1972.

Simondon, G., *Individuation in Light of Notions of Form and Information*, translated by T. Adkins, Minneapolis, MN, University of Minnesota Press, 2020.

Simondon, G., *On the Mode of Existence of Technical Objects*, translated by C. Malaspina and J. Rogove, Minneapolis, MN, University of Minnesota Press, 2017.

Smith, B. K., *Reflections on Resemblance, Ritual, and Religion*, Delhi, Motilal Banarsidass, 1998.

Soothill, W.E., *The Three Religions of China: Lectures Delivered at Oxford*, Oxford, Oxford University Press, 1929.

Spengler, O., *The Decline of the West*, translated by C.F. Atkinson, New York, NY, Knopf, 1926.

Spinoza, B., *Ethics*, translated by W.H. White and A.H. Stirling, Ware, Wordsworth Editions, 2001.

Staal, F., *Ritual and Mantras: Rules without Meaning*, New Delhi, Motilal Banarsidass, 1996.

Staniloae, D., *The Experience of God: Orthodox Dogmatic Theology*, 6 Vols., translated by I. Ionita and R. Barringer, Brookline, MA, Holy Cross Orthodox Press, 1989–2013.

Strauss, L., *Myth and Meaning*, Abingdon, Routledge, 2001.

Strauss, L., *The Raw and the Cooked: Mythologiques*, translated by J.D. Weightman, Chicago, IL, The University of Chicago Press, 1969.

Tacitus, *Agricola and Germany*, translated by A. Birley, Oxford, Oxford Universty Press, 1999.

Tertullianus, *Ante-Nicene Christian Library: Translations of the Writings of the Fathers*, vol. 7, *Tertullianus Against Marcion*, edited and translated by A. Roberts, Edinburgh, T&T Clark, 1868.

Thera, N.M., *A Manual of Abhidhamma*, Kuala Lumpur, Buddhist Missionary Society, 1987.

Thomas, D., *The Collected Poems of Dylan Thomas: The Centenary Edition*, London, Weidenfeld & Nicolson, 2016.

Townsend, C., *Malintzin's Choices: An Indian Woman in the Conquest of Mexico*, Albuquerque, NM, University of New Mexico Press, 2006.

Tronti, M., *Workers and Capital*, translated by D. Broder, London/New York, Verso, 2019.

Trubetzkoy, N.S., *Principles of Phonology*, translated by C.A.M. Baltaxe, Berkeley, CA, University of California Press, 1971.

Tucci, G., *Storia della Filosofia Indiana*, Bari, Laterza, 2005.

Tyack, Rev. Geo. S., *The Cross in Ritual Architecture and Art*, London, William Andrews & Co., 1900.

Unamuno, M. de, *Tragic Sense of Life*, translated by J.E. Crawford Flitch, New York, NY, Dover Publications, 1954.

Ungaretti, G., *Selected Poems*, edited and translated by A. Frisardi, Manchester, Carcanet, 2003.

Varadpande, M.L., *History of Indian Theatre: Loka Ranga: Panorama of Indian Folk Theatre*, New Delhi, Abhinav Publications, 1992.

Vasari, G., *Le Vite de' piu' eccellenti pittori scultori e architetti italiani*, Firenze, Sansoni, 1966.

Verga, G., *Cavalleria Rusticana and Other Stories*, translated by G.H. McWilliam, London, Penguin, 1999.

Virgil, *Aeneid*, I–VI, London, Bristol Classical Press, 2002.

Vitruvius, *The Ten Books on Architecture*, translated by M.H. Morgan, Cambridge, MA, Harvard University Press, 1914.

Viveiros de Castro, E., *Cannibal Metaphysics*, edited and translated by P. Skafish, Minneapolis, MN, Minnesota University Press, 2014.

Viveiros de Castro, E. and D. Danowski, *The Ends of the World*, translated by R. Nunes, Cambridge, Polity, 2017.

Wallace-Hadrill, J.M. (ed.), *The Fourth Book of the Chronicle of Fredegar: With Its Continuations*, Santa Barbara, CA, Praeger, 1981.

Warburg, A., *The Renewal of Pagan Antiquity*, edited by K.W. Foster, translated by D. Britt, Los Angeles, CA, Getty Research Institute, 1999.

Weil, S., *Simone Weil's the Iliad or the Poem of Force: A Critical Edition*, edited and translated by J.P. Holoka, New York, NY, Peter Lang Publishing, 2006.

Weil, S., *Waiting for God*, translated by E. Craufurd, New York, NY, Harper and Row, 1973.

Weizman, E., *The Least of All Possible Evils: Humanitarian Violence from Arendt to Gaza*, London/New York, Verso, 2011.

Wind, E., *Giorgione's 'Tempesta' with Comments on Giorgione's Poetic Allegories*, Oxford, Oxford University Press, 1969.

Yates, F., *The Art of Memory*, London, The Bodley Head, 2014.

Zolla, E., *Che Cos'e' la Tradizione*, Milan, Adelphi, 1998.

ARTICLES

Berardi 'Bifo', F., 'Communism Is Back but We Should Call It the Therapy of Singularisation', *Generation Online*, 2009. Online at http://www.generation-online.org/p/fp_bifo6.htm

Berardi 'Bifo', F., 'The End of Prophecy', *e-flux journal*, no. 95, November 2018.

Bunnag, A., 'Why Time Is Unreal: From Buddhism to J. E. McTaggart', *Veridian E- Journal International*, vol. 9, no. 5, 2016, pp. 83–94.

Daumal, R., 'L'origine du Théâtre de Bharata', *Mesures*, IV, 5 October 1935.

Davidson, M., 'Speech Work', *We Do Not Believe in the Good Faith of the Victors*, 2019, a one-off publication by Fraile Press, London. Online at: https://socialtextjournal.org/speech-work/

Hussey, J.M., 'The Byzantine Empire in the Eleventh Century: Some Different Interpretations', *Transactions of the Royal Historical Society*, 4 s., XXXII, 1950.

Reynolds, M., 'Nicely Combed', *London Review of Books*, vol. 25, no. 23, 4 December 2003.

Smith, B.K., 'Sacrifice and Being: Prajapati's Cosmic Emission and its Consequences', *Numen*, vol. 3, Fasc. 1, Jul. 1985, pp. 71–87.

Summers, D., 'Michelangelo on Architecture', *The Art Bulletin*, vol. 54, no. 2, June 1972, pp. 146–57.

Virgilio, *Eneide* (dual language edition), Turin, Einaudi, 2014.

OTHER PUBLICATIONS

A/traverso, Bologna, December 1976.

Internationale Situationniste, no. 1, June 1958.

Robinud, Sesto San Giovanni (MI), Re Nudo, 1974.

MUSIC

H. Eisler and J.R. Becher, *Auferstanden Aus Ruinen*, anthem of the Deutsche Demokratische Republik, 1949.

INDEX